THE
AVENGERS
DOSSIER

By the same authors:

THE NEW TREK PROGRAMME GUIDE – The Next
Generation and Deep Space Nine Episode by Episode

X-TREME POSSIBILITIES – A Paranoid Rummage
Through The X-Files

THE AVENGERS DOSSIER

Paul Cornell, Martin Day & Keith Topping

Virgin

First published in 1998 by
Virgin Books
an imprint of Virgin Publishing Ltd
332 Ladbroke Grove
London W10 5AH

ISBN 0 86369 754 2

Printed and bound in Great Britain by
Cox & Wyman Ltd, Reading

Acknowledgements

The authors of 'The Avengers Unpulped' would like to thank the following for their help: Ian Abrahams, Ian Atkins, Paola Brandolisio, Colin Brockhurst, Anthony Brown, Paul Condon, Nick Cooper, Mark Cullen, Peter Darvill-Evans, Gary Finney, Lisa Gaunt, Jeff Hart, Graham Howard, Adam Jezard, Rebecca Levene, Penny List, David McIntee, Anthony McKay, Dave Matthews, John McLaughlin, Mary Milton, Stephen O'Brien, Kate Orman, Andrew Pixley, Steve Purcell, Michael Richardson, Gareth Roberts, Dave Rogers, Paul Simpson, Gary Spain, Susannah Tiller, Lily Topping, Martin Wiggins, and the staff of Newcastle upon Tyne Central Library.

Acknowledgement is also made to the following books: *A for Andromeda to Zoo Time: The TV Holdings of the National Film and Television Archive 1936–1979* by Simon Baker and Olwen Terris (eds) (BFI), *British Television Drama Research Guide 1950–1995* by Richard Down and Chris Perry (eds) (Kaleidoscope), *The Encyclopedia of TV Science Fiction* by Roger Fulton (Boxtree), *The Ultimate Avengers* by Dave Rogers (Boxtree), *British Television: An Illustrated Guide* by Tise Vahimagi (Oxford University Press), and our own *The Guinness Book of Classic British TV* (Guinness); to the following newspapers and magazines: the *Daily Mail*, *DreamWatch*, the *Guardian*, the *Journal*, *On Target*, *625*, *Starburst*, *Stay Tuned*, *Thermal Lance*, *Time Screen*, *The Times*, *TV Times*, the *Viewer*; and to the following Web sites: Harry Knowles' Ain't It Cool News (http://www.aint-it-cool-news.com/coolnews.html), James Dawe's Avengers Page (http://www.ee.ualberta.ca/~dawe/avengers.html), David Fakrikian's Chapeau Melon et Bottes de Cuir (http://perso.club-internet.fr/fakirpro/tv/avengers.htm), Corona (http://198.53.172.4/~corona/films/details/avengers.htm), and Alistair McGown's Elan (http://www.mech.gla.ac.uk/~alistair/bowler/menu.htm).

Dedicated . . .

To Jac (PC)

To Donald McFarlan – wherever you are! – without whom . . . (MD)

To Colin and Maureen Topping, with love and thanks (KT)

CONTENTS

Introduction

The Avengers: the name summons up so many images. As this book will show, the series was one of television's great chameleons, able to change style, content and even format to fit in with changing times, attitudes and viewing habits.

Thanks to the recent video releases by Lumiere Pictures Ltd, a whole new generation is being introduced to the delights of *The Avengers*. The aim of this book is to provide a useful reference guide to this varied and continually surprising series. Lumiere have stated that they intend to release all of the existing episodes, which means everything bar the first season, of which only one episode ('The Frighteners') is known still to exist.

This book is written in a less analytical way than various other television episode guides, for three reasons. Firstly, readers may be about to see the episodes for the first time, and we wouldn't dream of giving away every single twist ending and plot detail. Secondly, such a dry approach would be indescribably boring for both you and us. Thirdly, there was never a programme less suited to the 'plot-cast list-producer's assistant' approach than *The Avengers*.

In September 1960, ABC Television, who provided programmes for several ITV regions at weekends, began transmitting *Police Surgeon*, a thriller series starring Ian Hendry as Dr Geoffrey Brent. The series seemed to lack something, though Hendry was obviously destined for great things. Thankfully, one of television's great innovators intervened.

Sydney Newman was a Canadian television executive who'd been headhunted by ABC (they offered him £8,500 a year, a Jaguar and a free mortgage) in an attempt to make their television more 'modern'. He gave them *Armchair Theatre* and *The Avengers*, not so much a format as a great title, since he had no idea who should be avenging what. (The BBC took him on

1

a couple of years later and got *Doctor Who*, another back-of-the-envelope idea that ran forever.) Newman fleshed out the idea with writers Ray Rigby and Brian Clemens, the latter of whom would come to dominate the way the programme was made, with results both positive and negative. This time around, Hendry would be Dr David Keel, avenging the death of his girlfriend with help from secret service spook John Steed, played by Patrick Macnee.

Macnee wasn't the star of the series, but he was well placed to emerge as its defining presence. The stylish actor was more mature than most leading men of his day, having a young child to look after, and having spent time as a television producer. This gave him the authority to quietly shape the show as it progressed, especially in the matter of the support he gave his various leading ladies against those who wanted to make them more 'feminine'. If we might indulge in a little amateur psychology, it is tempting to think that Macnee's bizarre upbringing (he was raised as a girl, a trait he shares with that other combative icon of the 60s, Bruce Lee) might have contributed to the rather before-its-time respect that John Steed as a character shows to women. Macnee himself comes over as a kind, witty and humble man ('I work on the lower slopes,' he once said while praising Diana Rigg's acting talents). He does himself down. As a television actor, an early example of a new breed, he is constantly watchable, communicating directly to the audience and capable of a great degree of subtlety. When *The Avengers* is at its worst, Patrick Macnee is still there making it interesting. He is greatly responsible for its longevity.

After *The New Avengers* finished production, Brian Clemens tried to resurrect the format three times. A pilot script for *The Avengers USA* was eventually made as the TV movie *Escapade* by Quinn Martin Productions. In 1980, Clemens and Dennis Spooner collaborated on a potential TV movie with CBS in mind (John Cleese was strongly tipped to play the villain), but

2

nothing came of it. Finally, in 1985, a pilot for *The Avengers International* was commissioned by Taft Entertainment, but didn't make it to production. Rumours frequently surface in the popular press about a major Hollywood movie based on Steed and Mrs Peel, usually involving Mel Gibson. Perhaps we should make our position clear. *The Avengers* stars Patrick Macnee as John Steed. Without him, it's clearly something else.

How to use the guide

The Avengers Programme Guide discusses the 161 episodes of the series made between 1961 and 1969, and also the 26 episodes of *The New Avengers* made in 1976 and 1977. The two series were made in nine blocks of episodes, or 'seasons'. For example, the first season of *The Avengers* was the block of 26 episodes made between January and December 1961. Some other books have chosen to lump together seasons five and six (the 24 colour Diana Rigg episodes) as one season, but these episodes were made in two distinct batches (sixteen and eight episodes respectively) and broadcast as such, with a five month gap between 'Who's Who???' and 'The Return of the Cybernauts'. For this reason, you may see the Tara King episodes incorrectly described as season six elsewhere. We insist that they form the seventh season.

Sorry about all that. Good form, you know.

We give each season a general introduction, recording transmission information, production and casting notes, and an overview of how the show was developing. We've also included a 'top five episodes' list to provoke a few arguments. We finish with two critical essays on the series.

The format for our guide to an individual episode is as follows:

Episode number
Title
Date (and time) of transmission
Working Title and/or approx. production dates

By-line

The by-lines – a short, witty episode description – appeared on screen after the episode title in the fifth season. These were used for publicity purposes during the Cathy Gale era, and continued into the seventh season in *TV Times*, although not on screen. If we're aware of the by-line, we show it. The time of transmission for a particular group of episodes, if known, is shown once (for example, at the start of a season), and is only indicated again when the time of transmission changes.

Writer

Among celebrated TV writers who wrote for *The Avengers* were Dennis Spooner (creator of *The Champions*, *Randall and Hopkirk (Deceased)* and *Department S*), Robert Banks Stewart (creator of *Shoestring* and *Bergerac*), and Terry Nation (*Blake's 7, Survivors*). As Brian Clemens notes, 'Between the mid-60s and the early 70s all the episodic film series in this country were being written by about eight writers . . . We'd say to one of them "Can you do us a quick script?" We tended to lean on each other.'

Director

The old videotaped episodes were directed by TV stalwarts like Bill Bain and Don Leaver, but when we get to film, and thus exterior shoots, bigger budgets and greater opportunities for artistic tomfoolery, various important names get in on the act. Ealing comedy veteran Charles Crichton (*A Fish Called Wanda*), Leslie Norman (Barry's Dad) and Robert Fuest (60s pop-art designer and director of *The Final Programme*) become some

4

of the names in the tight little group of directors the show employed.

Guest Cast

Including some surprisingly big names. If somebody appeared in a minor role before going on to wider fame we've often drawn attention to this via a separate category, 'With A Young . . .'. Our information is derived, where ever possible, from on-screen credits.

Brief Plot Description

Then we look at various aspects of the episode in greater detail. The various subheadings we use change somewhat from season to season, often reflecting the changing nature of the programme. We've taken care to provide an indication of the relative importance of the four Important *Avengers* Things in each episode, namely Wit, Kinkiness, Champagne and Fights.

Wit: The series can be seen as a reaction to the late 50s advance of 'kitchen sink drama', even amongst its own writers. The fact that a writer like James Mitchell, who created *When the Boat Comes In* and *Callan*, could also work extensively on an escapist spy series (albeit in the early years) indicates that perhaps there was some element of release from the abiding social concerns of the time, of 'having fun', as it were. First season episodes tended to be more gritty than witty, with their own wry and cynical humour. However, as early as the second season, writers like Roger Marshall and Martin Woodhouse were introducing verbal repartee and satire. (The show was often competing with *That Was the Week That Was* on Saturday nights, and trying to lure the same young, urbane audience.)

In 1964, the series moved from videotape to film, and Emma Peel arrived. Brian Clemens and Philip Levene took *The*

Avengers right to the edge, and hopped precisely and success-fully along that fine line between 'witty' and 'stupid'. Unfor-tunately, when Tara arrived, Clemens fell right over the other side. Many fans regard the seventh season as a failure because it was 'silly', but in fact the problem is exactly the opposite. The scripts suddenly become bereft of wit and verbal humour, and in their place we get ever more bizarre concepts, humorous visual conceits and laboured character play. The character of Mother, widely criticised for being a 'comedy sidekick', is in actual fact a very serious man in a wheelchair. He just happens to be surrounded by surreal visuals and bizarre incidents, pumped up to try and inject some interest into a series of flat and stone-faced scripts.

Kinkiness Factor: So much for political correctness. *The Avengers* was kinky. Sometimes very kinky. Sometimes very feminist as a result, bizarrely. Strong female characters in leather dish out stylised violence to men. And, erm, get tied up a lot. We've listed all this with a sort of resigned glee. Please don't hurt us. Well, not too much anyway.

Champagne: One of the icons on which the series was based, but surprisingly this (very expensive) commodity doesn't really arrive until it becomes part of the title sequence in season five. Of course, it's all over the place in the Tara season as the people in charge make a desperate effort to make it *Avengers*-ish. When there's no champers, we've mentioned other impor-tant alcohol-related things. With all of this boozing going on, it's a wonder the characters weren't too legless to catch the Diabolical Masterminds.

Fights: *The Avengers* made an important contribution to soci-ety in that it popularised the idea of self-defence for women, making it stylish instead of unfeminine. It also introduced a whole new vocabulary to that most visual of artforms, the on-screen punch-up. In Cathy Gale, television had its first fighting woman. In Emma Peel, it had its second. In Tara King it had somebody who could do some damage with a brick in her handbag, but only if her dress didn't get in the way. By the time 'Fights' became 'Violence' in *The New Avengers*, different rules applied. The series was then starting to follow, rather than create, the trends.

60s Concerns: Aspects of particular episodes that either reflected or, in some cases, predicted, what was going on in the real world. The series was made in an era when global mass communication was starting to make society's problems into world affairs. In other words, you don't need to live in England to understand the people in *The Avengers*, because in the 60s the English agenda was suddenly everybody's agenda. The series as a whole tackled sexism, the cold war and class politics, usually by ignoring such issues completely in circumstances where any sane series would have raised them. That's what we call a tackle. *The New Avengers* had less obvious material to work with, and most of their '70s concerns' are hangovers from the 60s. Like the hippy children they were, they're an unhappy breed.

Strangeness: Another standard element of the filmed episodes. We have tried to highlight both intentional strangeness (aspects of surrealism and general strangeness) and unintentionally odd aspects of visual style, script, set designs, etc.

Eccentrics: The mid-period *Avengers* likes to include several per episode, but they thin out before and after. Eccentrics often have names that reflect their obsessions, and occupy uncommercial little shops or stately homes in green-belt Hertfordshire. They either want to rule the world (as Steed says, 'What's

7

so good about that job anyway?') or are killed by those that do.

Medical Subplots: In the David Keel/Martin King episodes, someone often had to get injured in an unusual way to justify Steed involving his GP mates. After a season of this, Cathy or Venus just 'being there' was a welcome change.

Scenes In a Nightclub: Mainly applicable to the Venus episodes (where she'd do a full number with the Dave Lee Trio as a sort of bizarre musical interlude), as it's surprising how few times Emma and Tara went out grooving. Too busy chasing Diabolical Masterminds, no doubt.

Other Categories: Most of our other whims are largely self-explanatory. 'They Leave' refers to the final scene of each fourth-season episode, where Steed and Emma would trundle off in a variety of different modes of transport. *The New Avengers* utilises such headings as 'Gambit's Conquests', 'Fashion Victims' and 'Porno Funk Music Factor' because . . . Well, just because.

Notes: These are used to highlight an episode's strengths or weaknesses, and to provide information on continuity (there is a little) and character development. We also seek to highlight unique elements and running themes, and note the real-life locations of certain episodes or scenes. Most of the location filming was done in the area surrounding Borehamwood. Possibly the most famous *Avengers* location is the bridge that Tara runs across in the season seven title sequence (Emma walks along its wall in 'The Hour That Never Was', and it's also in 'Two's a Crowd', 'You Have Just Been Murdered', 'They Keep Killing Steed' and the sweet opening sequence of 'Honey for the Prince'). It crosses the river Colne just outside

8

Borehamwood. The tiny village of Aldbury, for example, also makes several appearances, becoming Swingingdale in 'Dead Man's Treasure', while nearby Bushby provided the locations for, amongst others, 'Death's Door'. These charming English rural settings no doubt help to explain the continuing fascination with the series, particularly in America.

Occasionally we also feature a 'Trivia' heading for real *Avengers* buffs.

German/French Titles: Dubbed, the series was massively popular in both countries. In Germany it was *Mit Schirm, Charme und Melone* ('With Umbrella, Charm and Bowler') and in France *Chapeau Melon et Bottes de Cuir* ('Bowler Hat and Leather Boots'). Clearly, both preferred titles that reflected aesthetic elements rather than Sydney Newman's more subtle vision. (It could have been worse. *Man in a Suitcase* in France became *Un Homme dans une Valeise*!) We've included some of the odder German and French episode titles.

THE
AVENGERS

First Season

Introduction

It is common knowledge that *The Avengers* began life as a spy-thriller with few of the elements that went on to make it famous across the globe, and yet one remains surprised by just how different this first season is from that which followed. It would be wrong to apply retrospective criteria to it and to criticise it for not being 'proper' *Avengers* from the start, but when episodes deal with the effects of a hurricane or a shipment of rotten fruit, you do begin to wonder what on earth a British agent and his medical 'helper' are doing investigating such rubbish.

Even such gentle questioning is partly misplaced. It is true that such areas would be of trifling importance in the fantasy-land of later *Avengers* seasons, but, of course, in the real world such concerns are of the utmost importance to the individuals involved. And the series wasn't about a shadowy agent and the doctor who helped him, but about a doctor who, after the death of his fiancée, developed an increasing knack for discovering subterfuge and danger in the course of his medical duties. At such times Dr Keel would go to Steed for help. Patrick Macnee's Steed *became* the vital element, and as the series progressed episodes would tend to alternate their emphasis between the two main characters, sometimes being given 'assignments' by Steed's superiors. However, right until the end of this season, Ian Hendry as Dr Keel was the starring performance and, indeed, at the heart of the programme's existence.

The genesis of *The Avengers* lay in the decision of Howard Thomas, the Managing Director of ABC, to approach Sydney Newman, Head of Drama, with a request for something a little lighter than Newman's *Armchair Theatre* to further fill out the schedules. It was 1960, and the style considered was somewhere between Hitchcock's films and the James Bond books (*Dr No*, the first Bond film, was not released until two years later). Ian Fleming's books – like the earliest Bond movies – were gritty, powerful thrillers, tempered by a likeable leading character, glamorous locations and a hint of the unusual. (As with *The Avengers*, the gadget-driven comic-book tomfoolery came later.) *The Avengers* should, Newman felt, bring such a style to television and, whilst there simply wouldn't be the money there to go jetting around the world, Newman always believed that nothing was too difficult if one poured enough enthusiasm and energy into a project.

It seems that the source of that energy was Ian Hendry, already popular through *Police Surgeon*. Patrick Macnee, in a letter to *TV Zone* magazine, described Hendry as 'the fountainhead – the inspiration, the genius'.

Police Surgeon ran for thirteen 30-minute episodes between September and December 1960, with Hendry playing the compassionate Dr Geoffrey Brent. Despite Hendry, though, it seemed to be going nowhere fast, and the style was too mundane, too cops-and-robbers. However, Newman perceived some added frisson in Hendry continuing to play a doctor. He and the producer of the later episodes of *Police Surgeon*, Leonard White, created the character who was to be Dr Keel's link with the Secret Service, John Steed. Other links between the two series include Ingrid Hafner, who appeared in both shows, writer Richard Harris and many technical personnel (directors Don Leaver and Guy Verney, designer Alpho O'Reilly).

Comparing the stories that ensued to Newman and White's 'vision' – at least if White's internal memos are anything to go by – it almost seems that the writers were reticent to fully take on board the ethos that the show was intended to have. A lot of the early plots were fairly conventional and rather too dark; the locations and characters were mundane. Far from featuring 'beautiful, attractive, unusual women', many stories were masculine power-struggles and almost dull to boot. Of 'wit, humour and grace' there was little. In addition, those episodes concentrating on Keel proved much more difficult to write. Although the characters of Keel and Steed were interesting, with their long macs and their tendency to puff on fags they were hardly discernable from other fictional spies of the time.

And yet . . . There was something there. Despite the dull plots involving arson and small-time crooks, the clichéd gangsters and thugs, the occasional groaning lack of wit, White's insistence as to what *The Avengers* should be began to pay off. Dennis Spooner's two scripts stand out as at least fulfilling White's desire to have unusual locations and 'something to intrigue the intelligence, however lightly'. Despite that, and the slightly odd attempts of Peter Ling and Sheilagh Ward to bring glamour into this very male world, the tone was effectively set by the first two stories, which interlocked well with their grim tale of competing drug-peddling gangs. Max Marquis's 'Diamond Cut Diamond' almost seemed to try to out-grit those stories around it, with Steed accused of murder whilst on a 'stake out' in a bungalow once owned by a suicide in One-Ten's department. Of champagne and kinkiness we find, to no one's real surprise, barely a trace. Macnee's insight into the first season is interesting, and again plays up Hendry's unique role: 'It started live, and was entirely based on the skills of Sydney Newman, Peter Hammond, Don Leaver but most of all Ian Hendry because he wasn't just an actor, he was a writer, an innovator – a great and talented man . . . I once saw him take a script and rewrite it from scratch. The writers we had on *The Avengers* were great writers but Ian treated them like hacks, which only made them work harder. We also had some of the best designers in the world: Jim Goddard, Tim O'Brian, Bob

Fuest, just an incredible design department. Together, they helped to create shows that captured the British public's fancy.'

Logic indicates that *The Avengers* should have sunk without trace: after the first season, the star left, and the show had proved only partly successful at bringing its 'unique selling point' to life. It didn't vanish from our screens, and, at its best, the first season gives a tiny hint why.

Transmission Details

The transmission details are as ABC. ABC were almost the only region to broadcast all 26 episodes. Other ITV regions joined during February and March 1961, transmitting recordings of 'Hot Ice' and 'Brought to Book' before joining the ABC networked episodes. From March to September 1961 the series alternated with *Deadline Midnight*. An Equity strike caused the delay between 'Kill the King' and 'Dead of Winter'.

26 b&w episodes (60 mins)
ABC Television

Producer: Leonard White

Script Editors: Patrick Brawn, John Bryce
and Anthony Read (?) (all uncredited)

The Avengers theme composed and
played by Johnny Dankworth

Regular Cast: Ian Hendry
(Dr David Keel, episodes 1–25),
Patrick Macnee
(John Steed, episodes 1–5, 7–20, 22–26),

Ingrid Hafner (Carol Wilson,
episodes 2 – 4, 6 – 3, 15, 16, 18, 20, 22–25)
Douglas Muir (One-Ten, episodes 7, 14, 17, 20, 24).

1

'Hot Snow'

7 January 1961, 10.00pm
Recorded: 30 December 1960
Writer: Ray Rigby
(based on a story by Patrick Brown)
Director: Don Leaver
Guest Cast: Philip Stone (Dr Richard Tredding),
Catherine Woodville (Peggy), Gordon Quigley (Spicer),
Murray Melvin (Charlie), Charles Wade (Johnson),
Alister Williamson (DS Wilson),
Moira Richmond (Stella), Astor Sklair (Sgt Rogers),
June Monkhouse (Mrs Simpson).
Uncredited: Robert James (Ronnie Vance).

Following the death of his fiancée, Peggy, at the hands of a gang of heroin smugglers, Dr David Keel vows to track down the killers and avenge his lost love. He is aided in his quest by a mysterious stranger, John Steed.

Wit: Well, hardly. We've got drug smugglers and the death of a potential female leading character in the opening scenes. There's precious little humour about anything here.

Kinkiness Factor: Keel gives Peggy a playful smack on the bum, but they're engaged, so that's hardly kinky, is it?

Champagne: None.

Fights: ☆☆☆ The climax of the episode sees the shooting of the driver of the gang's car. The others – including the assassin Spicer and the leader 'Big Man' (later revealed to be Ronnie Vance) – escape before the police arrive.

60s Concerns: The availability of, and dangers of involvement with, heroin.

Medical Subplot: In what was to become something of a standard for the early episodes to follow, Keel uses his medical connections to follow a trail to Dr Treading, a recently struck-off GP. It was he – rather than Keel's senior partner Dr Tredding – who was supposed to receive the consignment of 'snow'.

Notes: An intensely grim and gritty first episode to set the series going. Keel begins the episode as a happy-go-lucky young doctor in private practice with a beautiful fiancé, and ends it a more cynical, depressive figure following Peggy's death. At this stage Steed is barely defined: a shadowy figure, through with many of his later traits well intact ('I'm on the side of the angels,' he says at one point).

Interestingly, it is not *explicitly* indicated that Steed saves Keel from the gang, and he plays his 'role' as a gang member right until the last moment. A promising, if somewhat down-beat, start.

Macnee married Woodville in 1965.

2
'Brought to Book'
14 January 1961
Recorded: 12 January 1961
Writer: Brian Clemens

Director: Peter Hammond
Guest Cast: Lionel Burns (Prentice),
Clifford Elkin (Pretty Boy),
Charles Morgan (Nick Mason),
Godfrey Quigley (Spicer),
Philip Stone (Dr Tredding),
Joyce Wong Chong (Lila),
Robert James (Ronnie Vance),
Alister Williamson (DS Wilson),
Michael Collins (Detective Sgt).

Steed has infiltrated a gang, led by Mason, which is implicated in Peggy's murder. Steed asks Keel to establish contact with a rival gang, and the doctor discovers that Vance's hitman, Spicer, has been sent to kill Steed.

Wit: ☆ A rather gloomy tale, typical of first-season *Avengers*, punctuated by Steed's increasingly sardonic wit.

Kinkiness Factor: An almost entirely male story.

Champagne: None: Steed and Keel are more interested in Scotch.

Fights: ☆☆ Keel and Steed have a mock fight in order to capture Spicer. Dr Keel gets a confession out of Spicer by threatening him with a deadly hypodermic.

Medical Subplot: The hypodermic isn't deadly after all, containing a harmless barbituate (a trick the doctor uses on several occasions this season). Keel is asked to attend to Vance's brother, Pretty Boy, who has been flick-knived by Mason.

18

Notes:
    'What's this?'
    'Heroin, old boy. Sit down and I'll tell you the rest.'
The episode begins with a voice-over (Philip Stone) explaining the events of the previous episode as, until the final *New Avengers* season, these first two stories are as close as *The Avengers* ever came to a two-part story. Steed describes himself as a 'kind of civil servant'.

3
'Square Root of Evil'
21 January 1961, live
Writer: Richard Harris
Director: Don Leaver
Guest Cast: Heron Carvic ('5'),
Cynthia Bizeray (Secretary),
George Murcell (Hooper), Vic Wise (Jackie Warren),
Alex Scott (The Cardinal), Delphi Lawrence (Lisa).

Steed impersonates Riordan, a forger soon to be released from prison, and gains the trust of gang-leader Hooper. Things seem to be going well until Hooper's second-in-command, known as the Cardinal, announces that Riordan's girlfriend is outside waiting to see him.

Wit: ✩✩ 'Timothy James Riordan. Oh my little Irish mother. Profession: master forger. Delicate fingers – I'd better get a manicure.'

Kinkiness Factor: The Cardinal 'teaching his wife a lesson' is unpleasant rather than kinky. According to the dialogue, Steed was unable to intervene.

Champagne: Steed, 'playing' forger Riordan, refuses a drink. When he injures his hand he asks Carol for a double Scotch, though.

Fights: ☆☆☆ A large-scale fight towards the end in a printing room.

Strangeness: '5' (*Prisoner*esque), the Cardinal: the names are getting just a little bizarre. '5' is Steed's first boss, and is briefly referred to as One-Five. The Cardinal (real name Jimmy Bishop) dresses as a Chicago gangster.

Medical Subplot: Steed makes the most of his injured hand in order to contact Keel.

With a Young . . . : John Woodvine (Steve Bloom).

Notes: As with many stories this season, Steed's department's relationship with the (uniformed) police is a good deal more straightforward than it later became.

4
'Nightmare'
28 January 1961, live
Writer: Terence Feely
Director: Peter Hammond
Guest Cast: Gordon Boyd (Williams),
Helen Lindsay (Faith Braintree),
Michael Logan (Commander Reece),
Robert Bruce (Dr Brown), Redmond Bailey (Dr Jones),
Robert Sansom (Dr Miller).

Keel receives a phone call from one of his patients, and ends up assuming the identity of her missing husband, a scientist engaged in secret research. Shot in the chest, Keel needs a minor operation – but the anaesthetist has tampered with the oxygen.

Kinkiness Factor: ☆ Carol is tied up for the first time.

Fights: ☆☆

Medical Subplot: For once, Keel is on the receiving end of an operation.

Notes: Early signs that the series was a little different from those around it emerge in this story, with its complex plot concerning a fake MI5 agent and a deadly anaesthetist.

5
'Crescent Moon'
4 February 1961, live
Working Title: 'Kidnapping by Consent'
Writers: Geoffrey Bellman and John Whitney
Director: John Knight
Guest Cast: Patience Collier (Senora Mendoza),
Harold Kasket (Bartello),
Bandana Das Gupta (Carmelite Mendoza),
Nicholas Amer (Luis Alvarez), Jack Rodney (Fernandez),
Roger Delgado (Vasco), George Roderick (Policeman).

A young girl, Carmelite Mendoza, has been kidnapped from a Caribbean island, but Steed suspects a political motive. His suspicions are confirmed when Vasco, the Mendoza family retainer, is observed killing the original kidnapper and abducting the girl himself.

Fights: ☆

Medical Subplot: Keel tends General Mendoza in London.

With a Young . . . : Eric (*Magic Roundabout*) Thompson (Paul).

Notes: In a great liberal statement, a large number of ethnic actors were employed for this episode.

6
'Girl on the Trapeze'
11 February 1961, live
Working Title: 'The Man on the Trapeze'
Writer: Dennis Spooner
Director: Don Leaver
Guest Cast: Delena Kidd (Vera),
Naja Regin (Anna Danilov), Kenneth J. Warren (Zibbo),
Howard Goorney (Supt. Lewis),
Edwin Richfield (Stefan).

Keel, reviving a young woman who has jumped into the Thames, is led to the Radeck State Circus, where the trapeze girl is guarded, her face covered by bandages because of an accident. The 'trapeze girl' proves to be the daughter of a defecting scientist, who will be used to force her father to return home. When Keel discovers this, he and Carol are captured by Zibbo the Clown, who will shoot Carol if the police investigation is not called off.

Wit: ☆

Fights: ☆

Strangeness: Trust Dennis Spooner to bring just a hint of weirdness to what was fast becoming a standard spy romp. It was at about this time that Leonard White drew up a memo for the writers reminding them, among other things, that the locales should be unusual and exciting. The introductory sequences – with a young woman jumping into the Thames and a different girl being pulled out – also carried more than a hint of the paradoxical quirkiness that was to come. A good solo episode for Keel.

7
'Diamond Cut Diamond'
18 February 1961, live
Writer: Max Marquis
Director: Peter Hammond
Guest Cast: Sandra Dorne (Fiona Charles),
Hamlyn Benson (Dr Collard),
Joy Webster (Stella Creighton).

Steed, attempting to break a gang of international diamond smugglers, is living in a bungalow near Heathrow Airport which was once owned by a suicide whom One-Ten suspects of involvement. Steed awakes one morning, somewhat the worse for drink, when a phone call advises him to check the morning paper: the police are tracking a hit-and-run driver. Steed checks his car: it is damaged, and the front is covered with dried blood.

Wit: The central ideas are much too nasty.

Champagne: Probably not even at the hypothetical 'party the night before'.

Fights: ☆

Medical Subplot: Keel runs a series of tests on Steed and concludes that he was given a massive dose of barbiturates the previous night and therefore couldn't have driven the car.

Notes: The first episode to feature One-Ten.

8
'The Radioactive Man'
25 February 1961, live
Writer: Fred Edge
Director: Robert Tronson
Guest Cast: George Pravda (Marko Ogrin),
Christine Pollon (Mary Somers),
Gerald Sim (Dr Graham).

Dr Keel is asked to help in the search for a man who has picked up a radioactive isotope, not knowing that it will quickly kill him and harm anyone else he comes into contact with. But Marko, fearing that the police want to find him because of his forged passport, has already gone into hiding.

Fights: Not a sausage: at the end Keel and Marko's girlfriend are able to persuade the man away from a shoot-out with the police.

60s Concerns: The deadly effects of radiation.

Medical Subplot: Keel learns the true extent of the danger posed by the isotope from Dr Graham, head of the top-secret Medical Research Laboratory.

Notes: As *Edge of Darkness* and various real-life cases have shown, this tale had a strong hint of reality about it. It also managed to portray the plight of the immigrant worker with some degree of sympathy.

9
'Ashes of Roses'
4 March 1961, live
Writers: Peter Ling and Sheilagh Ward
Director: Don Leaver
Guest Cast: Olga Lowe (Olive Beronne),
Mark Eden (Jacques Beronne),
Peter Zander (Johnny Mendelssohn),
Hedi Erich (Denise).

Steed, investigating a number of probable arson cases, is led to the hairdressing salon of Olive and Jacques Beronne. He asks Keel to let Carol investigate the salon, but, after she enters, there is an explosion from within.

Fights: Hardly: a salon assistant is strangled off-screen and Steed knocks out Mendelssohn before he can light an incendiary bomb.

Notes: A year before *Compact* and three before *Crossroads*, Peter Ling introduces a hint of glamour into the drab world of the early *Avengers*. Still, it's all a bit predictable, with the salon owners hoping to avoid bankruptcy by claiming on the insurance when the place is burnt down. Emma Peel wouldn't even lower herself to investigate such a cheesy establishment. Steed endangers Carol's life in an attempt to trap the arsonist, and Keel berates him for this. However, Keel ends up taking Steed's Great Dane, 'Puppy', for a walk so that Steed and Carol can go out for the evening.

The *TV Times* reported that the filming of this story afforded Hendry the opportunity to mince around with scissors and comb to keep the cast amused.

10
'Hunt the Man Down'
18 March 1961
Recorded: 12 March 1961
Writer: Richard Harris
Director: Peter Hammond
Guest Cast: Maurice Good (Paul Stacey),
Melissa Stribling (Stella Preston),
Susan Castle (Nurse Wyatt).

Frank Preston is released from prison and is intent on reclaiming the hidden proceeds of his robbery. So is Steed, who has been ordered to follow the man. So are a couple of thugs, who kidnap Carol. So is Preston's scheming wife, eager to get her hands on the £100,000 hidden somewhere in the sewers.

Kinkiness Factor: ✩ Carol is tied up and kidnapped. Again. Perhaps we should describe her in future as Keel's secretary and everybody else's hostage? Little wonder that in mid-season it was ordered that her role be 'beefed up' a little.

Fights: ✩ Steed rescues Frank Preston, who's on the receiving

26

end of a damn good going-over from the thugs, Stacey and Rocky. And, though it doesn't really count, there are some nice chases through the sewers.

Medical Subplot: Keel tends to Frank Preston's wounds. Twice.

Notes: This episode, the first in its new fortnightly format, saw a *TV Times* cover in some regions and a new set for Keel's surgery.

11
'Please Don't Feed the Animals'
1 April 1961, 8.35pm
Recorded: 30 March 1961
Writer: Dennis Spooner
Director: Dennis Vance
Guest Cast: Tenniel Evans (Felgate),
Carole Boyer (Christine), Harry Ross (Kollakis),
Alastair Hunter (Renton-Stephens),
Catherine Ellison (Yvonne),
Genevieve Lyons (Sarah), Mark Baker (Barman),
Richard Neller (Evans), Charles Bird (Harrigan).

Steed trails a blackmailed civil servant to Brinkley House, a private zoo, only to observe the man throwing a package of money into the reptile pit. The package soon vanishes. The man is then ordered to steal a top secret file.

Wit: ✩✩ Almost loses a point for the 'How do porcupines make love?' joke at the end.

Kinkiness Factor: ✩✩✩ Strip clubs and strippers.

Fights: ✩✩ A mock-drunken fight at the strip club, and a tussle at the end.

Strangeness: The 'contact' is a trained monkey.

Eccentrics: Jimmy the monkey, probably.

Medical Subplot: Steed and Keel sport bruises after saving Felgate from the blackmailers at the strip club. Carol asks Steed if he's seen a doctor . . .

Notes: Steed allows himself to be compromised at the Bromango Strip Club in Soho so that he too can be 'blackmailed' (he has an 'adventure' with Yvonne, a stripper). That shouldn't have been too much of a struggle for him. Once again, all credit to Dennis Spooner: you can keep your hair salons and smelly sewers, let's have a subversive monkey and blackmailing strippers!

12
'Dance with Death'
15 April 1961, 10.00pm
Recorded: 13 April 1961
Writers: Peter Ling and Sheilagh Ward
Director: Don Leaver
Guest Cast: David Sutton (Trevor Price),
Angela Douglas (Beth Wilkinson),
Ewan Roberts (Major Caswell),
Pauline Shepherd (Valerie Marne),
Diana King (Mrs Marne), Norman Chappell (Porter).

Dr Keel resuscitates Elaine Bateman, the owner of a ballroom dancing school who has narrowly survived a murder attempt by gassing. When he returns to the school after dropping his scarf, he is arrested: his scarf has been used to strangle the woman.

Kinkiness Factor: Electrocuting a woman in a bath is just too 'real life' and nasty.

Fights: Good grief, this is partly set in a school for ballroom dancing, and you expect fights?

Medical Subplot: Only in as much as his treatment of Elaine Bateman gets Keel embroiled in the whole sordid mess. Don't you think he should take up an alternative career? Would you be his patient?

With a Young ... : Caroline Blakiston (Elaine Bateman), Geoffrey Palmer (Philip Anthony).

13
'One for the Mortuary'
29 April 1961
Recorded: 26 April 1961
Writer: Brian Clemens
Director: Peter Hammond
Guest Cast: Peter Madden (Benson),
Ronald Wilson (Scott), Dennis Edwards (Pallaine),
Malou Pantera (Yvette Declair),
Frank Gatliff (Dubois), Irene Bradshaw (Maid),
Toke Townley (Bernard Bourg).

When Keel attends a health conference in Geneva he is unaware that he is carrying, in microdot form, a vital new medical formula – unaware, that is, until he is arrested for murder.

Wit: ☆

Medical Subplot: Keel treats a girl on the plane over to Geneva and for once she doesn't come to a sticky end five minutes later.

14
'The Springers'
13 May 1961
Recorded: 11 May 1961
Writers: John Whitney and Geoffrey Bellman
Director: Don Leaver
Guest Cast: David Webb (Pheeney),
Charles Farrell (Straker), Brian Murphy (Haslam),
Arthur Howard (Mr Groves),
Margo Andrew (Caroline Evans),
Donald Morley (Neame).

Steed is trying to track down the organisers of a group who offer to spring any convict – even the dangerous ones – from prison if they're paid the right money. Keel impersonates a prisoner, and the trail seems to lead to a girl's finishing school . . .

Kinkiness Factor: None, but one can only wonder what would have happened to this plot if it were made later.

Fights: ☆

15
'The Frighteners'
27 May 1961
Recorded: 25 May 1961
Writer: Berkely Mather
Director: Peter Hammond
Guest Cast: Willoughby Goddard (The Deacon),
Philip Gilbert (Jeremy de Willoughby),
David Andrews (Nigel),
Stratford Johns (Sir Thomas Waller),
Dawn Beret (Marilyn Waller), Doris Hare (Mrs Briggs),
Godfrey Jones (Nature Boy), Neil Wilson (Beppi),
Eric Elliot (Butler), Ann Taylor (Secretary),
Ralph Tovey (Waiter), Benn Simons (Insp. Foster).
With: Eleanor Darling, Benny Nightingale,
Victor Charrington, Frank Peters, Charles Wood.

To stop his daughter seeing suspected conman Jeremy de
Willoughby, Sir Thomas Waller has hired arch criminal the
Deacon to 'put the frighteners on'. Steed is on the trail of the
Deacon and, with the aid of Dr Keel, stops two thugs from
seriously wounding de Willoughby. They set a trap for the
Deacon . . . and the lovers.

Wit: ☆☆☆ 'I suffer under the disability of a public-school
eduction,' notes Steed, forcing entry into a chemist's. One of
Steed's snouts, Nature Boy, is dressed as a bus conductor and,
having given his information, asks Steed: 'Know where I can
get a bus to Wembley Park?' Keel, after he has been asked to
take the unconscious Moxon and de Willoughby back to his
surgery, notes: 'We'd better get these boys there quickly before
anybody else passes out. It's only a small surgery!'

Kinkiness Factor: Moxon enjoys his violence but little else.

Champagne: ☆ A first for the series. Keel has a bottle for de Willoughby and Marilyn. Steed, however, prefers 'a large brandy with a small soda'!

Fights: ☆ A stagey (almost balletic) attack on de Willoughby by Moxon and croney (with knuckle-dusters) before Steed and Keel arrive and beat off the thugs. Keel chillingly threatens the Deacon with hydrochloric acid for information (the hypodermic really contains lemonade) and convinces Moxon that he has a broken neck with a load of medical double-speak.

60s Concerns: Extortion rackets.

Strangeness: Keel meets Steed in the back of 'Fred's taxi' for briefing. The Deacon's headquarters are in a vault behind a chemist's. Steed and Keel pet a stray cat in Chelsea as they hunt their quarry. Nigel, de Willoughby's friend, plays classical guitar while de Willoughby explains his plans of deception.

Medical Subplot: Keel has to treat Moxon after laying him out. When threatening Waller with exposure over his use of criminals, Keel tells the industrialist to get his blood pressure checked.

With a Young . . . : Philip Locke (Moxon).

Notes: 'Give 'im the real frighteners!' One of the few early episodes to have survived, this is great fun. There is much (seemingly authentic) use of criminal-speak, a superb villain in the Deacon, and a complex finale in which Steed and Keel outwit everybody with the help of an actress and the police. Steed speaks Italian fluently when arresting the shop owner

Beppi. Lovers of later *Avengers* episodes should note that both a uniformed policeman *and* a black man appear in successive scenes.

16
'The Yellow Needle'
10 June 1961
Recorded: 8 June 1961
Writer: Patrick Campbell
Director: Don Leaver
Guest Cast: Andre Dakar (Sir Wilberforce Lungi),
Eric Dodson (Insp. Anthony),
Margaret Whiting (Jacquetta Brown),
Bari Johnson (Chief Bai Shebro), Wolfe Morris (Ali).

After an unsuccessful murder attempt against Sir Wilberforce Lungi, Steed asks Keel, an old friend of the pro-Western African leader, to investigate Lungi's secretary, Jacquetta Brown. Meanwhile, Steed flies to Africa to meet Lungi's tribalist rival, Shebro.

60s Concerns: Independence movements in Africa.

Strangeness: Black people and non-Western issues in *The Avengers* (even early *Avengers*) is a tad odd.

17
'Death on the Slipway'
24 June 1961, 8.50pm
Recorded: 22 June 1961

Writer: James Mitchell
Director: Peter Hammond
Guest Cast: Peter Arne (Kolchek),
Frank Thornton (Sir William Bonner),
Nyree Dawn Porter (Liz Wells),
Paul Dawkins (Sam Pearson), Sean Sullivan (Fleming),
Redmond Bailey (Geordie Wilson),
Robert G. Bahey (Jack),
Barry Keegan (Insp. Georgeson),
Gary Watson (Pardoe), Patrick Conner (PC Geary),
Hamilton Dyce (Sgt Brodie), Billy Milton (Chandler).

An agent has been killed at the secret dockyard where submarines are built. Steed investigates, and finds that a foreign spy has been arranging 'accidents' for him.

Fights: ☆ There's a bit of a tussle towards the end involving a gun and a bomb-laden briefcase.

With a Young . . . : Tom Adams (PC Butterworth).

Notes: The location of this tale is not dissimilar to Mitchell's scripts for *The Troubleshooters* some years later.

18
'Double Danger'
8 July 1961
Recorded: 6 July 1961
Writer: Gerald Verner
Director: Roger Jenkins
Guest Cast: Charles Hodgson (Mark Crawford),
Robert Mill (Harry Drew), Peter Reynolds (Al Brady),

Ronald Pember (Bert Mills),
Vanda Hudson (Lola Carrington),
Kevin Brennan (Bruton),
Gordon Phillott (Bartholomew).

Keel, called to deal with a man seriously injured by an accident, quickly discovers that the man is suffering from gunshot wounds, and that he may be implicated in a recent diamond robbery.

Fights: ☆ In which Keel escapes from the bad guys. Hurrah!

Medical Subplot: Does Keel ever deal with mundane injuries? Anyway, when forced to treat Mace, the injured man, Keel is able to send a prescription to Carol, including the cryptic phrase 'Fonus Equus': 'Phone Steed'. Geddit?

19
'Toy Trap'
22 July 1961
Recorded: 20 July 1961
Writer: Bill Strutton
Director: Don Leaver
Guest Cast: Hazel Graeme (May Murton),
Tony van Bridge (Henry Burge),
Nina Marriott (Alice), Sally Smith (Bunty Seton),
Ann Tirard (Mrs McCabe), Brandon Brady (Freddie),
Brian Jackson (Johnnie), Lionel Burns (Photographer),
Tex Fuller (Lennie Taylor), Mitzi Rogers (Ann).

Keel is asked by the improbably named Bunty to help her find her missing friend. What is the connection between the department store where the women work and a call-girl racket?

Kinkiness Factor: ☆☆ Pretty tame by today's standards perhaps but in 1961 even the suggestion of a call-girl racket was hot stuff.

60s Concerns: Call-girl rackets, of course.

Medical Subplot: Bunty just so happens to be the daughter of a country doctor who Keel knows.

Notes: One of the first instances of *The Avengers* getting in ahead of reality. It would be another two years before the Ward/Profumo case brought the sleazy twilight world of the call-girl into public focus. We can only speculate on Steed's interest in such a case. The conclusion takes place in the toy department of a large store (thus the title), and sees Keel almost give Steed a long overdue thumping for his callous treatment of others, in this case Bunty.

20
'The Tunnel of Fear'
5 August 1961
Recorded: 3 August 1961
Writer: John Kruse
Director: Guy Verney
Guest Cast: Stanley Platts (Maxie Lardner),
John Salew (Jack Wickram),
Murray Hayne (Harry Black), Doris Rogers (Mrs Black),
Nancy Roberts (Madame Zenobia),
Miranda Connell (Claire), Douglas Rye (Billy),
Morris Perry (Sergeant).

Top-secret information is finding its way into the wrong hands, and the source seems to be a south coast fairground. Steed succeeds in getting hypnotised and winds up in the ghost- train tunnel. With frightening results, of course.

Kinkiness Factor: Steed and Claire get tied up in said tunnel, but let's not clutch at straws.

Fights: ☆ Steed pretends he has an explosive cigarette.

Strangeness: It's set in Southend.

Medical Subplot: Keel is treating someone for cuts, and - guess what? – it's not little Jimmy Smith who's fallen over and grazed his knee. It's escaped con Harry Black. Well, of course.

Notes: Kruse submitted a script to *The Avengers* production team in January 1965 entitled 'The Day It Rained Poets', which was turned down.

21
'The Far Distant Dead'
19 August 1961
Recorded: 14 August 1961
Writer: John Lucarotti
Director: Peter Hammond
Guest Cast: Reed de Rouen (Luis Garcia),
Katharine Blake (Dr Ampara Alverez Sandoval),
Francis de Wolff (Hercule Zeebrugge),
Tom Adams (Rayner), Andrew Malandrinos (Godoy),
Michael Mellinger (Mateos),
Guy Deghy (Insp. Gauvreau).

Dr Keel, treating the victims of a cyclone-struck Mexican village, uncovers a number of food-poisonings: emergency cooking oil is, in fact, hydraulic fluid.

Strangeness: Hercule Zeebrugge. What a great name.

Medical Subplot: Not surprisingly, the attempts made by Keel and fellow doctor Sandoval to treat the victims of the disaster.

Notes: Sandoval tries to kill the financier who caused all the deaths; Keel – not directly employed by the forces of law and order, of course – lets her go before calling the police to deal with the crook. Sydney Newman was, apparently, not enamoured of Lucarotti's tough, solo-Keel script.

22
'Kill the King'
2 September 1961
Recorded: 30 August 1961
Writer: James Mitchell
Director: Roger Jenkins
Guest Cast: Burt Kwouk (King Tenuphon),
James Goei (Prince Serrakit),
Patrick Allen (Gen. Tuke), Lisa Peake (Mei Li),
Moira Redmond (Zoe Carter),
Ian Colin (Major Harrington),
Carole Shelley (Ingrid Storm), Andy Ho (U Meng),
Eric Young (Suchong).

A visit to London to sign an oil treaty from a monarch whose life is under threat brings Steed and Keel into the world of dissidents and assassinations.

Wit: ☆

Fights: No, but lots of guns . . .

60s Concerns: Political assassination.

Strangeness: The use of the sound of a helicopter to draw the King and his party on to their hotel balcony. Obvious, but effective.

Medical Subplot: None except for the confirmation that Serrakit has been shot, and you hardly need to be David Keel to work that out.

With a Young . . . : Peter Barkworth (Crichton-Bull).

Notes: An unusual subject in 1961, James Mitchell's script took on a macabre predictability two years later when another complex plot centred on the shooting of a world statesman. A large proportion of oriental actors is in evidence, very liberated for the era. Mitchell and Jenkins would later work together extensively on *The Troubleshooters*.

23
'Dead of Winter'
9 December 1961, 10.00pm
Working Title: 'The Case of the Happy Camper'
Recorded: 7 September 1961
Writer: Eric Paice
Director: Don Leaver
Guest Cast: John Woodvine (Harry),
Blaise Wyndham (Syd), Carl Duering (Schneider),

David Hart (Dr Brennan), Sheila Robins (Inez),
Michael Sarne (Willi), Zorenah Osborne (Margarita),
Neil Hallett (Weber), Norman Chappell (Ted),
Arnold Marle (Kreuzer).

The discovery of the body of Schneider, a wanted Nazi war criminal, deep-frozen in a consignment of meat at London docks brings Steed and Keel into the shadowy world of Phoenix, a new and terrifying Fascist party in Britain.

Wit: ☆

Fights: ☆☆ At the docks, Steed is attacked by Kreuzer's henchmen until his patriotic speech to the dockers, Harry and Syd (whose accents match their obviously working-class names), has the desired effect.

60s Concerns: The return of Fascism. Cryogenics.

Medical Subplot: An autopsy is arranged for the frozen body but, when Steed and Keel arrive at the mortuary, they find the body gone and the pathologist dead.

Notes: A serious subject treated somewhat lightly, especially at the end when having destroyed Phoenix, Steed rescues Keel from his cold-room prison where he was to be the next recipient of Kreuzer's cryogenic experiments. The doctor's only after-effect is a cold.

24
'The Deadly Air'
16 December 1961
Recorded: 20 September 1961
Writer: Lester Powell
Director: John Knight
Guest Cast: Ann Bell (Barbara Anthony),
Michael Hawkins (Dr Philip Karswood),
Keith Anderson (Heneger),
Richard Butler (Hervert Truscott),
Allan Cuthbertson (Dr Hugh Chalk),
John Stratton (Dr Owen Craxton),
Cyril Renison (Dr Harvey),
Anthony Cundell (Ken Armstrong),
Geoffrey Bayldon (Professor Kilbride).

An experimental vaccine is stolen, and the subsequent test proves deadly. Steed and Keel, suspecting that the human 'guinea pig' did not die directly from the vaccine, volunteer to be the next subjects.

60s Concerns: Vaccines.

Medical Subplot: The whole episode is set in a top secret medical facility.

25
'A Change of Bait'
23 December 1961
Recorded: 27 September 1961
Writer: Lewis Davidson
Director: Don Leaver

Guest Cast: Victor Platt (Archie Duncan),
John Bailey (Lemuel Potts),
Henry Soskin (Peter Sampson),
Robert Desmond (Herb Thomson),
Graham Rigby (Nat Fletcher), Gary Hope (Barker),
Arthur Barrett (André), Norman Pitt (Bryan Stubbs),
Gillian McCutcheon (Ivy), Harry Shacklock (Charlie),
Michael Hunt (Steed's Helper).

An epic and sprawling tale of heart disease, industrial unrest, and a consignment of rotten bananas. Honest.

Strangeness: That this entire plot is based around a man with a serious heart complaint who wants to sell a shipment of bananas. A perfect example of the mundane nature of some of the things that Steed and Keel investigate.

Medical Subplot: Keel tends to Archie when he has a heart attack.

26
'Dragonsfield'
30 December 1961
Working Title: 'The Un-Dead'
Recorded: 18 October 1961
Writer: Terence Feely
Director: Peter Hammond
Guest Cast: Sylvia Langova (Lisa Strauss),
Alfred Burke (Saunders),
Ronald Leigh-Hunt (Reddington),
Barbara Shelley (Susan Summers),
Thomas Kyffin (Jack Alford),

**Amanda Reeves (Secretary),
Eric Dodson (One-Fifteen), Steven Scott (Boris),
Michael Robbins (Landlord), Herbert Nelson (Peters),
Morris Perry (Second Technician).**

How has a research centre developing radiation-proof material managed to irradiate one of its scientists? Once more, Steed submits himself to scientific testing.

Fights: Some minor skirmishing, including Susan trying to strangle Lisa at the end.

Eccentrics: None in the story itself, but the episode's designer was called Voytek.

With a Young . . . : Keith Barron (Technician).

Second Season

Introduction

Evolution, not revolution. That's what the second season of *The Avengers* is all about. Despite the first season coming to an abrupt halt, the intention was to begin a new batch of episodes under the heading 'business as usual'. There was one new development, although it was originally planned for the 27th episode of the 39 episode first season that an Equity strike curtailed after 26: the introduction of Venus Smith. She was a nightclub singer, and very much an innocent in the spying games perpetuated by Steed. Her episodes would begin to alternate with Keel's, an implicit acknowledgement that the series had become Steed's.

The auditions were held in August 1962, and amongst the 51 applicants were Kathy Kirby, Shirley Eaton, Sally Bazely, Anita Harris and Millicent Martin. Angela Douglas, Vera Day and Julie Stevens were shortlisted, although Douglas, the first choice, proved to be unavailable. The following month Julie Stevens signed up to play Venus Smith.

With the departure of Ian Hendry between seasons to pursue a cinema career, producer Leonard White had a number of Keel stories already on his desk. Some were given to a new doctor character, Martin King, which explains why he doesn't really get an introductory story. In 'Mission to Montreal', his first story, it's as if Steed and King have known each other for years, much to the viewer's puzzlement.

In addition, one suspects that Leonard White was keen to gently push the series in a quirkier, more immediately attention-grabbing direction. In the second season, then, we see an increase in odd characters, strange locations and introductory sequences to really grab the attention of the viewers. Of course, this happens in a fairly piecemeal fashion, with some episodes definitely looking to the grim escapades of the first season for inspiration, whilst others, notably 'Death of a Great Dane', would not have been out of place in subsequent seasons. (It's hardly surprising that 'Great Dane' was re-made in the second colour Rigg season.) But White, with another 26 episodes at his disposal, was happy for such changes of emphasis to take place gently.

Evolution, not revolution – with one important exception, the Gale Force called Cathy. Circumstances conspired to produce what was probably the only valid way of creating a strong female character at that time: giving an actress a man's lines. The character was created by White and Newman, and three actors were shortlisted: Fenella Fielding (who later appeared in 'The Charmers'), Honor Blackman (whom Newman did not want), and Nyree Dawn Porter (whom Newman did). Prior commitments meant that Porter was unable to accept the role; Newman returned from a holiday in June 1962 to find that Blackman had been signed up for four episodes, with the possibility of a further twelve by January 1963.

Honor Blackman playing an action-orientated, decision-making Keel-equivalent in scripts that were already written proved to be revelational, a rare example of television challenging the preconceptions of an age. However, the moment the writers knew they were writing for a woman, the scripts became soft and flaccid and in need of strong, radical input (which, thankfully, they usually received). Over a period of time, with Mrs Gale on the screen, the writers knew exactly what they were doing. One can only say that Honor Blackman seemed to know what she was about from the very start.

In early-60s TV (and one might sometimes cynically think things often aren't different today) a woman might scream if attacked, and that was about it. If she had a brain, it was a quirky

45

anomaly rather than something to be expected. Imagine, then, a woman striding through a thriller/spy series, efficiently shooting the villains. The ridiculous practicalities of this – miniature pistols in handbags or a gun tucked into a garter (by golly that's feminist) – combined with the morality of her character (unlike Steed she is not a cold professional) eventually led her to dispense with firearms. Their place was taken by judo, i.e. a woman actually flinging a man about. This was exponential radicalism.

Patrick Macnee has spoken in some detail about Cathy Gale's impact on the series: 'Women are not women but persons. The fact that we're the opposite sex just enables the race to continue and causes, hopefully, a lot of pleasure between both parties. So that shows in *The Avengers*. On the other hand, we had our own caprices. We had Honor Blackman in black leather, partly because it was better than wearing skirts when she was doing lots of violent action. It was an idea before its time to show women in the positive sense and not in the repressive, submissive sense, and I found that exciting and interesting. We used a lot of sexual fetishes – leather, bondage, whatever – in a very, very light way. In other words we titillated.'

Equally important was the fact that this (sexual) force came from a woman who, from the start, was portrayed as being PhD material were it not for the practicalities of life (in this case, falling in love with a white African farmer). If this cosy yet adventurous domesticity (which came to a tragic end) can be perceived as diluting Mrs Gale as a radical statement, it did at least allow a background in which she would have acted like a man (e.g. used guns and mended engines) in a very male world. Without Mrs Gale it is impossible to speculate how popular *The Avengers* would have been, or how long it would have lasted: but it would certainly have been a very different show.

Top five episodes: 'Death of a Great Dane'
                      'Warlock'
                      'Bullseye'
                      'Mr Teddy Bear'
                      'The Decapod'

Transmission Details

The transmission details are as ABC, and the season was generally networked.

26 b&w episodes (60 mins)
ABC Television

Producer: Leonard White (episodes 27–40),
John Bryce (episodes 41–52)

Story Editors: John Bryce (episodes 27–40, 44),
Richard Bates (episodes 41–43, 45–52)

The Avengers theme composed and played
by Johnny Dankworth

Regular Cast: Patrick Macnee (John Steed),
Honor Blackman (Catherine Gale,
episodes 27, 28, 30, 33, 34, 36–39, 41, 42, 44,
45, 47, 49, 51, 52),
Julie Stevens (Venus Smith,
episodes 29, 32, 43, 46, 48, 50),
Jon Rollason (Dr Martin King,
episodes 31, 35, 40),
Douglas Muir (One-Ten,
episodes 27, 32, 39, 42, 44).

27
'Mr Teddy Bear'

29 September 1962, 10.05pm
Recorded: 4 August 1962
Writer: Martin Woodhouse
Director: Richmond Harding
Guest Cast: Tim Brinton (Interviewer),
Kenneth Keeling (Col. Wayne-Gilley),
John Horsley (Dr Gilmore),
Michael Collins (Technician), Michael Robbins (Henry),
Bernard Goldman (Mr Teddy Bear),
Sarah Maxwell (Café Girl),
John Ruddock (Dr James Howell).

A man is murdered whilst being interviewed on live television. One-Ten is sure that it is the work of the ruthless assassin Mr Teddy Bear, and he asks Cathy Gale to trap the man – by arranging for him to murder Steed.

Wit: ☆☆

Kinkiness Factor: ☆ An honorary star for being the first episode to feature Gale and the leather 'action suit'.

Fights: Mr Teddy Bear is much too clever to engage in mere fisticuffs.

60s Concerns: Hired killers.

Strangeness: When Cathy steals Mr Teddy Bear's cigarette case it carries only the fingerprints of a chimp. His plan to kill Steed is great: covering a telephone with poison and then ringing up Steed to tell him that, in picking up the phone, he's now dead . . .

Eccentrics: Mr Teddy Bear, who communicates to Cathy through (of course) a voice-link to a toy teddy.

Cathy Undercover?: Not really.

Notes: An excellently plotted thriller. The season begins as it ought to have gone on: a chilling introductory sequence, a hint of weirdness, a great villain.

28
'Propellant 23'
6 October 1962
Recorded: 21 July 1962
Writer: Jon Manchip White
Director: Jonathan Alwyn
Guest Cast: Frederick Schiller (Jules Meyer),
Justine Lord (Jeanette), Michael Beint (Co-Pilot),
Geoffrey Palmer (Paul Manning),
Catherine Woodville (Laure),
Trader Faulkner (Jacques Tissot),
John Crocker (Lt 'Curly' Leclerc),
John Dearth (Siebel), Ralph Nossek (Roland),
Barry Wilsher (Pierre), Graham Ashley (Gendarme),
Deanne Shenderey (Shop Assistant), John Gill (Baker).

At Marseilles airport, Steed and Cathy find the courier they were due to meet dead. His sample of new liquid rocket fuel has been taken. Facing an array of enemy agents, the duo must recover the flask of Propellant 23.

Wit: ☆☆☆ Steed, waiting for the airport to clear so that he can break in: 'Come on, come on, haven't you got homes to go to?'

Cathy: 'Do you always arrange to take your calls in the lingerie department?'

Steed: 'If humanly possible.'

Kinkiness Factor: ☆☆☆ As you have probably guessed, Steed and Cathy meet in the lingerie department of a Paris store. Steed fondles a pair of lace knickers while Cathy glares at him and tells him that black is so 'obvious'. Cathy, keeping her gun in her garter, flashes some thigh.

Champagne: No, but some French wine.

Fights: ☆☆ Steed is attacked by the agent Siebel whilst breaking into the room where the briefcase is being kept by the police. At the climax, Steed disarms Manning with a blow from his umbrella.

60s Concerns: Cheap fuel.

Strangeness: Steed and Cathy discover the hotel tout, Jacques, getting drunk in a deserted bakery.

Eccentrics: Lieutenant 'Curly' Leclerc, a bald French police officer who is given a bottle of hair-restorer which secretly contains the rocket fuel. Needless to say all of his hair falls out at the climax.

With a Young . . . : Nicholas Courtney (Capt. Legros).

Notes: A well-presented Riviera setting. Much use of red herrings with various different characters possessing flasks which they believe contain the rocket fuel. A French farce, no doubt? Cathy is staying with friends in Toulon and gives Steed a lecture on Third World famine in which Steed shows rather callous disinterest. Justine Lord has a smashing French accent but most of the other characters speak perfect Queen's English!

29
'The Decapod'
13 October 1962
Recorded: 12 August 1962
Writer: Eric Paice
Director: Don Leaver
Guest Cast: Pamela Conway (Girl in Shower),
Paul Stassino (Yakob Borb), Philip Madoc (Stepan),
Douglas Robinson/Valentino Musetti (Bodyguards),
Valerie Stanton (Cigarette Girl),
Lynne Furlong (Edna Ramsden), Wolfe Morris (Ito),
Raymond Adamson (Harry Ramsden),
Harvey Ashby (Guards Officer) and the Dave Lee Trio.

Borb, the president of the Balkan Republic, is visting London to sign a military deal. His private secretary is killed as she emerges from a shower by a masked wrestler, the Decapod. Steed is assigned to augment the president's bodyguards, but the wrestler continues to kill those close to Borb.

Wit: ☆☆☆ Venus Smith (on Yakob Borb's name): 'Sounds like a beat poet.'

Borb (observing Venus's slinky dress): 'I see you have no hidden weapons.'

Steed (to Borb): 'Just how many bodyguards do you get through in a week?'

Kinkiness Factor: ☆☆ Borb's secretary is glimpsed none-too-subtly through the shower curtain at the beginning. Steed tucks his card into Venus's cleavage, and, as he leaves the club, slaps a cigarette seller on the bum.

Champagne: ☆ It appears that Steed is drinking champagne in the club.

Fights: ☆☆ Some reasonable wrestling scenes, especially at the end when the real Decapod takes on the imposter.

60s Concerns: The reality (or otherwise) of wrestling: 'They're not really hurting one another.'

Strangeness: At the climax Borb is shot twice but there isn't a spot of blood.

Scenes in a Night Club: As this is the first Venus Smith story there are many. Venus is singing in a small jazz club, and Steed thinks she will be a perfect replacement for Borb's secretary. He doesn't tell her this, of course, but spins out a yarn about Borb being an impresario.

Notes: Venus is a likeable enough character, saying 'Heel!' and 'What do you want now, a biscuit?' to Borb's 'goons'. Unfortunately, the script avoids having a confrontation between Steed and Venus, the former manipulating her terribly from start to finish.
Venus: 'Don't do it again.'
Steed: 'As if I would.'
Steed is able to recognise her legs after just a few meetings.

30
'Bullseye'
20 October 1962
Working Title: 'Dead on Target'
Recorded: 20 September 1962
Writer: Eric Paice
Director: Peter Hammond
Guest Cast: Mitzi Rogers (Jean),
Judy Parfitt (Miss Ellis), Charles Carson (Brigadier),
Robin Wentworth (Foreman),
Ronald Radd (Henry Cade), Felix Deebank (Young),
John Frawley (Reynolds), Graham Bruce (Shareholder),
Bernard Kay (Karl), Laurie Leigh (Dorothy Young),
Fred Ferris (Inspector).

Shareholders in Anderson's, small-arms manufacturers, are being killed one by one whilst a tycoon plans a take-over. Rifles and other weapons, possibly manufactured by Anderson's, are being smuggled into Africa. Cathy Gale joins the board with a 20 per cent share in order to investigate.

Wit: ☆☆ Steed (observing the Stock Market): 'Ooh, they're so greedy.'
Gale 'interviews' Cade: 'How would you describe your taste in decor?'
'Vulgar.'
'I see you are a frank, straightforward man.'
'No, I'm cunning and devious.'

Kinkiness Factor: Some rather needless close-ups of Gale's and a secretary's legs, but nothing unusual for the era.

Champagne: No. Brandy, possibly.

Fights: There's a brief tussle between Karl and Gale, but it doesn't amount to much.

Eccentrics: Cade's apartment is set to the temperature of his abode in the Bahamas, complete with artificial sunlight and huge plants. He wears sunglasses. If you're that rich we suppose that this hardly counts as eccentricity.

Cathy Undercover?: As Miss Catherine Grey, reporter of *Woman About London* magazine. (She purposefully chooses a magazine owned by Cade so that he can check up on her and find her to be a fraud but, intrigued, will still allow her to see him.)

Notes: A straightforward tale of boardroom power struggles and smuggling, but superbly done. Gale adds bullets to the body of Reynolds behind the target she is aiming at and is thus suspected by the police. According to the dialogue, Steed impersonated Gale's window-cleaner. Steed does maths on a steamed-up mirror in a phone box towards the end and works out that Mrs Gale's dabble in the Stock Market has brought in £6,000.

31
'Mission to Montreal'
27 October 1962
Working Title: 'Gale Force'
Recorded: 12 May 1962
Writer: Lester Powell
Director: Don Leaver
Guest Cast: Patricia English (Carla Berotti),
Harold Berens (Film Director), Pamela Ann Day (Peggy),
Alan Curtis (Brand), Angela Thorne (Secretary),

Eric McCaine (Pearson), Mark Eden (Nicholson),
Peter Mackriel/William Swan (Stewards),
Gerald Sim (Budge), John Bennett (Marson),
Malcolm Taylor/Terence Woodfield/
Leslie Pitt (Reporters), William Back (Photographer),
Iris Russell (Sheila Dowson), Gillian Muir (Judy),
John Frawley (Passenger), Allan Casley (Barman).

A film star's stand-in is murdered, and microfilm of North American early warning systems has been stolen. The film star, despite an aversion to travelling by sea, proceeds to Montreal on a luxury liner. In an attempt to find the microfilm Dr King is assigned as her personal doctor, and Steed goes under cover as a steward.

Champagne: ☆☆☆ Berotti takes her pills with champagne. Much Moët is consumed during a party thrown by the film star.

Fights: ☆ Steed vs. funny-bearded one-eyed killer Brand.

60s Concerns: The price of fame.

Notes: A slightly dull story, despite the good characterisation of the neurotic film star, Carla Berotti. She's a sex symbol, adored throughout the world, but she is also a neurotic hypochondriac. (A reporter asks her if she's frigid as well, but we don't get an answer to that.) The script, originally written for Dr Keel, seems hardly to have been rewritten, which means that there is no real introduction for Dr King: the story appears to assume that his working relationship with Steed will (somehow) already be familiar to the viewers. King sees tolerance as a great virtue and does not castigate Carla for her drinking. There's a good scene when Carla says that she won't dance with Steed because she is on a British ship and it's hardly the done thing for First Class passengers to dance with stewards. Steed looks wonderfully crestfallen at this missed opportunity to get close to a beautiful woman.

32
'The Removal Men'
3 November 1962
Working Title: 'The Most Expensive Commodity'
Recorded: 4 October 1962
Writers: Roger Marshall and Jeremy Scott
Director: Don Leaver
Guest Cast: Reed de Rouen (Jack Dragna),
Edwin Richfield (Bug Siegel), Donald Tandy (Godard),
Patricia Denys (Cecile Dragna),
George Roderick (Binaggio),
George Little (Waiter), Hugo de Vernier (Jailer),
Edina Ronay (Nicole Cauvin), Hira Talfrey (Charlie),
Ivor Dean (Harbour Officer) and the Dave Lee Trio.

Steed is trying to infiltrate a group of assassins currently based in the South of France. He robs the leader of some jewellery in order to impress him, then waits for them in the local club. It just so happens that Venus Smith is singing there.

Wit: ☆ Cecile (trying to seduce Steed): 'Why so shy?'
Steed (knowing that this is probably another 'test'): 'Retiring nature.'
Cecile: 'What does that mean?'
Steed: 'It means I want to live long enough to retire.'

Kinkiness Factor: ☆☆ Cecile Dragna comes to investigate Steed's burglary wearing a pair of fluffy slippers and nothing else. (Her modesty is covered, firstly, by a pair of saloon-style doors, and then by a robe that Steed offers her.) Steed then locks her in the toilet. Very Freudian. Oh, and Nicole wears an incredible black-and-white-squared bikini on the beach near the end. One-Ten seems (understandably) quite taken by her.

Champagne: ☆☆ Steed asks for champagne while being held at gunpoint in the club, and gets it, too. It's all part of his cunning plan.

Fights: ☆ The plan is to distract Siegal and Dragna's attention, and is augmented by Venus's singing. Contrary to what has been written elsewhere, Venus doesn't directly distract the villains: she's much too upset.

Strangeness: Some of the accents (French, American, Australian) are horridly strange. And trying to recreate the French Riviera within the confines of the studios is bound to be good for a laugh.

Scenes in a Nightclub: Getting on for half of the story, actually. Julie Stevens proves quite capable in this department, which doubtless held her in good stead when subsequently she sang songs to Humpty and friends on *Play School*.

Notes: Not a huge amount happens in this story, which is probably why there is a five-minute sequence of the Dave Lee Trio playing. Or does it just feel like it lasts five minutes? Steed is wonderful, though, and continuity is maintained as Venus is still annoyed with Steed's deception (see 'The Decapod'). He then proceeds to lie to her. Again. What a swine.

33
'The Mauritius Penny'
10 November 1962
Recorded: 18 October 1962
Writers: Malcolm Hulke and Terrance Dicks
Director: Richmond Harding
Guest Cast: Philip Guard (Goodchild),
Harry Shacklock (Peckham), Anthony Rogers (Boy),
David Langton (Gerald Shelley),
Edward Jewesbury (Maitland), Alfred Burke (Brown),
Richard Vernon (Lord Matterley),
Raymond Hodge (Porter), Alan Rolfe (Burke),
Edward Higgins (Andrews), Grace Arnold (Charlady),
Edwin Brown (Lorry Driver),
Anthony Blackshaw (Lorry Driver's Mate),
Delia Corrie (Miss Power), Sylva Langova (Sheila Gray),
Theodore Wilhelm (Foreign Delegate).

The owner of a stamp shop is murdered when excitedly talking on the phone to a contact about the rare Mauritius Penny that has turned up on a list. Cathy Gale applies for a job in the shop, and she and Steed witness another murder in an auction room.

Wit: ☆☆ Cathy Gale: 'To have a stamp like that offered on a list is like seeing a Leonardo da Vinci painting advertised for sale on your local newsagent's board.'

Steed: 'You'd be surprised at the artwork my newsagent sells.'

Later, Steed examines Goodchild's wallet: 'Membership cards to three strip clubs and a ticket for a Turkish baths. Obviously a clean-living young man.'

Steed (to his Dalmatian after a slightly strained conversation with Mrs Gale): 'Oh Freckles, I'll never understand your sex.'

Fights: ☆ There are some, but they are very anaemic and slow.

60s Concerns: The rise of totalitarian extremists.

Notes: Another fair Steed story (we get to see into his wine cabinet, and it is revealed that he was in Young's House at Eton), especially when he follows a lead found in Goodchild's dairy and ends up at a dentist. (Wouldn't it be great if that were a genuine red herring? It isn't, of course.) There are also some nice scenes between Steed and his housekeeper, Elsie. The New Rule logo looks like two inter-locked Ks (a subtle nod to the KKK, perhaps?). The end is rather rushed and a bit silly, with the viewer left wondering what happened in all the other countries.

34
'Death of a Great Dane'
1 December 1962
Recorded: 1 November 1962
Writers: Roger Marshall and Jeremy Scott
Director: Peter Hammond
Guest Cast: Billy Milton (Minister),
Herbert Nelson (Gravedigger), Leslie French (Gregory),
Clare Kelly (Mrs Miller),
Dennis Edwards (First Assistant),
Anthony David (Second Assistant),
Frederick Jaeger (Getz), Frank Peters (Miller),
Michael Moyer (Policeman),
John Laurie (Sir James Mann),
Eric Elliott (First Winetaster),
Roger Maxwell (Second Winetaster),
Kevin Barry (Man from Kennels).

A man involved in a car crash is found to have £50,000 of diamonds in his stomach. Steed investigates the man's joke shop, Big Laugh, and then the offices of multi-millionaire Litoff. The burial of one of Litoff's Great Danes is not quite what it seems . . .

Wit: ☆ Steed comments that Dancer, the second Great Dane, probably 'hasn't seen a decent tree for years'.

Kinkiness Factor: None, although when Steed and Mrs Gale are imprisoned Cathy starts pulling back the sheets on the bed, provoking Steed to comment: 'This is neither the time or the place.' (She's going to tie the sheets together to make a rope, of course.)

Champagne: No, but a wine-tasting, complete with a man muttering about a 'distinct taste of candle grease'. (Mrs Gale shocks Stead by gulping back a glass.)

Fights: ☆

Eccentrics: Gregory, the Butler, is mildly odd, being most upset when the dog is buried at the Happy Hunting Grounds Pets [sic] Cemetery. He is, despite his manner, implicated in the plot: 'It's the power that excites me, sir. I want to be rude and ill-mannered and order people about.'

Notes: 'In the final analysis, everyone's corruptible. It's just a question of price.' A clever story, with a slight prophetic hint that the monetary dealings of one man could destabilise the financial basis of an entire country (cf. Black Wednesday).

35
'The Sell-Out'
24 November 1962
Working Title: 'Traitor'
Recorded: 9 September 1962
Writers: Anthony Terpiloff and Brandon Brady
Director: Don Leaver
Guest Cast: Carleton Hobbs (Roland),
Anthony Blackshaw (Policeman),
Storm Durr (Gunman), Arthur Hewlett (One-Twelve),
Michael Mellinger (Fraser),
Frank Gatliff (Harvey), Anne Godley (Lilian),
Gillian Muir (Judy), Cyril Renison (Customer),
Richard Klee (Workman), Henry Rayner (Reporter).

Steed's department is guarding M. Roland, a UN negotiator in London for important talks, but cannot prevent an assassination attempt. Indeed, it seems that one of Steed's colleagues is selling secrets – and Steed finds that even he is under suspicion.

Fights: ☆ Dr King executes a perfect rugby tackle on a would-be killer.

Medical Subplot: Steed calls in Dr King to examine the man mistakenly shot instead of Roland, and then uses Harvey's illness (suitably 'amplified' by a pill dropped into his drink) to get the doctor admitted to the man's house.

Notes: 'Who's to guard the guards themselves?' Despite the unusually high usage of exterior filming there is little to distinguish this basic tale of spies and counter-spies. (One-Twelve's name is listed as One Twelve in the credits.)

36
'Death on the Rocks'
1 December 1962
Working Title: 'Pillar of Salt'
Recorded: 9 January 1962
Writer: Eric Paice
Director: Jonathan Alwyn
Guest Cast: Annette Kerr (Mrs Ross),
Ellen McIntosh (Liza Denham),
Jack Grossman/Vincent Charles (Diamond dealers),
Hamilton Dyce (Max Daniels),
Richard Clarke (Van Berg), Haydn Ward (Painter),
Gerald Cross (Fenton), David Sumner (Nicky),
Meier Tzelniker (Samuel Ross),
Toni Gilpin (Jackie Ross), Douglas Robinson (Sid),
Naomi Chance (Mrs Daniels).

Illegal diamonds are swamping the market. The wife of a diamond merchant is murdered. Time for Steed and Cathy Gale to feign marriage . . .

Wit: ☆

Kinkiness Factor: Not unless you find the very idea of Steed and Mrs Gale pretending to be married faintly gratifying.

Fights: ☆☆☆ Stuffed animal head as offensive weapon? We find that fairly offensive.

Strangeness: In the opening sequence Mrs Ross is killed by a quick-hardening face pack – the sort of scene that launched a thousand *Department S* episodes. (OK, a handful, then.)

Cathy Undercover?: Yes, with Steed.

37
'Traitor in Zebra'
8 December 1962
Recorded: 29 November 1962
Writer: John Gilbert
Director: Richmond Harding
Guest Cast: Richard Pescud (Escorting Officer),
Noel Coleman (Nash), Danvers Walker (Crane),
June Murphy (Maggie), Ian Shand (Mellors),
Michael Browning (Wardroom Steward),
Richard Leech (Franks),
John Sharpe (Rankin), Katy Wild (Linda),
Jack Stewart (Thorne).

Secrets are finding their way from HMS *Zebra*, a naval base, to the enemy, rendering the Navy's missile-tracking equipment useless. Steed and Mrs Gale investigate, and find their attention drawn to the local sweet shop.

Wit: ☆

Fights: ☆

Strangeness: Information is passed via the dartboard at the Inn.

Cathy Undercover?: Yes, in the base's control room where the missile-tracking equipment is kept. Steed goes undercover as well as a psychiatrist, playing snooker with Graham, a friend of the man initially accused of treachery.

With a Young . . . : William Gaunt (Graham).

38
'The Big Thinker'
15 December 1962
Recorded: 13 December 1962
Writer: Martin Woodhouse
Director: Kim Mills
Guest Cast: Walter Hudd (Dr Clemens),
David Garth (Prof. Farrow), Tenniel Evans (Dr Hurst),
Marina Martin (Janet Lingfield),
Allan McClelland (Broster), Penelope Lee (Clarice),
Ray Brown (Blakelock).

Plato, the most advanced computer in the world, which could be used to target intercepting missiles, keeps breaking down. The body of a professor on the team is found within: very cold, and very dead.

Fights: ☆☆ Cathy teaches Broster a lesson he won't forget in a hurry.

60s Concerns: For the second week running, hi-tech missile equipment.

Cathy Undercover?: As a language specialist.

With a Young . . . : Anthony Booth (Dr Kearns, a mathematical genius).

39
'Death Dispatch'
22 December 1962
Recorded: 13 December 1962

Writer: Leonard Fincham
Director: Jonathan Alwyn
Guest Cast: Hedger Wallace (Baxter),
Alan Mason (Pasco),
Geoff L'Cise/Arthur Griffiths (Thugs),
Richard Warner (Miguel Rosas),
Valerie Sarruf (Anna Rosas), David Cargill (Monroe),
Bernice Rassin (Chambermaid),
Michael Forrest (Rico), Maria Andipa (Singer),
Jerry Jardin (Customer), Gerald Harper (Travers).

A British courier is attacked in Jamaica, and he protects the contents of his diplomatic bag at the expense of his life. But why? The case only contains mundane documents.

Kinkiness Factor: ☆ See below.

Fights: ☆☆

Cathy Undercover?: Yes, as a hotel chambermaid.

Notes: Straightforward runaround, the studios trying to become, in turn, Jamaica, Chile and Argentina. An internal memo shows that Leonard White enjoyed this episode but felt that the style 'encroached on the locale and storyline seen in Associated Rediffusion's *Top Secret*'. The first Blackman episode to be recorded.

40
'Dead on Course'
29 December 1962
Working Title: 'The Plane Wreckers'
Recorded: 9 May 1962
Writer: Eric Paice
Director: Richmond Harding
Guest Cast: Trevor Reid (Pilot),
Bruce Boa (Bob Slade), Margo Jenkins (Margot),
John McLaren (Freedman),
Elisabeth Murray (Deidre O'Connor),
Janet Hargreaves (Sister Isobel),
Peggy Marshall (Mother Superior),
Nigel Arkwright (Hughes),
Liam Gaffney (Michael Joyce),
Donal Donnelly (Vincent O'Brien),
Edward Kelsey (Gerry).
With: Wilfred Grove, Mollie Maureen, Denis Cleary.

A plane crashes in Ireland in suspicious circumstances, and the bodies are taken to the nearby St Mary's Convent. Steed calls in Dr King to check up on the circumstances of death, while he samples Irish hospitality and bad deeds at Shamrock Airport.

Wit: ☆☆ Steed: 'I'm counting on you to keep her alive.'
Dr King: 'Thanks for reminding me.'
Later, Steed's description of King to nuns: 'A man.'

Fights: ☆ Gun-wielding Mother Superior killed by King using a Molotov cocktail. Actually not as fun as it sounds.

60s Concerns: Cool methods for stealing cash shipments.

Medical Subplot: King brought in to examine crash victims.

Notes: Steed bosses nuns about and strangles a villain into submission. He's a qualified pilot, though not of airliners. King is rather a good character, a harassed young intern, but very overshadowed by Steed. The whole episode is a world's-worst-Irish-accent contest, won by a man searching the wreckage. Visibly badly directed, with an ending that must have looked great on paper, but falls so flat it's actually embarrassing. Leonard White was concerned about the violence in the script, particularly the garrotting of an air stewardess with her waist cord. In the finished episode – recorded first in the season – this scene is somewhat played down.

41
'Intercrime'
5 January 1963
Recorded: 29 December 1962
Writers: Terrance Dicks and Malcolm Hulke
Director: Jonathan Alwyn
Guest Cast: Donald Webster (Palmer),
Rory MacDermot (Sewell), Alan Browning (Moss),
Julia Arnall (Hilda Stern), Charlotte Selwyn (Trusty),
Bettine Milne (Prison Officer Sharpe),
Kenneth J. Warren (Felder), Jerome Willis (Lobb),
Patrick Holt (Manning),
Angela Browne (Pamela Johnson),
Paul Hansard (Kressler).

Steed wants Mrs Gale to impersonate Hilda Stern, a recently arrested assassin about to be used by the trans-national crime syndicate Intercrime. Things go swimmingly, until the real

Hilda Stern breaks out of Holloway and confronts the imposter.

Wit: ☆

Fights: ☆☆

60s Concerns: None, though a 1980s audience might be concerned by a horrid blonde called Hilda . . .

Cathy Undercover?: As the aforementioned assassin.

Notes: Uniformed policemen alert! Uniformed policemen alert! At the end, Steed is mistakenly arrested for being a member of Intercrime, and Cathy visits him in his cell. He'll be out *fairly* soon . . . John Bryce regarded this episode highly, particularly the fact that 'there is nothing specific about it which would bring Tenpin Bowling into disrepute'. Er, yes.

42
'Immortal Clay'
12 January 1963
Recorded: 10 January 1963
Writer: James Mitchell
Director: Richmond Harding
Guest Cast: Gary Watson (Allan Marling),
Didi Sullivan (Mara Little),
James Bree (Miller), Rowena Gregory (Anne),
Bert Palmer (Josh Machen), Steve Plytas (de Groot),
Frank Olegario (Blomberg).

Marling Ceramics, run by Cathy's friends Richard and Allan Marling, claim to be on the verge of creating an unbreakable china. However, when Steed arrives to investigate, a body is discovered in a tank of clay.

Wit: ☆☆ 'I'll sell to anyone who'll buy. Politics doesn't come into this. I make cups and saucers not H-bombs.' And a special mention for Mara's brilliant observation that 'there are no secrets in a pottery!'

Kinkiness Factor: ☆ Mara, in a catsuit, practices ballet moves against a stair rail and describes Steed as 'dreamy'. Only slightly kinky, admittedly . . .

Champagne: Steed and Cathy share a whisky in the pub.

Fights: ☆☆ Several small skirmishes involving the huge Blomberg who knocks out Steed and Allan before Cathy overcomes him by kneeling on his chest.

Strangeness: Steed meets One-Ten in a sauna. De Groot plays solo chess whilst being massaged by Blomberg (strange *and* homoerotic!).

Cathy Undercover?: As a buyer of unbreakable ceramics to smoke out de Groot. Steed claims to be from the Ceramics Research Council.

With a Young . . . : Paul Eddington (Richard Marling).

Notes: 'It'll be great not to break a cup every time I wash up but I don't see what that's got to do with security.' Plytas is excellent as the scheming de Groot, a Dutchman from Leipzig!

Trivia: Cathy is researching a book on fine china.

43
'Box of Tricks'
19 January 1963
Recorded: 17 January 1963
Writers: Peter Ling and Edward Rhodes
Director: Kim Mills
Guest Cast: Ian Curry (Gerry),
Jacqueline Jones (Henrietta),
Dallas Cavell (Manager), April Olrich (Denise),
Maurice Hedley (General Sutherland),
Jane Barrett (Kathleen Sutherland),
Edgar Wreford (Dr Gallam).

Classified information is finding its way into the wrong hands (again), and Steed feels sure that this has something to do with the death of the magician's assistant at the club where Venus Smith is working (why, of course). Steed investigates the lethal vanishing cabinet.

Wit: ☆

Kinkiness Factor: No, although Steed does go undercover as a masseur.

Fights: ☆

60s Concerns: Faith healers, especially bogus ones.

Scenes in a Nightclub: With Venus Smith and a lethal magician on the bill, what more could you ask for?

Notes: The original script features both Venus and Cathy.

44
'Warlock'
26 January 1963
Recorded: 7 July 1962
Writer: Doreen Montgomery
Director: Peter Hammond
Guest Cast: Peter Arne (Cosmo Gallion),
Allan Blakelock (Neville),
Olive Melbourne (Mrs Dunning),
John Hollis (Markel), Pat Spencer (Julia),
Philip Mosca (Mogam), Brian Vaughan (Doctor),
Gordon Gardner (Pathologist),
Christina Ferdinando (Miss Timson),
Susan Franklin (Barmaid), Herbert Nelson (Pasco).

Steed is entrusted with the safe-keeping of a new fuel formula when its inventor is found in a coma. The scientist had been involved in a black magic circle which leads Steed and Cathy into the world of hexes and magic powers.

Wit: ☆☆ Steed, handing a feather to Cathy: 'I think this is called a "hex symbol"!'
Steed and Cathy, back-to-back in peril: 'Do you come here often?'
'My first visit. I don't think I'll be asked again.'

Kinkiness Factor: ☆☆☆☆ A (mostly implied) orgy at Gallion's, with apprentice witch Julia (in a microdot swimsuit) in especially 'abandoned' form. Steed chats up a barmaid claiming to be a palmistry expert. Wicked.

Champagne: Brandy and soda (Steed). Gin and tonic (Cathy).

Fights: ☆☆ Steed fights a possessed dog (on film) and one of Gallion's minions. Cathy and Mogam wrestle over a knife in the sacrifice scene.

60s Concerns: The occult.

Strangeness: The opening scene, complete with a pentacle and hooded-figures, is accompanied by a strange voodoo soundtrack and looks like something out of a 90s rave party. Steed meets Cathy in the Natural History Museum. She's holding up a skull when he arrives. 'I know the face but I can't place the name.' Each time Gallion invokes a hex, there is a weird spinning light and discordant music, giving the impression that something supernaturally horrid is about to happen.

Cathy Undercover?: As a psychic investigator interested in voodoo to gain admittance to Gallion's circle. Steed claims to be a physicist but Gallion thinks his 'aura is all wrong'.

Notes: 'Do what thou will is the *whole* of the law!' A story of the erotic attachment to occultism (featuring an extremely memorable dance sequence) which was one of *The Avengers'* first stabs at kinkiness. An interesting 'Is witchcraft real or not?' script seems to conclude that it probably is. Cathy Gale's date and time of birth are revealed as being midnight on 5 October 1930 (not 1932 as often stated).

45
'The Golden Eggs'
2 February 1963
Recorded: 31 January 1963
Writer: Martin Woodhouse

Director: Peter Hammond
Guest Cast: Donald Eccles (Dr Ashe),
Pauline Delaney (Elisabeth Bayle),
Gordon Whiting (De Leon), Irene Bradshaw (Diana),
Robert Bernal (Hillier), Peter Arne (Redfern),
Louis Haslar (Campbell), Charles Bird (Hall).

A burglar steals two gold-plated eggs from Dr Ashe, not knowing that they contain a deadly virus. The man quickly falls ill, but refuses to indicate where the case containing the eggs is buried.

Wit: This is actually quite a grim tale, with the thief, De Leon, eventually dying in a fake ambulance that crashes in flames.

Fights: ☆

Cathy Undercover?: No.

Notes: An interesting episode, marred by a slightly implausible ending.

46
'School for Traitors'
9 February 1963
Recorded: 9 February 1963
Writer: James Mitchell
Director: Jonathan Alwyn
Guest Cast: John Standing (East),
Melissa Stribling (Claire Summers),
Richard Thorp (Roberts), Reginald Marsh (Higby),
Frederick Farley (One-Seven),

**Anthony Nicholls (Dr Shanklin),
Frank Shelley (Professor Aubyn),
Terence Woodfield (Green), Ronald Mayer (Proctor),
Janet Butlin (Barmaid) and the Kenny Powell Trio.**

Steed, investigating the suicide of a University tutor, discovers that the man seems to have shot himself with a gun with a silencer attached. Venus is sent a tub of acid 'face cream', and there is another mysterious suicide.

Wit: ✩ One-Seven (on learning that Steed's 'cover' will be research into the life of Dr Johnson): 'Your cover usually has a large element of wishful thinking.'

Champagne: Nope. Steed drinks a lot of Scotch.

Fights: ✩

60s Concerns: For one per cent of the population, the fear of being 'sent down' from Oxbridge must have been a great concern.

Scenes in a Nightclub: None: Venus is singing during Rag Week.

Notes: Despite two songs with the Kenny Powell Trio and one with East playing Spanish guitar, Venus comes across rather well, with a shorter haircut giving her a quirkier edge.

This is quite a good story, and notable for one scene which appears to have Stevens fluffing her lines and Macnee ad-libbing brilliantly. (This isn't too surprising given that the story was filmed on the day of its transmission.) John Standing was mooted as a possible new regular by sexist ABC executives worried by the show becoming 'hag-ridden'.

47
'The White Dwarf'
16 February 1963
Recorded: 16 February 1963
Writer: Malcolm Hulke
Director: Richmond Harding
Guest Cast: Keith Pyott (Richter),
Daniel Thorndike (Minister),
Peter Copley (Henry Barker),
Philip Latham (Cartwright),
Vivienne Drummond (Fuller), Paul Anil (Rahim),
George Rubicek (Luke),
George A. Cooper (Maxwell Barker),
Bill Nagy (Johnson),
Constance Chapman (Miss Tregarth),
John Falconer (Butler).

Astronomer Professor Richter believes that the sun's stellar companion, a white dwarf, is returning to the solar system. If it does, that's the end of everything. So why on Earth would anybody want to murder him now?

Wit: ☆ 'It won't be the end of the world.'

Fights: ☆ An armed Steed pursues and fights the villain on the observatory roof.

60s Concerns: Popular astronomy.

Eccentrics: Miss Tregarth, owner of a vegetarian B&B in Cornwall. In those days, eccentric; these days, a going concern.

Cathy Undercover?: Dr Gale, astronomer.

Notes: The science is very accurate, Cathy delivering a little lecture to Steed, who's got all his knowledge from *The Boy's Book of Astronomy*. He owns a little dog, as, it seems, all the bright young things did, called Sheba, and reveals that he hasn't got a brother. Steed's accent through some of this episode is strange, as if he's recovering from a dental anaesthetic. Perhaps he's already started 'having myself a good time while there's still time to have it.' Cathy confirms that she was born on 5 October. The observatory is well-designed, with great attention to realism. The story's pretty good, too, with some thought given to what people would do in the face of impending doom, and a pair of star-crossed astronomer lovers. However, the ending is rather rushed, and it's not made absolutely clear that Cathy has *tricked* the villains into thinking that the solar system really is about to be destroyed, and that everything is actually okay. Without a bit of thought, the subsequent tag scene seems a touch bleak.

48
'Man in the Mirror'
23 February 1963
Recorded: 22 February 1963
Writers: Geoffrey Orme and Anthony Terpiloff
Director: Kim Mills
Guest Cast: Daphne Anderson (Betty),
Ray Barrett (Strong), Julian Somers (Brown),
Rhonda Lewis (Jean), Hayden Jones (Trevelyan),
Frida Knorr (Iris).

Venus has her camera and films stolen whilst taking pictures in a fun fair. One film is missed, however, and when developed a face can be seen in the Hall of Mirrors: that of Trevelyan, the cypher clerk who has committed suicide. But Venus's photograph was taken after the man's death.

Fights: ☆

Strangeness: Venus's hat is pretty strange.

Scenes in a Nightclub: Surprisingly (and thankfully), no.

Notes: As with many stories this season, the puzzling introduction eventually gives way to a standard blackmail/treason plot.

49
'Conspiracy of Silence'
2 March 1963
Recorded: 1 March 1963
Writer: Roger Marshall
Director: Peter Hammond
Guest Cast: Artro Morris (James),
Alec Mango (Sica), Robert Rietty (Carlo),
Sandra Dorne (Rickie),
Ray Purcell (Gutman), Leggo (Himself),
John Church (Terry), Tommy Godfrey (Arturo),
Willie Shearer (Professor), Ian Wilson (Rant).

The Mafia aren't about to let Steed get in the way of their lucrative drug-smuggling operation between Britain and North America, and arrange for him to be assassinated. Steed survives, and tracks his intended killer to a circus, where some of the clowns prove to be anything but figures of fun.

Wit: ☆☆

Fights: ☆

Cathy Undercover?: Yes, as a journalist.

Notes: Roger Marshall's first solo script shows yet more evidence of a developing talent for odd characters playing against an unsettling backdrop. As Dennis Spooner discovered back in the first season ('Girl on the Trapeze'), *The Avengers* works very well in a circus setting.

50
'A Chorus of Frogs'
9 March 1963
Recorded: 8 March 1963
Writer: Martin Woodhouse
Director: Raymond Menmuir
Guest Cast: Makki Marseilles (Staphanopoulus),
Michael Gover (One-Six), Eric Pohlmann (Mason),
Yvonne Shima (Anna), Frank Gatliff (Pitt-Norton),
John Carson (Ariston), Colette Wilde (Helena),
Alan Haywood (Jackson).

A holiday for Steed in Greece is, of course, no straightforward affair. A deep-sea diver dies in mysterious circumstances, whilst bathyscope experiments are taking place on the yacht where Venus is singing.

Wit: ☆

Fights: ☆☆

Scenes in a Nightclub: None.

Notes: By this stage of the season one is reminded that the problems of writing for Venus Smith (and the advantages of Mrs Gale) are not just those that arise from intrinsic character differences, but from the series of ridiculous coincidences that the writers are called upon to invent in order to get Venus involved in a story. Cathy's reasons for involvement were always much more straightforward.

Director Ray Menmuir would end up producing the later seasons of Clemens' *The Professionals*.

51
'Six Hands Across a Table'
16 March 1963
Recorded: 15 March 1963
Writer: Reed R. De Rouen
Director: Richmond Harding
Guest Cast: Philip Madoc (Julian Seabrook),
John Wentworth (Sir Charles Reniston),
Campbell Singer (George Stanley),
Guy Doleman (Oliver Waldner),
Ian Cunningham (Butler),
Edward De Souza (Brian Collier),
Freda Bamford (Lady Reniston),
Sylvia Bidmead (Rosalind Waldner),
Gillian Barclay (Miss Francis),
Frank Siemen (Bert Barnes), Ilona Rogers (Receptionist).

What should have been a quiet weekend at the home of an old friend soon turns into a thick web of treachery and scheming, which throws Cathy into the world of shipbuilding, cross-company romance, mysterious 'accidents' and misguided nationalism.

Cathy Undercover?: No.

With a Young . . . : Stephen Hancock (Draughtsman): one for ageing *Coronation Street* fans.

Notes: Reed De Rouen played Garcia in 'The Far Distant Dead' and Dragna in 'The Removal Men', and crafts an unadventurous tale with more than a hint of some of the mundane episodes from the first season. John Bryce commented in an internal memo that the story was based around an 'extremely interesting idea. Unfortunately the author seems to be a bit woolly-minded and it is difficult to sort out who is on which side of the battle between opposing shipyard owners. One or two possible libels should be eradicated.'

52
'Killer Whale'
23 March 1963
Recorded: 22 March 1963
Writer: John Lucarotti
Director: Kim Mills
Guest Cast: Patrick Magee (Pancho Driver),
Morris Perry (Harry), Kenneth Farrington (Joey),
John Tate (Willie), Frederick Abbott (Sailor),
John Bailey (Fernand), Julie Paule (Angela),
Lyndhall Goodman (Receptionist),
Christopher Coll (Laboratory Assistant),
Robert Mill (Brown).

Cathy is managing the boxer Joey Frazer, but Pancho Driver's gym, where the man is training, is, Steed suspects, the centre for shipments of illegal ambergris.

Fights: ☆☆☆ Both inside the ring and out.

60s Concerns: Saving the whales, no doubt.

Strangeness: Various dead sailors.

Third Season

Introduction

'People use the 1960s in a very loose way. We were using computers, machines that controlled, electronics way before it became fashionable... This was the time of *That Was the Week That Was*; the 60s wasn't just a decade, it was a time when people experimented. The Beatles and the start of rock and roll all began around that time and we were just fortunate to be part of it.'

Patrick Macnee's perceptive view of the consciousness in which *The Avengers* flourished recognises the changes that were both affecting and influencing the series. By 1964 Sydney Newman's weird little show was becoming something else entirely. A much quoted newspaper review stated boldly that *The Avengers* 'keeps the Bright Young Things of Belgravia and Chelsea home on Saturday nights'. If nothing else, this captures the sense of freshness that surrounded the third season of *The Avengers*. Here was something bright, witty and absolutely unlike *anything* else on television.

Leonard White left for *Armchair Theatre* midway through the second season, leaving John Bryce in charge of production. Bryce and his script editor Richard Bates had at their disposal some of the best writers in television and a team of stylish, innovative directors. As Brian Clemens noted, *The Avengers* 'was one of the youngest shows on television'. It had an energy that its youth made inevitable.

Subtle changes took place in the series' structure during the third season. Steed especially was reshaped both in terms of his image (the Edwardian dress style, bowler hat and umbrella began to appear more and more) and character. Despite this, as

Macnee himself would later acknowledge, 'the whole reason for the success of the show during this period was Honor Blackman'. For this season it was just Steed and Cathy Gale. Honor Blackman's wardrobe was now designed by Frederick Starke.

Patrick also noted that 'We had inspiration. We had a lot of talented people. Paul Eddington, Peter Bowles, Donald Sutherland . . . I could think of many more. We were very privileged to have them. The reason we got them was that they wrote the parts wonderfully well. You see we worked on the edge of madness.'

The taping schedule was ten days' rehearsal followed by two in the studio. 'They had three cameras,' noted Macnee, 'which needed a lot of skill to make the thing work. We just raced from one scene to another, changed our clothes and hoped for the best.'

During the first half of the season, *The Avengers* was in direct competition with the BBC's influential *That Was the Week That Was*. In those pre-video days it's interesting to speculate on the number of arguments across the country surrounding which side to watch at 9.50pm on Saturday night. On 23 November the episode 'The Medicine Men' was broadcast several minutes late due to the extended news coverage of the assassination of President Kennedy the evening before. On 22 November, 'The White Elephant' was being completed in the studio. It would be interesting to know if the cast and crew were actually working when the news came through (around eight o'clock London time).

So the programme was changing, and its audience was changing with it. Wit and strangeness had always been present to some degree but now, with episodes like 'The Charmers' and 'The Wringer', *The Avengers* was on the verge of surrealism. Other elements – the hidden 60s agenda regarding the rise of high technology – started to creep in. The almost object-orientated style adopted by many of the directors, notably Peter Hammond, gave the series a cutting-edge, which ensured that the programme always looked (even) more expensive that it actually was. 'You'd always know you were on a Peter Hammond show because there would be strange mirror shots, strange keyhole shots, something wild and unusual,' said Honor Blackman. Macnee called Hammond 'far and away the best director of his time'.

Fights: 'When the fights proved so successful, they tried to include two in each show,' noted Honor. This is *the* season for fights, including such famous set pieces as the remarkable Blackman/Jackie Pallo confrontation in 'Mandrake' and the balletic ballroom antics of 'Man with Two Shadows'.

Strangeness: This is where the show really began to mutate. If one looks at the innovative content, such as Cathy joining a motorcycle gang in 'Build a Better Mousetrap' (a Brian Clemens story that borrowed heavily from the biker-movie genre) and the madcap antics of 'The Grandeur that was Rome', amplified by the weird set design of stories like 'Second Sight', it is not hard to see why the series was suddenly able to put itself on a completely different level to the television around it.

In 1963 Louis de Rochemont, US film producer, approached ABC with regard to working on a 140-minute 70mm *Avengers* film. At around the same time, Cheryl Crawford, an American play producer, expressed interest in a musical. Neither, of course, got off the ground. But there was some positive input from the States.

Towards the end of the season, ABC made the decision that future seasons of *The Avengers* would be made on film. *The Times* announced that the series had been sold to the American ABC network along with 14 other countries (the deal was eventually concluded in November 1965). Howard Thomas, (British) ABC's managing director, said 'I have no doubt this is only the beginning'. Julian Wintle was appointed to handle the transfer whilst the series' most prolific writer Brian Clemens (who had worked extensively on filmed series such as *Danger Man*) and his new partner Albert Fennell became Associate Producer and 'In Charge of Production' respectively. Although Honor Blackman's contract expired at the end of the season, it was anticipated that she would join the team moving to Associated British at Borehamwood. But she didn't. Offered the role of Pussy Galore in *Goldfinger* she left at the height of both the series and her own fame. (A Macnee ad-lib in 'Lobster Quadrille' had Cathy 'pussy-footing around on some foreign island', whilst a reference is made to her presence at Fort Knox in the next season's Christmas episode.) Meanwhile, ABC put together a batch of episodes from seasons two and three for repeat in the ITV regions under the title *The Best of The Avengers* in 1964.

Critique: Writing in the Oxford University newspaper *Isis*, Nigel Rees admired 'Mandrake' for 'a graveyard fight that for sheer expertise in presentation would have done credit to any film editor'. On the other hand *The Critic* radio series felt the series was 'as empty as a dry skull'. A report in *The Times* in March 1964 stated that in a survey the boys of Eton had voted *The Avengers* their favourite television programme.

'Shy girls, cool girls, sexy little schoolgirls . . . ': I supposed we'd better get this out of the way. 'Kinky Boots' (quite possibly the worst record ever made by anyone) was recorded in late 1963 (according to Blackman directly after filming an episode). Released on the Decca label in February 1964 (Decca F 11843) with 'Let's Keep It Friendly' on the b-side (much less famous, this was another spoken-sung effort about there being 'no hanky panky' between Steed and Cathy), the record, predictably, sank without trace. The fact that it was a top ten hit 25 years later says less about the quality of the record and more about the state of the charts in 1990. Patrick, apparently, now regrets being involved in the project. Blackman recorded an LP for Decca shortly afterwards (*Everything I've Got*). For lovers of 60s kitsch, it's worth around 20 quid in mint condition. On a more serious musical note, Johnny Dankworth's jazz theme and the title sequence were also revamped for the third season.

Top Five episodes: 'Esprit de Corps'
                                  'Man with Two Shadows'
                                  'The Charmers'
                                  'Don't Look Behind You'
                                  'Death of a Batman'

Transmission Details

Broadcast details are as ABC, and the season was generally networked.

26 b&w episodes (60 mins)
ABC Television

Producer: John Bryce

Story Editor: Richard Bates

The Avengers theme composed and played
by Johnny Dankworth

Regular Cast: Patrick Macnee (John Steed),
Honor Blackman (Catherine Gale).

53
'Brief for Murder'

28 September 1963, 9.50pm
Recorded: 1 May 1963
Steed is tried at the Old Bailey for the murder of
Catherine Gale
Writer: Brian Clemens
Director: Peter Hammond
Guest Cast: Alec Ross (Westcott),
June Thrody (Dicey), Fred Ferris (Marsh),
Anthony Baird (Wilson),
Helen Lindsay (Barbara Kingston),
Harold Scott (Miles Lakin),
John Laurie (Jasper Lakin), Robert Young (Judge),
Michael Goldie (Bart), Pamela Wardel (Maisie),
Alice Fraser (Miss Prinn),
Waller Swash (Foreman of the Jury).

Thanks to the clever briefing of the Lakin brothers a man charged with treason is found not guilty. Mrs Gale believes that Steed is implicated, and contacts the newspapers. Steed threatens her: withdraw her allegations or pay the consequences. Soon Steed is on trial for Gale's murder . . .

Wit: ☆☆ Steed, visiting a centre for meditation, talks to the principal, Miss Prinn.
    Prinn: 'I take it you believe in absolute purity, Mr Steed.'
    Steed: 'Couple of baths a day, a good soap . . . '
    Later, Steed talks to the Lakins.
    Miles: 'Tape recorders, you know. They make them devilishly small nowadays . . . [They] make everything smaller.'
    Steed: 'Except lawyer's fees, maybe.'

Kinkiness Factor: ☆ Half a point for the nubile young things meditating by standing on their heads, and for Gale's interesting tights and Dicey's leotard; and half for Dicey's line 'I'm playing the Green Cockatoo next week. I do interesting things with stuffed snakes.'

Champagne: Nope. The Lakins drink from the largest brandy balloons in the world, though.

Fights: ☆

Strangeness: Steed is locked up in a graffiti-covered police cell. One scrawled slogan seems to be 'Raffle Your Soul'.

Cathy Undercover?: As the brunette Miss Patchett.

Notes: An interesting way to start a season (heralded by another *TV Times* cover), seeming to pit Steed and Gale against each other. The direction is inventive, and Clemens's script is careful and crafty, with the Lakins providing Steed with all the legal and technical advice necessary to commit murder and get away with it.

Trivia: A lot of information about Steed's background is highlighted during the trial. It is stated that Steed is the younger son of a younger son of a noble family, but is regarded as something of a 'black sheep'. His Eton schooling is mentioned, as is his distinguished Navy career, where he commanded a torpedo boat. Later Steed worked for the Civil Service and as an economic adviser in the Middle East to Sheikh Akbar Ben Sidi Ben Becula. However, some of this information (particularly the military career) is contradicted by several other stories which suggest that this background is a tissue of lies.

54
'The Undertakers'
5 October 1963
Recorded: 2 August 1963
Steed meets an undertaker – Cathy joins the
millionaires
Writer: Malcolm Hulke
Director: Bill Bain
Guest Cast: Howard Goorney (Green),
Patrick Holt (Madden), Lally Bowers (Mrs Renter),
Lee Patterson (Lomax), Ronald Russell (Wilkinson),
JanuaryHolden (Paula), Mandy Miller (Daphne),
Marcella Markham (Mrs Lomax),
Helena McCarthy (Mrs Baker), Denis Forsyth (Reeve).

All of the occupants of a rest home, Adelphi Park, are multi-
millionaires. And most of them are refusing to see anyone,
including Professor Renter who was due to fly to America with
Steed to show off his latest invention. His wife is unable or
unwilling to help and, curiously, the neighbour, Madden,
another millionaire, is missing.

Wit: ☆☆ When Madden is shot, all of the undertakers remove
their hats.
Steed: 'I'll send you a postcard.'
Cathy: 'This time put a stamp on it!'
Cathy says that the death duties on a million pounds would
be over four-fifths, leaving the widow with *only* £200,000.
'There's always national assistance,' notes Steed.

Kinkiness Factor: ☆ Lomax and Paula enjoy a couple of
passionate moments – but surely something could have been
done with Daphne, the busty young daughter hot-foot from a

Swiss finishing school?

Champagne: ☆ Two bottles in Cathy's flat (one of which is drunk at the end with Mrs Renter). Steed also drinks a five-star Napoleon brandy.

'You'll enjoy it Mr Steed.'

'I'm sure I shall!'

Fights: ☆ Steed fights an undertaker and batters him into a coffin with his brolly. Cathy judo-throws Lomax impressively.

60s Concerns: Death duties.

Strangeness: Undertakers as assassins, keeping guns in the First Aid cupboard. Yep, this is a strange one! Steed gives Cathy a jar of 'jellied bumble bees' (made in Japan): not so much strange as disgusting. Madden's HQ is a hidden room beneath his coffin.

Eccentrics: Mrs Renter, a batty old dear whose husband has been bumped off by the undertakers with her approval. *And* she gets away with it at the end! There's no justice . . .

Cathy Undercover?: First she claims to be from the Architects' Friendly Society of Great Britain, then she applies to become assistant matron at the Adelphi Park rest home (Steed tells the matron about her criminal past to ensure she gets the job). Steed, meanwhile, is 'Mr Small', a funeral director.

Notes: 'Has he retired for life?'

'Yes, that's what retired means!' The climactic chase is done on film through a maze of bushes and is a little prediction of the quality of the filmed episodes to come. Could the champagne in the final scene have gone to Patrick's head? He nearly fluffs his lines but recovers to deliver one of the best closing lines in the series' history: 'Big girls!'

55
'Man with Two Shadows'
12 October 1963
Recorded: 21 June 1963
Steed hides from himself – Cathy is ordered to kill him
Writer: James Mitchell
Director: Don Leaver
Guest Cast: Daniel Moynihan (Gordon),
Paul Whitsun-Jones (Charles),
Terence Lodge (Borowski),
Douglas Robinson (Rudi), George Little (Sigi),
Gwendolyn Watts (Julie), Geoffrey Palmer (Dr Terence),
Philip Anthony (Cummings), Anne Godfrey (Miss Quist),
Robert Lankesheer (Holiday Camp Official).

Agent Borowski has been brainwashed by the enemy, but between moments of multiple-personality disorder he tells Steed that three 'doubles' have been created. Steed tracks down one likely replacement to a holiday camp, but then discovers that he, himself, is about to be replaced.

Wit: ☆☆ 'What I'm looking for, Mr Steed, is security.'
'Aren't we all!'
Cathy is discussing trust with Charles: *'Sed Quis Ipsos Custodiet!'* ('But who is to watch the watchers?')
Cathy shows Steed what equality is all about: 'What's for breakfast?'
'Cook it and find out.'

Kinkiness Factor: Not really. Despite being in a holiday camp, we only get to hear about the 'Miss Lovely Legs' competition.

Champagne: No, whisky.

Fights: ☆☆ Steed brutally interrogates the deranged Borowski in his cell. Cathy knocks Rudi around the holiday camp ballroom to a Viennese waltz.

Strangeness: Gordon opens his wardrobe to find his double about to shoot him. Charles (Steed's superior) arrives to brief Cathy with a tub of ice-cream which they eat while listening to tapes of Borowski.

Cathy Undercover?: Yes, to befriend Julie, Gordon's girlfriend.

Notes: 'I found out about the doppelgangers!' A handsome episode, and an early indication of the militant strangeness that was to come, although the plot could be said to have been inspired by *Invasion of the Body Snatchers*. This is still set with one foot in the real world (Newcastle upon Tyne is mentioned). There's a great 'end of part one' break as Steed's double first appears. Honor Blackman almost fluffs her lines at one point but such criticism is churlish of an excellent yarn. There is an interesting denouement as Steed allows Gordon to believe that he has got away with his deception. Steed intends to 'feed' the traitor false secrets.

Trivia: Steed was captured by the other side and held for four days before escaping. The duplicate Steed has studied the real thing for five years. He describes Cathy as 'one of Steed's stablemates'. Cathy has an uncle called Joseph.

56
'The Nutshell'
19 October 1963
Recorded: 10 May 1963
Steed hunts a traitor, and finds himself fighting Cathy

Writer: Philip Chambers
Director: Raymond Menmuir
Guest Cast: Edina Ronay (Elin Strindberg),
Patricia Haines (Laura),
Edwin Brown (Military Policeman),
John Cater (Disco), Charles Tingwell (Venner),
Christine Shaw (Susan), Ian Clark (Anderson),
Jan Conrad (Jason), Ray Brown (Alex).

The Director of Operations (Disco) of the Nutshell, a subterranean World War III bunker, tells Steed and Cathy that Big Ben, a file giving details of all their double agents, has been copied. Security cameras point to a young girl, but she is later found dead. Evidence implicates Steed, and Disco orders that he be apprehended.

Wit: ☆

Kinkiness Factor: ☆ Edina Ronay gets a point for being very cute.

Fights: ☆☆ Including a fight in which Cathy is able to slip Steed a gun.

Notes: Elin Strindberg is another poor unfortunate to be filed under the heading 'Used by Steed; comes to a sticky end'.

57
'Death of a Batman'
26 October 1963
Recorded: 14 August 1963
Steed is named in a will – Cathy goes into Big
Business
Writer: Roger Marshall
Director: Kim Mills
Guest Cast: Kitty Attwood (Edith Wrightson),
Andre Morrell (Lord Teale),
Philip Madoc (Van Doren), Ray Browne (Cooper),
Katy Greenwood (Lady Cynthia),
Geoffrey Alexander (Gibbs).

At the reading of the will of Wrightson, Steed's former batman, the man's family are shocked to discover his estate is worth a fortune. Steed and Cathy set out to find out where a £20-per-week draughtsman acquired such a huge amount of money, and whether it was legal.

Wit: ☆☆☆ Steed, after he has passed himself off as a kennel maker: 'I thought that was rather good. Steed's Dog Kennels. Concealed entrances, perfect for ambushing postmen!'

An exchange between Van Doren and Cooper:

'You're an optimist.'

'That's why I'm a banker!'

Kinkiness Factor: ☆ Steed meets Lady Cynthia. 'Don't I know your face?'

'No, I think it's my knees you recognise!'

Cynthia calls Wimbledon 'kinky' and they flirt when Steed tells her they once shared a taxi after a drunken party. Steed calls her 'a naughty girl'. Oh dear . . .

Champagne: ☆ Steed tells Lady Cynthia she didn't miss much at the 'Campbell-Cunninghams' party. Flat champers!'

Fights: ☆ Steed and Cathy get a fight each, to pounding percussion. Steed talks down a lethal confrontation with Van Doran whilst the banker holds a gun on him.

60s Concerns: Investment in electronics.

Strangeness: Lady Cynthia's shop has a Venus de Milo in a prominent position. 'That's what you get for biting your nails,' notes Steed.

Eccentrics: Lady Cynthia Bellamy, a charming scatterbrained heiress. She adores wrestling ('all those big strong men grunting at each other').

Cathy Undercover?: As a secretary at Teale–Van Doran. Steed, as noted, poses as the owner of a company making dog kennels.

With a Young . . . : David Burke (John Wrightson).

Notes: 'At the time of making the will the estate stood at the sum of £180,000.' A smashing Roger Marshall story. Many details are revealed about Major Steed's army career which contradicts all of the details about Lieutenant Steed's Navy career established in 'Brief for Murder' just a couple of months previously.

Trivia: Steed was based in Munich in 1945 where Wrightson was his batman. Cathy speaks fluent Spanish on the phone to Madrid. Steed is attempting to buy some polo ponies whilst 'a very important person' is also involved in the negotiations.

58
'November Five'

2 November 1963
Recorded: 27 September 1963
Steed buys a firework - Cathy stands for
parliament
Writer: Eric Paice
Director: Bill Bain
Guest Cast: John Murray Scott (Returning Officer),
Gary Hope (Dyter), Ric Hutton (Mark St John),
Frank Maher (Farmer), Aimeé Delamain (First Lady),
David Langton (Major Swinburne),
David Davies (Arthur Dove), Joe Robinson (Max),
Ruth Dunning (Mrs Dove).

Michael Dyter, the newly elected MP for South-East Anglia, is shot shortly before making his acceptance speech in which he had threatened to expose a major scandal involving the government. Steed knows that the subject of this was the recent theft of a nuclear warhead near London. So was Dyter killed to keep him quiet, and if so, by whom?

Wit: ☆☆☆☆ Steed: 'Michael Dyter held the seat for exactly one and a half seconds.'

Cathy: 'Must be the shortest political career on record!'

Steed, on Cathy standing for MP: 'You'd be very good. I'd vote for you. I'll pay your deposit. I'll even kiss a few babies for you!'

Cathy, on Steed's speech-writing: 'Couldn't I write my own clichés?'

Kinkiness Factor: ☆ A lingering shot of Cathy pulling on her boots.

Champagne: ☆ St John and Swinburne share a glass in the members' bar at the House of Commons.

Fights: ☆☆ Cathy fights a heavy in the ski school and judo-throws Max. Steed saves London from nuclear holocaust by shooting Dyter before he can activate the bomb ('I suppose you know it's an offence to set off those things within 50 yards of the street?').

60s Concerns: Political assassination ('That sort of thing doesn't happen in this country,' says Major Swinburne). Nuclear blackmail.

Strangeness: Cathy visits the ski school and fitness centre run by Fiona and frequented by many MP's wives. One of Steed's snouts is an old lady who slips him information at the House whilst on a conducted tour ('If you trip over a missing warhead let me know').

Eccentrics: Mark St John, image consultant and publicity agent.

Cathy Undercover?: Only as a parliamentary candidate!

With a Young . . . : Iris Russell (Fiona).

Notes: 'Oh dear, I hope he isn't one of the opposition; you can never tell these days!' A modern day Guy Fawkes tale of political evil and a nuclear warhead hidden in the House of Commons to be detonated at midnight on 5 November. Although no political parties are specified, Dove is clearly supposed to be an Aneurin Bevan-style Labour MP and Swinburne a Tory-shire rebel with his eye on the leadership. John Bryce commented (before filming): 'In my opinion this script, at worst, brings the House of Commons and its members into disrepute and could prove embarrassing. It seems to be tinged with political bias and by implication rakes up the Ward case where security is concerned and Keelerism where the suggested behaviour of certain MPs is concerned.' Given such nervousness, it seems remarkable that the episode was even made. Twenty days after its transmission political assassination became a horribly topical subject.

59
'The Gilded Cage'
9 November 1963
Recorded: 25 October 1963
Steed masterminds a robbery – Cathy is framed for murder
Writer: Roger Marshall
Director: Bill Bain
Guest Cast: Neil Wilson (Groves),
Patrick Magee (J.P. Spagge),
Norman Chappell (Fleming),
Fredric Abbott (Manley), Allan Haywood (Westwood),
Margo Cuningham (Wardress),
Edric Connor (Abe Benham),
Martin Friend (Hammond), Terence Soall (Peterson),
Geoff L'Cise (Gruber), Douglas Cummings (Barker).

Steed's trap for criminal mastermind J.P. Spagge involves a brilliant plan to steal a million pounds in gold bullion. But when two detectives arrive at Steed's flat and arrest Cathy for Spagge's murder things don't seem to be going to plan.

Wit: ☆☆☆☆ A typical Roger Marshall double act between

Spagge and his butler Fleming provides many fine moments.

'Was he carrying a gun?'

'In a suit like that he couldn't have carried another fountain pen!'

'I do believe you're a snob, Fleming.'

'Naturally, sir, that's what I'm paid for!'

Kinkiness Factor: ☆☆ Cathy: 'You're a slave-driver.'

Steed: 'I've got my whip on the kitchen table!'

Later, one of the gang holds up one of Cathy's leather boots.

'Don't you go trying them on,' quips another.

Champagne: ☆ Cathy drinks a glass while Steed tucks into a salad.

Fights: ☆☆ A rather confusing, scrappy affair at the episode's climax.

60s Concerns: Bullion robbery. Drugs.

Strangeness: Cathy, having been apparently arrested for Spagge's murder, wakes up in the condemned cell at Holloway. But, of course, it's all a trick.

Eccentrics: J.P. Spagge, wheelchair-bound master-criminal with a Germanic accent.

Cathy Undercover?: Once she has realised she is being tested in the prison mock-up, Cathy brilliantly reverts to her under-cover role, describing Steed as 'a man about town. He has money but doesn't seem to do much for it!'

Notes: 'How long have you been in gold?' A complex and clever episode, almost a dry run for Honor Blackman's later gold fetish at Fort Knox. Realism: Spagge uses amyl nitrate to counteract his angina. The Great Train Robbery is mentioned. West Indian actor Edric Connor plays the leader of the gang. He sculpts Cathy whilst questioning her. When this episode was repeated on Channel 4's *TV Heaven* in 1992, host Frank Muir noted it was rare in the early 60s to see such an interesting role for a black actor on television.

Trivia: Cathy's address is given as 14 Primrose Hill.

60
'Second Sight'
16 November 1963, 8.55pm
Recorded: 11 October 1963
Steed fights in the dark – Cathy exposes a
millionaire's precious light
Writer: Martin Woodhouse
Director: Peter Hammond
Guest Cast: Steven Scott (Dr Vilner),
Peter Bowles (Neil Anstice), Judy Bruce (Dr Eve Hawn),
John Carson (Marten Halvarssen),
Ronald Adam (Dr Spender), Terry Brewer (Steiner).

The cornea grafts that will, hopefully, restore the sight of blind millionaire Marten Halvarssen fascinate Steed: they're rumoured to be coming from a live patient, one Hilda Brauer. Steed suspects that all is not what it seems and so sends a (somewhat unwilling) Cathy to Switzerland to oversee the operation.

Wit: ☆☆ Steed on the eye operation: 'I, on behalf of the government, and sterile as well, am supposed to observe.'

Dr Spender, an old friend of Steed's family, on the agent's chosen career: 'I never took you for the Whitehall type, Steed.'

Kinkiness Factor: ☆ Anstice and Eve indulge in several passionate (and illicit) clinches, accompanied by conspiratorial jazz, but by 1964 standards this is tame stuff.

Fights: ☆ Little until the climax when Steed puts out the lights to even up the odds in the showdown. Cathy and Anstice grapple while Steed disarms Eve, a further example of the series' bulldozer tactics when it came to gender roles.

60s Concerns: New surgical techniques.

Strangeness: Memorably, there is much use of strange, minimalist design. The opening shot is brilliant, the reflection of several characters in a mirrored table. Halvarssen's living quarters are ambiently lit with various wooden blocks studding the ceiling to allow the blind man to make his way around. Clever stuff.

Eccentrics: Halvarssen can shoot by soundwave (which aids our heroes in the climactic fight).

Cathy Undercover?: Yes, as 'Mrs Gale', a biochemist researcher with a special interest in optical medicine.

Notes: 'With the right resources, nothing is impossible'. Somewhat disappointingly, this witty, literate script ends up as just another diamond-smuggling caper. A weird story of obsession and greed with a sterling performance by the young Peter Bowles as the episode's villain.

61
'The Medicine Men'

23 November 1963, 9.50pm
Recorded: 8 November1963
Cathy takes a Turkish bath to help Steed prove the
value of good soap
Writer: Malcolm Hulke
Director: Kim Mills
Guest Cast: Peter Barkworth (Geoffrey Willis),
Newton Blick (John Willis),
Harold Innocent (Frank Leeson),
John Crocker (Taylor), Monica Stevenson (Fay),
Brenda Cowling (Masseuse), Joy Wood (Miss Dowell),
Peter Hughes (Edwards).

Willis-Sopwith, a top pharmaceutical firm, is being drained by
cheap imitations of its products in foreign markets. The death
of a member of staff while investigating the fraud brings Steed
and Cathy face to face with a deadly artist and a plot to poison
children.

Wit: ☆☆ 'What Lord Beaverbrook is to New Brunswick, I am
to Reykjavik!'

Kinkiness Factor: ☆☆ Several scenes of Cathy in the Turkish
baths (being massaged and taking a shower). Cathy stands on
Miss Dowell while Steed tackles Leeson.

Fights: ☆☆ Steed and Cathy tackle two thugs in the printers'
after breaking in. Steed also carries a gun and shoots Geoffrey
Willis.

60s Concerns: The consumer society. Industrial espionage.

Strangeness: An oriental woman suffocated with a towel in the steam room. A man hanging in a stationery cupboard.

Eccentrics: Leeson ('I get ideas like electric shocks!'), a murderous 'action' painter.

Cathy Undercover?: As a business efficiency consultant and as a model for Leeson. Steed also goes undercover as a cigar-smoking Icelandic-accented art critic.

Notes: 'Let's hope you can keep it secret.' A clever, witty episode. Cathy suffers an eye injury and spends half of the episode in an eyepatch.

62
'The Grandeur that was Rome'
30 November 1963, 8.55pm
Working Title: 'The Glory that Was Rome'
Recorded: 19 July 1963
Steed attends a Roman orgy – Cathy is offered as a
human sacrifice
Writer: Rex Edwards
Director: Kim Mills
Guest Cast: Hugh Burden (Bruno),
John Flint (Marcus), Ian Shand (Estow),
Colette Wilde (Octavia), Kenneth Keeling (Appleton),
Raymond Adamson (Lucius), Colin Rix (Barnes).

Strange diseases are being reported in various parts of the world, and Steed's suspicion is that somebody has been tampering with the insecticides and fertilisers of United Foods and Dressings. Cathy Gale is captured whilst investigating, and will be the 'guinea pig' for a test on the new strain of bubonic plague.

Wit: ☆

Fights: ☆☆

Eccentrics: Sir Bruno Lucer, who has a 'thing' about the Caesars. And then there's Marcus and Octavia and, indeed, a 'senate' from around the world.

63
'The Golden Fleece'
7 December 1963
Recorded: 24 May 1963
Steed hunts a modern Robin Hood – Cathy joins the Army
Writers: Roger Marshall and Phyllis Norman
Director: Peter Hammond
Guest Cast: Warren Mitchell (Capt. Jason),
Tenniel Evans (Major Ruse),
Barry Lineham (Sgt Major White),
Yu Ling (Mrs Kwan), Robert Lee (Mr Lo),
Lisa Peake (Esther), Michael Hawkins (Jones),
Ronald Wilson (Private Holmes).

Steed and Cathy eat at a Chinese restaurant, but, as ever, it's not just for fun: Steed suspects the owner, Mr Lo, of gold smuggling. He also seems to be allied with Army types who are smuggling ammunition to support ex-servicemen.

Wit: ☆☆

Fights: ☆

Cathy Undercover?: No. Steed asks her to investigate Captain Jason but she can't as she's just got a job in a military museum. (There ends up being a link between the museum and the smuggling, of course.)

Notes: Odd that a series with such a marked aversion to ethnicity seemed to have no problems with the Chinese (cf. 'Kill the King', 'Lobster Quadrille', etc.). Perhaps they're more exotic (and therefore 'unreal') than Africans, Asians or West Indians. Cathy and Steed assure Captain Jason and the others that their ex-colleagues will never discover the illegal nature of the financial support that they received.

64
'Don't Look Behind You'
14 December 1963
Working Title: 'The Old, Dark House'
Recorded: 5 July 1963
Steed takes a country drive – Cathy endures a
night of terror
Writer: Brian Clemens
Director: Peter Hammond
Guest Cast: Janine Gray (Ola),
Kenneth Colley (Young Man), Maurice Good (Man).

Invited to spend the weekend at the home of mediaeval costume expert Sir Cavalier Resagne, Cathy finds herself alone in the house, pestered by a young man who claims to be a film director, and haunted by her past. And where is Steed?

Wit: ☆☆ Steed tells Cathy he's spent the morning with his tailor. 'He has to tell me about Italian styles. I don't know how those fellers manage *la dolce vita* in such tight clothes!'

Kinkiness Factor: ☆☆ Steed thinks Cathy is on to a winner with her mediaeval fashion ideas, 'so long as you aren't thinking of reintroducing the chastity belt'.

Champagne: No, red wine ('blood red!').

Fights: Steed overpowers the villain at the climax with a karate chop.

Strangeness: A photo of Cathy is torn from a magazine and carefully cut into pieces by an unseen admirer. An iconic episode, with much use of flowers, masks, a rocking horse, etc.

Notes: 'Are you afraid of the dark? I love the dark!' *The Avengers* goes weird! We have the novelty of location filming in Steed's 'spanking new car'. This is Macnee's favourite episode and it's not hard to see why. The script would later be reworked for the fifth season as 'The Joker'. The villain of the episode is identified (in the script) as Martin Goodman. The young man tells Cathy that he is Daryl F. Zanuck. He's lying, of course.

Trivia: Cathy's article for *Hers: For the Fashion Woman of Today* is called 'Mediaeval Influence of Fashion and Adornment'.

65
'Death à la Carte'
12 December 1963
Working Title: 'Fricassee of Death'
Recorded: 14 June 1963
Steed turns Chef – Cathy tries to prevent a murder
Writer: John Lucarotti
Director: Kim Mills
Guest Cast: Henry Soskin (Emir),
Robert James (Mellor), Valentino Musetti (Ali),
David Nettheim (Umberto),
Gordon Rollings (Lucien), Ken Parry (Arbuthnot),
Paul Dawkins (Dr Spender), Coral Atkins (Josie).

Emir Abdulla Akaba is visiting London for his annual medical, and Steed suspects an assassination attempt. Despite Steed assuming the guise of a chef, the Emir seems to have been poisoned while eating a meal. (Or perhaps it's just Steed's cooking, ho ho.)

Wit: ☆☆

Fights: ☆☆

Eccentrics: Lucien and Umberto, stroppy gastronomic role-models for Lenny Henry in *Chef!*.

Notes: Umberto tries to prepare a lasagne for the Emir, who must be very cosmopolitan.

66
'Dressed to Kill'
28 December 1963
Recorded: 6 December 1963
Steed is quick on the draw – Cathy becomes a
highway woman
Writer: Brian Clemens
Director: Bill Bain
Guest Cast: Leon Eagles (Newman),
Peter Fontaine (First Officer),
Alexander Davion (Napoleon), Frank Maher (Barman),
Anthea Windham (Highway Woman),
Richard Leech (Policeman).

An incoming missile attack, which is detected by all but one of
the country's early warning stations, proves to be a false alarm.
Steed finds himself attending an exclusive New Year's Eve
fancy-dress party on a train. The train terminates at a remote,
deserted station, and a guest is killed with an arrow.

Wit: ☆☆ Steed: 'I did know someone who tried shooting a pair
of handcuffs off . . . Nowadays he's laughingly known as
Lefty . . . '

Kinkiness Factor: ☆☆ A close-up of Pussy Cat's derrière and
lots of saucy dialogue. When Steed grabs her tail she says
'You'll make me purr.' When Robin Hood tries she says 'Hey,
watch it, you'll have it off.' Freudian slip, surely.

Champagne: ☆☆ Loads at the party and a nice bottle of '45
once the business is sorted out.

Fights: ☆☆ An entertaining gunfight at the end, complete with

Western-style music.

60s Concerns: The comparative ease with which nuclear war could break out.

Strangeness: When Gale fights the barman she flings him at an old weighing/fortune-telling machine, which intones, 'You are six stone two and have a strenuous day ahead.'

With a Young . . . : Anneke Wills (Pussy Cat), John Junkin (Sheriff), Leonard Rossiter (Robin Hood).

Notes: ' 'Ere, it's a bit quiet for Wolverhampton, isn't it?' A most enjoyable story, with the deserted railway station location and the actions of the sinister ticketless monk coming across particularly well. The credits don't reveal the characters' names, although the dialogue indicates that 'Robin Hood' is Billy Cavendish, 'Pussy Cat' is Jane Wentworth, etc.

67
'The White Elephant'
4 January 1964, 9.10pm
Recorded: 22 November 1963
Steed tracks a white elephant – Cathy hunts big game
Writer: John Lucarotti
Director: Laurence Bourne
Guest Cast: Martin Freind (George),
Geoffrey Quigley (Noah Marshall),
Judy Parfitt (Brenda Paterson), Bruno Barnabe (Fitch),
Toke Townley (Joseph Gourlay),
Rowena Gregory (Madge Jordan),
Edwin Richfield (Lawrence),

Scott Forbes (Lew Conniston).

The disappearance of an albino elephant from Noah Marshall's zoo seems to be linked to Steed's investigations of ivory dust in a gun shop. Steed sets out to rescue Cathy from the tiger's cage, find Snowy – oh, and capture a few ivory smugglers, too.

Wit: ☆

Kinkiness Factor: Noah likes snakes, and Cathy is locked in a cage . . . ? Not really.

Fights: ☆

60s Concerns: Save the elephant.

Cathy Undercover?: As a big game hunter, of course.

Notes: Poor zoo-keeper George is found hanging on a hook in the meat store. Bleurghhh.

Trivia: A hornbill died of a brain haemorrhage during the recording of this episode.

68
'The Little Wonders'
11 January 1964
Recorded: 3 January 1964
Steed joins the clergy – Cathy follows a headless doll
Writer: Eric Paice
Director: Laurence Bourne
Guest Cast: Lois Maxwell (Sister Johnson),

**David Bauer (Bishop of Winnipeg),
Rosemarie Dunham (Gerda), Alex McDonald (Porter),
Frank Maher (Hasek), Harry Landis (Harry),
John Cowley (Big Sid), Kenneth Warren (Fingers).**

Bibliotek are a criminal organisation who are fronted as a church. A coming 'Bible class' will decide who runs Bibliotek. It could be Steed . . .

Wit: ☆ 'What a dirty cassock.'

Kinkiness Factor: ☆☆☆ Steed makes a model of a nude lady during the Bible class. Though much was made at the time of the first screen kiss between Steed and Cathy, it's actually an enforced snog for undercover purposes. Both agents seem terrifically embarrassed.

Champagne: None. Cathy and Fingers share a whisky.

Fights: ☆☆☆ Cathy kicks Hasek all round the doll shop. There's a big shoot-out at the end, with both Steed and Cathy carrying guns.

Strangeness: A gun hidden in a hymn book. The Bible class takes place in a school room during half-term.

Eccentrics: The clergy have wonderful names like Fingers the Frog ('The Bishop of T'wumba'), Big Sid and Harry from Bangkok.

Cathy Undercover?: No, but Steed (or 'Johnnie the Horse') becomes a bishop for the occasion.

With a Young . . . : Tony Steedman (Beardmore).

Notes: 'Did you hear the one about the vicar . . . ?' A 'gathering of the clans' episode that just about avoids farce. Steed is shot in the leg by Sister Johnson and spends the last third of the episode hobbling with a stick.

69
'The Wringer'
18 January 1964
Recorded: 20 December 1963
Steed is sentenced as a traitor – Cathy helps to
brainwash him
Writer: Martin Woodhouse
Director: Don Leaver
Guest Cast: Paul Whitsun-Jones (Charles),
Barry Letts (Oliver), Gerald Sim (Lovell),
Neil Robinson (Bethune), Terence Lodge (The Wringer),
Douglas Cummings (Murdo).

Six agents have died on an escape route through Hungary and Austria. Anderson, a friend of Steed's, has also gone missing. Steed finds his friend but is then accused of being a traitor and taken to a brainwashing unit in Scotland run by the Wringer.

Wit: ✩ Cathy: 'You've broken the rules.'
   Charles: 'They're our rules . . . '

Champagne: No, black coffee (apt).

Fights: ✩ Cathy knocks out a guard to help free Steed.

Strangeness: Anderson is holed up in a fire-spotting tower in Scotland. The character of the Wringer is wonderful; part beat-poet, part psychologist, all nutcase. 'Time is what you make it, baby. Reality is merely a causal affair, we all know that. In reality, there is only the void' – and several other astonishing pieces of dialogue. Steed's brainwashing is electronic surrealism and sonic disturbance.

Eccentrics: Lovell, a department operative undercover as a tailor.

With a Young . . . : Peter Sallis (Hal Anderson).

Notes: 'It's an ugly trade. Its rules aren't those of justice but expediency.' *The Avengers*' only statement on brainwashing, but a memorable one. Paul Whitsun-Jones makes his second appearance as Charles, head of operations (his first was in 'Man with Two Shadows').

70
'Mandrake'
25 January 1964
Recorded: 16 January 1964
Steed pulls crackers to help Cathy unearth a grisly racket
Writer: Roger Marshall
Director: Bill Bain
**Guest Cast: George Benson (Revd Wyper),
Philip Locke (Roy Hopkins), Robert Morris (Benson),
John Le Mesurier (Dr Macombie),
Jackie Pallo (Sexton), Madge Ryan (Mrs Turner),
Annette Andre (Judy).**

After attending the funeral of an old friend in a lonely Cornish village cemetery, Steed discovers a plot to poison millionaires.

Wit: ☆☆☆

Kinkiness Factor: ☆☆☆☆ If your bag is seeing a big strapping man being knocked senseless by a woman dressed in black leather then *this* is the episode for you!

Fights: ☆☆☆ *That* fight! Cathy tackles the sexton in a nighttime scene in the graveyard and knocks him into an open grave with a shovel. Legendary stuff.

60s Concerns: Murder for profit.

Strangeness: Numerous aspects of the entire story: Cathy is held at gunpoint by the local vicar, and there is the discovery that the murder victims are being poisoned with arsenic and then buried in an area with soil of a high arsenic content so that future postmortems would reveal nothing. (Marshall got this idea from reading a biography of pathologist Sidney Smith.)

Notes: The previously mentioned fight scene is one of the most important moments of the 1960s: that a woman (especially such a sexually attractive one as Honor Blackman) could smash the nose of wrestler Jackie Pallo and knock him unconscious for seven minutes on national television was front-page news. That aside, the episode is fast-paced and very witty.

71
'The Secrets Broker'
1 February 1964
Recorded: 19 October 1963

Writer: Ludovic Peters
Director: Jonathan Alwyn
Guest Cast: Avice Landon (Mrs Wilson),
Jennifer Wood (Julia Wilson),
Valentine Musetti (Bruno),
John Stone (Frederick Paignton),
Patricia English (Marion Howard),
Brian Hankins (Jim Carey),
John Ringham (Cliff Howard),
Ronald Allen (Allan Paignton), Jack May (Waller).

One of Steed's colleagues has been murdered, and the subsequent investigation takes Cathy to a top-secret research establishment and Steed (*quelle surprise*) to a wine merchants.

Wit: ☆

Champagne: Wine lists have a crucial bearing on the plot.

Fights: ☆☆

60s Concerns: Fake mediums (cf. *The New Avengers*' 'Medium Rare').

Cathy Undercover?: Yes, at Bridlingtons, the research centre.

Notes: Extra-marital flings leading to blackmail readily mix with microdots and a photographic studio beneath a false wine barrel in this tale with one foot in *The Avengers*' future and one foot in its more mundane past.

72
'Trojan Horse'
8 February 1964
Recorded: 30 January 1964
Steed goes horse racing – Cathy becomes the
favourite for murder
Writer: Malcolm Hulke
Director: Laurence Bourne
Guest Cast: Derek Newark (Johnson),
Geoffrey Whitehead (Rt Hon. Lucien ffordsham),
James Donnelly (Kirby),
Arthur Pentelow (George Meadows),
Basil Dignam (Major Ronald Pantling),
Lucinda Curtis (Ann Meadows),
T.P. McKenna (Tony Heuston),
John Lowe (Lynton Smith), Marjorie Keys (Tote Girl).

Jockeys and stable hands are being trained in the use of firearms and poisons, so Steed delves deep into the murky world of horse racing. Very Dick Francis.

Wit: ☆☆

Kinkiness Factor: Almost a point for Cathy in tight trousers.

Champagne: ☆ In Cathy's flat.

Fights: ☆

Cathy Undercover?: Cathy's mathematical knowledge so impresses Heuston, owner of a chain of betting shops, that he employs her.

116

73
'Build a Better Mousetrap'
15 February 1964
Recorded: 28 August 1963
Steed visits two witches – Cathy rides a motorbike to do the ton plus ten
Writer: Brian Clemens
Director: Peter Hammond
Guest Cast: Donald Webster (Dave),
Nora Nicholson (Ermyntrude), Athene Seyler (Cynthia),
Harold Goodwin (Harris), John Tate (Col. Wesker),
Alison Seebohm (Caroline), Allan McClelland (Stigant),
Marian Diamond (Jessy), David Anderson (Gordon).

What does Cathy joining a motorcycle gang, two elderly ladies who own a watermill and claim to be witches, and all of the clocks stopping at a local atomic research station have in common? They're all present in Brian Clemens's first great step into the bizarre.

Wit: ☆☆ 'Hooligans!'

Kinkiness Factor: ☆☆☆ Cathy on a motorcycle. Enough said!

Champagne: No, pints at the local inn.

Fights: ☆☆ *The Wild Angels* it isn't but there's a big fight at the climax with much exploding equipment.

60s Concerns: Hell's Angels. Atomic Research.

Strangeness: All clocks, engines, fridges and other mechani-

117

cal and electronic devices in the area stop with the arrival of the gang. The denouement reveals that the jamming device central to Colonel Wesker's plans is actually a failed attempt to 'build a better mousetrap'.

Eccentrics: Ermyntrude Peck, daughter of the late Professor Peck, inventor of the long-range jammer.

Notes: Generally regarded as the first true example of Brian Clemens's *Avengers*, although there would be more successful later ventures in this field. The start of the episode borrows heavily from the biker-movie genre. But not too heavily. Now there's a thought – *The Avengers* influenced by *Faster Pussycat (Kill, Kill)*!

Trivia: Cathy's motorbike has the numberplate 987 CAA.

74
'The Outside-In Man'
22 February 1964
Working Title: 'The Twice Elected'
Recorded: 12 February 1964
Writer: Philip Chambers
Director: Jonathan Alwyn
Guest Cast: James Maxwell (Mark Charter),
Virginia Stride (Alice), Ronald Radd (Quilpie),
Ronald Mansell (Jenkins), Anthony Dawes (Edwards),
William Devlin (Ambassador),
Basil Hoskins (Major Zulficar),
Beryl Baxter (Helen Rayner),
Arthur Lovegrove (Michael Lynden),
Philip Anthony (Sharp).

Abarain revolutionary Sharp is visiting Britain and Steed is put in charge of security. He thinks it is ironic that they are now protecting a man they were trying to kill five years before. Two agents were thought to have died during the violent bloodshed in Abarain but now one of them is very much alive.

Wit: ☆☆ 'Come into the fridge, there's something that needs to be done!'

Kinkiness Factor: ☆☆ Cathy's legendary 'garter gun' is featured.

Champagne: ☆ At the reception for Sharp.

Fights: No, diplomacy.

60s Concerns: Formerly imprisoned anti-British 'terrorists' becoming respectable figures in the world community.

Strangeness: Quilpie, another of Steed's bosses, is a prototype Mother whose office is hidden behind the cold room of a butcher's shop.

Cathy Undercover?: At the Abarain Embassy.

Notes: Steed plays the diplomat in a story about the break-up of the empire and trade agreements. Topical *and* another example of weirdness in *The Avengers*: Quilpie handing out cuts of meat whilst briefing agents. The expected 'revenge' plot actually turns out to be a clever trick by Steed.

75
'The Charmers'
29 February 1964
Recorded: 27 February 1964
Steed goes to charm school – Cathy joins forces
with the opposition
Writer: Brian Clemens
Director: Bill Bain
Guest Cast: John Barcroft (Martin),
Warren Mitchell (Keller),
Fenella Fielding (Kim Lawrence),
Vivian Pickles (Betty Smythe),
John Greenwood (Sam), Frank Mills (Harrap),
Malcolm Russell (Horace Cleeves),
Brian Oulton (Mr Edgar), Peter Porteous (Vinkel).

The opposition believe Steed is responsible for the death of
their agent Vinkel. Steed, however, had nothing to do with the
murder and, as a show of good faith, agrees to a swop of partners
with Keller in a bid to find the real killer.

Wit: ☆☆☆☆ 'Rather a theatrical murder, don't you think?'
'I don't see the Thespian qualities of a rubbish dump.'
'So you didn't kill Vinkel?'
'No, I haven't killed anybody all week!'
Steed and Kim force entry to a tie shop: 'This is burglary.'
'Breaking and entering is the technical term.'
'We could go to Holloway.'
'Do you think that could be arranged?'

Kinkiness Factor: ☆ Kim is bound, gagged and dumped in a
crate.

Champagne: No. Steed and Keller drink vodka.

Fights: ☆☆ Cathy has a swordfight at the charm school while Steed pins Edgar to the wall with his umbrella. 'It's supposed to be unlucky,' he says.

Strangeness: Keller has a wall chart showing 'Most Wanted Agents' (actually various members of the production crew). Steed's photo is missing. Steed tells Keller one of the agents is dead and another has retired. Four bowler-hatted men arrive at the tie shop and leave carrying the crate containing Martin's body.

Eccentrics: Horace Cleeves, owner of the 'executive tie shop'. Mr Edgar from the Academy of Charm. Perhaps the first signs of the classic *Avengers* eccentric.
Cathy Undercover?: No, she's just working for the other side.

Notes: 'What would a dentist want with a crate full of bowler hats?!' A Brian Clemens high-comedy and an Emma script before its time (it was later remade as 'The Correct Way to Kill'). Warren Mitchell brings exquisite comic timing to his role as the cowardly villain Keller while Fenella Fielding is wonderful as a dizzy actress who is passed off to Steed as a Soviet spy. Steed's angry reaction to the Soviets' use of Kim as an innocent pawn is interesting since it almost exactly mirrors his own cynical usage of Venus Smith. Still, the Ruskies are rotters and Steed isn't.

76
'Concerto'
7 March 1964
Recorded: 26 April 1963
Steed spars with an old opponent – Cathy protects
a young pianist
Writers: Terrance Dicks and Malcolm Hulke
Director: Kim Mills
Guest Cast: Bernard Brown (Peterson),
Valerie Bell (Polly White),
Geoffrey Colville (Burns), Nigel Stock (Zelenko),
Sandor Eles (Veliko), Dorinda Stevens (Darleen),
Carole Ward (Receptionist),
Leslie Glazer (Robbins).

Soviet–British trade talks are coinciding with the first London concert of the brilliant young pianist, Stefan Veliko. A young girl accuses Veliko of assault, and is then murdered. If someone wants to disrupt the talks by incriminating the pianist, they seem to be going about it in the right way.

Wit: ☆☆

Kinkiness Factor: ☆☆ Polly and Darleen work at a strip club, and various scenes take place there. Steed and Cathy prevent Veliko from being further compromised with some dodgy photos.

Fights: ☆☆

60s Concerns: The sexual misdemeanours of public figures.

Cathy Undercover?: Not as such, although she is put in charge of Veliko's security.

77
'Esprit De Corps'
14 March 1964
Recorded: 11 March 1964
Steed faces the firing squad – Cathy becomes
pretender to the throne
Writer: Eric Paice
Director: Don Leaver
Guest Cast: Douglas Robinson (Sgt Marsh),
Duncan Macrae (Brigadier Gen. Sir Ian Stuart-
Bollinger), Pearl Catlin (Mrs Craig),
Joyce Heron (Lady Dorothy Stuart-Bollinger),
Anthony Blackshaw (Private Asquith),
Hugh Morton (Admiral), James Falkland (Signaller),
George Alexander (Piper), Tony Lambden (Drummer),
George Macrae (Highland Dancer).

The mysterious death of Corporal Craig of the Highland
Guards sends both Steed and Cathy undercover into the army
ranks. There, Steed finds himself under court-martial, and
Cathy becomes second in line to the throne.

Wit: ✩✩✩✩ 'I suppose it's never occurred to you that you
don't put leather in a washing machine?'
   'Why not? Cows must get wet sometimes, they never run!'
   Private Jessop on execution by firing squad: 'It's dead
quick!'

Kinkiness Factor: ✩✩ Jessop explains to Steed how the
laundrette was bought for Craig's widow. 'The lads had a whip
round . . . The officers did most of the whipping.' Steed, hiding
behind a chair, gooses Cathy to catch her attention. It works.

Champagne: ✩✩✩ At the regimental dinner. Brigadier General Stuart-Bollinger drinks (inappropriately) 25-year-old whisky. Steed is given a glass of champagne at his last meal before execution. It's a rotten year (the '56).

Fights: ✩✩ Cathy and Trench tussle in a magnificently staged sequence.

60s Concerns: Military coups.

Strangeness: Steed is first seen in a laundrette reading *The Times*. He has to be shown how to use the machines by Angela Craig. Steed is forced to undergo a drumhead court-martial.

Cathy Undercover?: She enrols in Captain Trench's 'unarmed combat' course. Steed, meanwhile, claims to be writing a book on the regiment.

With a Young . . . : John Thaw (Capt. Trench), Roy Kinnear (Private Jessop).

Notes: 'You will be known to your subjects as Queen Anne II!' A very funny episode, despite the somewhat grim nature of the story. The scene in which Steed eats a meal while handcuffed to Jessop is priceless. Steed escapes execution by bribing Jessop with his diamond tie-pin (worth 750 guineas). Macnee plays his own ancestor in some photos.

Trivia: Cathy claims she was taught judo by an uncle in Edinburgh. She also claims that an ancestor fought with Bonnie Prince Charlie at Preston Pans – but these facts are later revealed to be lies.

78
'Lobster Quadrille'
21 March 1964
Recorded: 20 March 1964
Writer: Richard Lucas
Director: Kim Mills
Guest Cast: Gary Watson (Bush),
Corin Redgrave (Quentin Slim),
Norman Scace (Dr Stannage), Burt Kwouk (Mason),
Leslie Sands (Captain Slim),
Jennie Linden (Katie Miles).

When an agent investigating radioactivity levels in shellfish is killed in a beach hut fire, Steed and Cathy get involved in the heady worlds of nightclubbing, chess and lobster fishermen.

Wit: ☆

Kinkiness Factor: ☆ Cathy is secured to a chair.

Champagne: ☆☆ Bad champers at the Alice Club. 'It's very . . . nice.' Steed murmurs, later pouring it away. 'It's very non-vintage.'

Fights: ☆☆ Cathy buries her attacker under lobster pots.

Strangeness: Apart from the club and the chess shop, even the mortuary has a chessboard look. Scace forgets his lines at one point, and has to be forcibly prompted to finish the scene. Numbers on phones in the club: *Prisoner*esque? Perhaps not.

Eccentrics: Mason, Chinese chess shop owner who matches sets to clients.

Notes: Mason is treated with some respect. 'Not Confucius, please,' he interrupts Cathy when she begins a Chinese proverb. We get to see Steed's surprisingly rakish idea of a night out, ending with coffee at his flat: 5 Westminster Mews, within the sound of Big Ben. Elements of solemn family drama intrude into this slightly unfocused story. Oh dear. At the end, Steed presents Cathy, who has just survived a rather trying fire experience, with a swimsuit. He needs her for a job in the Bahamas. She turns him down, saying that she 'won't be pussy-footing on those beaches, but lying on them'. She's off on holiday. Steed calls up somebody else for the Bahamas job. Whoever she is, she's an old friend, suspicious of his wiles, and having trouble with her Salukis . . .

Fourth Season

Introduction

The most important make-or-break function of the fourth season was to introduce Steed's new companion successfully. She was originally going to be called Samantha, then Mantha, but no one liked the name. Marie Donaldson, the show's press officer, eventually came up with the gorgeous name they were looking for: Man Appeal = M Appeal = Emma Peel.

After Eleanor Bron refused the role of Emma the production team cast the well-known actress Elizabeth Shepherd. The first story, 'The Town of No Return', was completely filmed with Shepherd, and 'The Murder Market' had commenced shooting (with Wolf Rilla as director). Then Shepherd departed, and production halted while a new Emma Peel was found.

Eleven actresses, including Diana Rigg, Moira Richmond and Rosemary Martin, were short-listed for the role, and director Peter Graham Scott was hired to direct the screen tests. According to Clemens, Moira Richmond's screen test was even better than Diana Rigg's, but 'when we met Diana, it was *fait accompli*'. The final say in the casting of Rigg apparently went to Julian Wintle. Second time around, the casting of Emma Peel took just three days. (Shepherd went on to star in the disturbing Granada fantasy *The Corridor People*, a very *Avengers*esque production.)

The season premiered with a new title sequence and a brand new theme tune, composed by Laurie Johnson. It was hoped that both would convey a sense of the increasingly eccentric Englishness of the series, an emphasis adopted with an eye on the potentially lucrative American market.

Behind the scenes, things were a little more difficult. *The Times* on 12 March 1966 announced that the Writers Guild (which represented up to 95 per cent of film and TV writers) had banned its members from writing for the British Film Producers Association following a dispute over royalty payments for overseas sales of *The Avengers*. 'The only series in dispute is *The Avengers*,' said a spokesman for the Guild at the time. This perhaps goes some way to explaining the sudden disappearance of writers such as John Lucarotti and Malcolm Hulke from the series, although there are reports that Honor Blackman had not been keen on the latter's scripts. For whatever reason, the fifth season almost completely relied on Clemens and Levene.

There were considerable changes to the production team in the fourth season, many of the newcomers having previously worked on *The Human Jungle*. Despite the influx of personnel and the problems at the beginning of filming, on screen the fourth season of *The Avengers* proceeded with a confident calm.

The Steed of the fourth season is a schoolboy, eager to play a game or run his umbrella down railings, but equally capable of showing a sudden dangerous edge. He saw wartime action behind occupied lines, and sometimes gives the air of a man hiding some great sadness. He conceals it with the sheen of the British Gentleman, but he can only really enjoy himself with Emma. Initially, he tries to rekindle what might have been an old relationship, but they swiftly settle into the most idyllic male/female friendship imaginable.

Emma Peel knows everything about those areas where Steed knows nothing (which is basically everything bar the traditional studies of the gentry and intelligence knowledge). She's utterly confident thanks to her physical skills, and shares with him the precise ability to turn aside any hint of impropriety or tastelessness. On many occasions in this season, she's called upon to assume a Cathy Gale role undercover, but this tendency fades in the fifth season.

The Avengers at this point is consciously hip, appealing to its particular young audience, and trying to pre-empt them. Like *Moonlighting* in the 80s and *The Man From UNCLE* in the States (the latter of which certainly influenced the show, except that the filmed *Avengers* made the decision never to leave England and thus, oddly, looked a bit more expensive in its location shooting), the series knew exactly who to expect on the other side of the screen. The viewers wanted hip current references, wit that tried to go over their heads, and above all an absolute denial of the Cold War that was spoiling their party. *The Avengers* fought individualistic villains more and more, and governments less. Because the audience wanted lightness and laughter, heavily researched plots faded out, and quick cartoons started to take their place. This season, in the midst of that transformation, has one foot in reality and the other in *Avengers*land, and that makes it the best of the whole lot. It must have been a joy indeed to be part of the original audience, tuning into something this original, this intelligent, this radical, this varied, every week, and knowing that your whole peer group was tuning in too.

There's a scene at the start of 'Honey for the Prince' that sums up Steed and Emma, skipping back from a party carrying balloons. If anything, it's this relationship that made the series so popular in the public imagination. This is the fantasy: you and your best friend (of whichever sex) solving fun mysteries without a chance of getting hurt, physically or emotionally. Nobody gives them orders, they don't seem to need wages, and they are the wittiest, most beautiful people in the world. No wonder people still love it.

Wit: This season ranges between the Wildean (Marshall at his best) and the dull (Clemens at his worst). On occasion, scripters seem to think that off-the-peg eccentrics will suffice. On others, we get genuine witty exchanges, and sublime existential comedy. Rigg and Macnee bring everything up with timing and added gesture. At the end of each episode, they ride into the distance on some unusual form of transport, to the accompaniment of that jaunty theme. What fun!

Kinkiness Factor: There is an obvious tendency for Emma to get tied up in this season, but she rises above it with confidence and disdain. If anything, Emma Peel is a dominating rather than submissive character, but, to put this in perspective, she's a fantasy of female liberation rather than male sexuality.

Champagne: For a series later to become famed for it, not much. Postwar austerity leads even these two smart young things into preferring wine or spirits, or perhaps it's just that nobody with real class drinks the stuff at all hours of the day. Champagne appears in only four episodes.

Fights: Lots. Well choreographed, often without stunt doubles, and usually witty. There's no sadism here, but Emma's spinning of opponents reminds one more of a playground bout than *Batman*'s too-obvious theatrics.

The Writers: Brian Clemens develops his particularly cartoony and kinky kingdom of *Avengers*land. When it's very OTT, it becomes opulent and full of laughter, but it often veers into dull formalism and offensive extremes. Philip Levene does it a lot better, subverting SF and thriller clichés and using large doses of refined English wit (contrasting with Clemens's unsubtle, almost American, view of all things English). Roger Marshall contributes a number of witty, sometimes rather old-fashioned, in-depth scripts, which, like Martin Woodhouse's effort, add meat to the confection of the season. Tony Williamson fits in perfectly, showing a particular understanding of Steed, but maybe needing an ounce more plot. Robert Banks Stewart never seems to get the hang of it, John Lucarotti adds a rather inapt sense of artistry and care, and Malcolm Hulke and Colin Finbow (head of the London Children's Film Unit) contribute one little gem each.

Top Five Episodes: 'A Touch of Brimstone'
                    'Two's a Crowd'
                    'Dial a Deadly Number'
                    'The Grave-Diggers'
                    'Too Many Christmas Trees'

Transmission Details

Broadcast details as ABC. The season was partially networked. Associated Rediffusion transmitted the episodes one day earlier in London and affiliated regions.

26 b&w episodes (60 mins)
ABC Television

Producer: Julian Wintle
In Charge of Production: Albert Fennell
Associate Producer: Brian Clemens

Script Editor: Brian Clemens (uncredited)

Music: Laurie Johnson

Regular Cast: Patrick Macnee (John Steed),
Diana Rigg (Emma Peel).

79
'The Town of No Return'
2 October 1965, time not known
Originally filmed: November 1964
Refilmed: July 1965
US transmission: 1 September 1966
Steed finds a town full of ghosts - Emma gets into harness
Writer: Brian Clemens
Director: Roy Baker
Guest Cast: Alan MacNaughton (Brandon),
Jeremy Burnham (Vicar), Robert Brown (Saul),
Walter Horsborough (School Inspector).

Four agents have vanished, looking for each other, in Little Bazeley-by-the-Sea. Steed and Emma go in for the man who went in for the man who . . . and meet the odd local landlord, blacksmith and vicar. Are they more than they seem?

Wit: ☆☆ 'You could run out of agents.'

Kinkiness Factor: ☆☆☆☆ Emma poses as schoolmistress, with cane, and gets trussed up to a saddle with bridles and things.

Fights: ☆☆☆ Steed vs blacksmith with tools and metal bowler. We're expected to believe that Emma has a hard time against the fey Jill Manson, but at least she finishes off the vicar.

60s Concerns: Infiltration and subversion.

Eccentrics: Piggy Warren, ex-pilot landlord with handlebar moustache and Terry Thomas laugh.

·With a Young . . . : Patrick Newell (Smallwood), Terrence Alexander ('Piggy' Warren), Juliet Harmer (Jill Manson).

Notes: Some similarities to 'The Hour That Never Was' – derelict airfield, Emma's fading sarcasm, nostalgia for the war years – and to 'The Living Dead' in terms of plot. Steed reads a book called *Great Disappearing Acts* on the train to Bazely-by-the-Sea. This is an intro story for Emma: she and Steed fence, verbally and sportingly. She reveals that she writes for *Science Weekly*, and tells Steed to make his own coffee. Their relationship is very Gambit/Purdey, Steed actively trying to get his end away, and hurt by her shrewishness. Thankfully, other elements faded too. He tells her to stay in her room because it's too dangerous, and at this stage it looks like Emma is going to be another Cathy, with a disguise every week. Steed's character is well defined, with a schoolboyish glee, spinning on a round-about, and a dangerous edge, burning Piggy's moustache. Originally filmed with Liz Shepherd (in red flight suit) under the direction of Peter Graham Scott, and then remounted midway through the season. Some scenes from the original story remain in the Rigg equivalent, chiefly those with Macnee in Norfolk. This explains why it isn't Patrick Newell running across the dunes in one sequence. The shoreline sequences were filmed at Holkham Gap; the town scenes at Wighton.

They Leave: On a moped.

French Title: 'Voyage Sans Return'.

80

'The Grave-Diggers'
9 October 1965
Filmed: March/April 1965
US Transmission: 4 August 1966
Steed drives a train – Emma is tied to the tracks
Writer: Malcolm Hulke
Director: Quentin Lawrence
Guest Cast: Ronald Fraser (Sir Horace Winslip),
Paul Massie (Johnson),
Caroline Blakiston (Miss Thirlwell),
Victor Platt (Sexton), Charles Lamb (Fred),
Ray Austin (Baron), Bryan Mosley (Miller),
Lloyd Lamble (Dr Marlow).

Has the late Dr Marlow's proposed radar-jamming system been tested against British defences? If so, the dead scientist seems to be doing it from his grave. And what's the connection with the local hospital's bizarre operations and a train- crazy philanthropist?

Wit: ☆☆

Kinkiness Factor: ☆☆☆ Emma, as nurse, bandaged to an operating table and tied to a railway line. 'She'll break the engine.'

Champagne: None, although the villain does call for it at one point.

Fights: ☆☆☆ Steed vs villain in the coaches of a model train. Wonderful!

60s Concerns: Early-warning systems.

Eccentrics: Sir Horace, who runs a hospital for railwaymen, lunches on a simulation of a moving carriage, and lives in a station.

With a Young . . . : Wanda Ventham (Nurse Spray), Steven Berkoff (Sager).

Notes: Berkoff is a bit-part heavy. A happy, silly, fun episode. The railway scenes were filmed at Stapleford Park, Melton Mowbray, Leicestershire, on 4 April 1965. Pringby Church is actually Aldenham Church.

They Leave: On a model train.

81
'The Cybernauts'
16 October 1965
Filmed: March 1965
US Transmission: 28 March 1966
Steed receives a deadly gift – Emma pockets it
Writer: Philip Levene
Director: Sidney Hayers
Guest Cast: Michael Gough (Dr Armstrong),
Frederick Jaeger (Benson),
Bernard Horsfall (Jephcott), Burt Kwouk (Tusamo),
John Hollis (Sensai), Ronald Leigh-Hunt (Lambert),
Gordon Whiting (Hammond).

A vastly strong, bullet-proof killer homes in on and destroys several electronics executives. Could it have something to do

Dr Armstrong's automated workplace? Or with the activities of a nearby karate school? Go on, guess.

Fights: ☆☆☆☆ Emma, in a nice skirt, overcomes Oyuka (Katharine Schofield), a female karate expert in the right gear.

60s Concerns: Japanese electronics, automation.

Eccentrics: Dr Armstrong, wheelchair-bound automationist.

Notes: For once, an absolutely false trail is followed by Emma. Steed has a camera in his umbrella handle. Armstrong has no grand ideas, he's just using his Cybernauts (mainly one called 'Roger') to kill his business rivals. The robots are designed well, with that memorable *thwack* noise when they chop people, and the maintenance version wears overalls and a flat cap. Steed tries a cover story: 'I'm playing it as a journalist.' Cybernauts apart, it's really a bit obvious. Brian Clemens invited Philip Levene to contribute to the show after hearing a science fiction play of his on the radio.

They Leave: In separate cars.

82
'Death at Bargain Prices'
23 October 1965
Filmed: January/February 1965
US Transmission: 11 April 1966
Steed fights in Ladies Underwear – Emma tries
'feinting'
Writer: Brian Clemens
Director: Charles Crichton

**Guest Cast: Andre Morell (Horatio Kane),
T.P. McKenna (Wentworth),
Allan Cuthbertson (Farthingale),
George Selway (Massey), Harvey Ashby (Marco),
John Cater (Jarvis), Peter Howell (Prof. Popple),
Ronnie Stevens (Glynn), Diane Clare (Julie).**

When an agent is killed in the lift of Pinter's department store, Steed and Emma get involved with King Kane, a tycoon who lives in a penthouse above the store. Why is Prof. Popple, a missing atom scientist, being held in the bargain basement?

Wit: ☆☆ Steed to Emma, on having his breast pockets searched (he's carrying a gun): 'What have you got to lose?'

Kinkiness Factor: ☆ Emma tied up in a carpet roll.

Fights: ☆☆☆ Emma freaks out her adversary by finger clicking, then kicks him around the shop. Steed knocks a knife into a dartboard with a cricket bat: 'Straight drive to mid-on.'

60s Concerns: Department stores. (The episode conveys a sense of disgust at the way in which huge department stores depersonalise their customers. According to Malcolm Hulke, Brian Clemens got the idea from his and David Ellis's abandoned *Doctor Who* script 'The Big Store'.)

Eccentrics: Horatio Kane, living amongst his discontinued lines, planning to blackmail the country with an atom bomb.

Notes: Emma's disguises (a shopworker) are starting to be more offhand. A genuinely creepy lift scene, appearances by Yogi Bear, puppets from *Fireball XL5* and the Daleks, and the reappearance of Steed's metal bowler combine to make a suitably outrageous episode, even if Steed and Em are still acting like exes. There are prints of this episode with a different title sequence: a quartered screen with positive and negative shots of Steed and Emma.

They Leave: On a pair of bicycles.

German Title: 'Ausverkauf des Todes'.

French Title: 'Mort en Magasin'.

83
'Castle De'ath'
30 October 1965
Filmed: August 1965
US Transmission: 2 May 1966
Steed becomes a strapping Jock – Emma lays a ghost
Writer: John Lucarotti
Director: James Hill
Guest Cast: Gordon Jackson (Ian),
Robert Urquhart (Angus), Jack Lambert (McNab),
James Copeland (Roberton),
Russell Waters (Controller).

Why have all the fish vanished from the Scottish coastline? Does it have anything to do with a dead frogman, found stretched as if on a rack? Steed and Emma think so, which is why they're guests of Ian, the 35th Laird of Clan De'ath, and in danger of being caught by the gillies.

Wit: ☆ 'It's all to do with the price of fish.'

138

Fights: ☆☆☆☆ Emma throws a piper over a balcony. Steed vs the villain with kilt, claymore and shield.

Eccentrics: Amongst the whole mock-Scottish mob, Gordon Jackson turns in a really good, genuine performance as a sort of sad, romantic figure. Odd, really.

Notes: Steed, in his kilt, is undercover as McSteed and gets to solve the mystery by sailing a paper boat. Emma is referred to as 'the Mistress Peel' throughout. A villain advises his lackey: 'Just remember not to touch anything, especially those switches.' Satisfyingly silly script with romantic touches, an awful torture chamber, and an oddly genuine Scottish warmth. And there's a big hidden base. This was the last episode of the first shooting block, with Allington Castle, Maidstone, Kent, doubling for Castle De'ath.

They Leave: In an amphibian car.

84
'The Master Minds'
6 November 1965
Filmed: December1964/Jan 1965
US Transmission: 11 July 1966
Steed becomes a genius – Emma loses her mind
Writer: Robert Banks Stewart
Director: Peter Graham Scott
Guest Cast: Laurence Hardy (Sir Clive Todd),
Patricia Haines (Holly Trent),
Bernard Archard (Desmond Leeming),
Ian McNaughton (Dr Fergus Campbell),
John Wentworth (Sir Jeremy),

**Georgina Ward (Davinia Todd),
Manning Wilson (Major Plessey).**

A government official, dressed as one of the Horseguards, helps in a raid on secret files and is wounded. Recovering, he remembers nothing. Is his crime anything to do with his membership of Ransack, a club for those with high IQs? Emma can join, but Steed may have to cheat . . .

Wit: ☆

Kinkiness Factor: ☆ Emma as nurse (again).

Fights: ☆☆☆ Em fights the villains behind a screen showing a film of RAF Vulcans scrambling, and throws them through it.

60s Concerns: IQ testing, brainwashing.

Eccentrics: The Professor with an Einstein accent who stands on his head to get blood to his brain.

Notes: Bit of a botched attempt to follow *The Avengers* format, with Emma in disguise for no good reason. Steed reveals a surprising degree of anti-government sentiment, and, while her IQ is revealed to be over 145, we get a drooling head-to-foot pan of Emma's catsuit. The identity of the villain, and the means of villainy, are obvious right away. It's also very dull. Harvey Hall appears (uncredited) as the heavy in the teaser. Dorrington Dean School is Caldecote Towers, Bushey.

They Leave: In Steed's Bentley, actually.

French Title: 'Les Aigles'.

85
'The Murder Market'
13 November 1965
Originally filmed: November/December 1964
Refilmed: December 1964
US Transmission: not networked
Steed seeks a wife – Emma gets buried
Writer: Tony Williamson
Director: Peter Graham Scott
Guest Cast: Patrick Cargill (Mr Lovejoy),
Peter Bayliss (Dinsford),
Suzanne Lloyd (Barbara Wakefield),
Naomi Chance (Mrs Stone),
John Woodvine (Robert Stone),
Edward Undertown (Jonathan Stone),
Barbara Roscoe (Receptionist), John Forghom (Beale).

What could an outbreak of motiveless murders have to do with
the activities of a marriage bureau called Togetherness Inc.?
Well, think of Hitchcock's *Strangers on a Train* and you'll be
close. Steed and Emma seek their ideal partners . . .

Wit: ☆☆☆ Steed's choice of partner: 'Well, broadly speak-
ing, female.' Emma's choice of partner: 'With stamina.'

Kinkiness Factor: ☆☆ Trouserless photographic model.
Mention of nude Steed photo (at thirteen months . . .).

Champagne: ☆☆☆ Emma drinks it while feigning death in
a coffin, and becomes very tipsy.

Fights: ☆☆☆☆ Destruction of bridal boutique, with cake in
face, showers of confetti, etc.

60s Concerns: Computer-dating agencies.

With a Young . . . : Penelope Keith (as a young bride).

Notes: Tony Williamson's next job after this was script-editing the BBC's *Avengers* variant, *Adam Adamant Lives!*. That odd wedding/funeral image that appears several times in *The Avengers* features, probably because, as a show driven by icons, the two scenes use the same props. Emma plays the tuba on her sofa, until Steed puts a golf ball down it. The twosome have a rather out-of-character tiff about a death they could have prevented, and Steed gets to ask Emma, 'Isn't it high time you thought of marrying again?' The first filming, with Elizabeth Shepherd, was abandoned on 4 December 1964. The lyric for the song 'Togetherness' is by Herbert Kretzmer.

They Leave: In a hearse. Told you.

French Title: 'Coeur à Coeur'.

86
'A Surfeit of H_2O'
20 November 1965
Filmed: April/May 1965
US Transmission: not networked
Steed plans a boat trip – Emma gets very wet
Writer: Colin Finbow
Director: Sidney Hayers
Guest Cast: Noel Purcell (Jonah Barnard),
Albert Lieven (Dr Sturm), Sue Lloyd (Joyce Jason),
John Kidd (Sir Arnold Kelly),
Geoffrey Palmer (Martin Smythe).

A poacher drowns in a field during a freak storm, and Jonah, the village carpenter, starts building an ark. But Steed thinks it's all got more to do with the permanent cloud that hangs over Grannie Gregson's Glorious Grog factory.

Wit: ☆☆☆ Steed on buttercup wine: 'I always wondered why cows had that contented look ... Thought it must be something to do with bulls.'

Kinkiness Factor: ☆☆ Em, shackled under a wine press, is forced to listen to the villain explaining the plot. 'You diabolical mastermind, you.'

Champagne: An entire wine factory, but ...

Fights: ☆☆ Versus villains in a room where it's continually raining.

Eccentrics: Eli, weather doomsayer who lives in a house full of leaks, and the extraordinary Jonah, bearded ark-builder who talks to his dog and who gets the OTT Performance of the Decade award.

With a Young ... : Talfryn Thomas (Eli Barker).

Notes: The outline of the dead body is a wet patch with wellies remaining. Steed is in his Edwardian outfit some of the time. The cloud-seeding villain is called Sturm, in case you didn't get it, and Steed's bowler gets crushed in the wine press ('I don't think it suffered').

They Leave: On Emma's fashionable Minimoke.

87

'The Hour That Never Was'

27 November 1965
Working Titles: 'Roger and Out', 'An Hour to Spare'
Filmed: July 1965
US Transmission: 24 April 1966
Steed has to face the music – Emma disappears
Writer: Roger Marshall
Director: Gerry O'Hara
Guest Cast: Gerald Harper (Geoffrey Ridsdale),
Dudley Foster (Philip Leas), Roy Kinnear (Hickey),
Roger Booth ('Porky' Purser),
Daniel Moynihan (Corporal Barman),
Daniel Morrell (Wiggins), Fred Haggerty (Driver).

Following a motor crash, Steed and Emma explore the seemingly deserted RAF Hamelin, where they were heading for a party to celebrate the base's closure. Is this surreal landscape all a dream, or is it something worse?

Wit: ☆☆ On finding an unconscious bunny: 'What did it?' 'Rabbit punch?'

Kinkiness Factor: ☆☆ Emma is tied to a dentist's chair.

Fights: ☆☆☆ Emma and Steed vs dentist (with drill) and lackey. The dentist releases some laughing gas, with hilarious results.

60s Concerns: Closedown of airbases. Hypnotic conditioning.

Eccentrics: William Napoleon Hickey, tramp specialising in airbases. He's a conscientious objector who hates stamp collectors and is nostalgic for a war when 'dustbins were always full' and he had a ration book (there's a subversive thought!). Plus the dentist villain who found that the sound of his drill could hypnotise people. 'I'd like to say that it was my life's work, but it wasn't.'

Notes: Em is in great summer fashions. Steed used to be dropped into Europe from Hamelin during the war. We're encouraged, by manipulation of TV cliché, to think that this is going to be a 'dream episode'. Stately, elegant script (Marshall's idea evolved from a recce with Clemens to a deserted airfield in Norfolk for 'The Town of No Return'), and great direction. Incredibly, the Hickey character was written with Harold Pinter in mind. The scenes at RAF Hamelin were filmed at Bovingdon Airfield, and the bridge is at Tyke's Water Lake, Elstree.

They Leave: On a milkfloat, speeded up like something out of Benny Hill (a sequence which ABC wanted dropped).

88
'Dial a Deadly Number'
4 December 1965
Filmed: January 1965
US Transmission: 21 July 1966
Steeds plays Bulls and Bears - Emma has no option
Writer: Roger Marshall
Director: Don Leaver
Guest Cast: Clifford Evans (Henry Boardman),
Jan Holden (Ruth Boardman),
Anthony Newlands (Ben Jago), John Carson (Fitch),
Peter Bowles (John Harvey),
Gerald Sim (Frederick Yuill),

**Michael Trubshawe (The General),
Norman Chappell (Macrombie), John Bailey (Warner),
Edward Cost (Waiter).**

A series of sudden deaths in high finance leads Steed to dabble in shares while Emma investigates the makers of executive paging devices. Are companies being acquired through a simple and subtle form of murder?

Wit: ☆☆☆☆☆ 'I'm an optimist, I admire a woman with a past.'
  'What's optimistic about that?'
  'History may repeat itself.'
  'I recommend the blue chip special.'
  'Splendid, at least one of us will enjoy it.' And many, many more in a sparkling script.

Kinkiness Factor: ☆☆☆ Very kinky villain, who ties Em up in a cupboard.

Champagne: ☆☆☆☆ A flying cork is used to knock out John Harvey.

Fights: ☆☆ Steed uses his cape against motorcycle killers, then fires a gun at them (?!). There is a subdued battle amongst wine racks.

Eccentrics: An undertaker very into his trade, and the splendid villain, an assassin obsessed by time, who was taught in the war and stops a clock for every victim.

Notes: An old-fashioned script, with real research about the stock market on display, and thus not quite *Avengers*ish. But this is compensated for by a wine-tasting duel 'from the northern end of the vineyard', some wonderful writing and a great sense of depth. One of the few female *Avengers* villains is, of course, a sexual aggressor, but it's great anyway. Incidentally, Philip Norman's *Shout* describes the Beatles watching an episode of *The Avengers* at Newcastle City Hall in December 1965, and it is most probably this one.

They Leave: In a London taxi.

French Title: 'Meutre par Telephone'.

89
'Man-Eater of Surrey Green'
11 December 1965
Working Title: Man Eater of Ferry Green
Filmed: June 1965
US Transmission: 25 August 1966
Steed kills a climber – Emma becomes a vegetable
Writer: Philip Levene
Director: Sidney Hayers
Guest Cast: Derek Farr (Sir Lyle Peterson),
Athene Sayler (Dr Sheldon),
Gillian Lewis (Laura Burford),
William Job (Alan Carter), Edwin Finn (Prof. Taylor),
Harry Shacklock (Prof. Knight),
Ross Hutchinson (Dr Connelly),
John G. Heller (Lennon),
David Hutcheson (Wing Commander Davie),
Joe Ritchie (Publican), Donald Oliver (Bob Pearson),
Joby Blanshard (Joe Mercer).

Deaf botanist Alan Carter's fiancée walks away from their floral bliss under some strange influence, and is picked up by an entranced chauffeur. Has it got anything to do with the giant seed from outer space that has landed nearby? Of course it has.

Wit: ✩✩ Emma on her chances of survival: 'The plant's only man-eating.'
  One point deducted for Steed's 'I'm a herbicidal maniac.'

Fights: ✩✩✩ Steed fights a controlled Emma, to the point of exhaustion. They butt heads accidentally, and she gets knocked out, whereupon Steed covers her with herbicide and feeds her to the plant! Bastard!

60s Concerns: Invasion by giant plants from Outer Space. Erm . . .

Eccentrics: Peterson, the botanist who drapes mannequins with ivy and feeds bad model Venus fly-traps, and Sheldon, the lovely old lady botanist.

Notes: Emma goes alone into a pub and is given a pint. The low budget confines the plant appearances to vines and under a groundsheet. Steed is in a much more Edwardian bowler and cravat, and is nearly killed by a poisonous cactus on his car seat. Bad acting award: the RAF boss. This story is (along with the Cybernauts stories) as close as *The Avengers* gets to pure SF. It's very, very like the (later) *Doctor Who* story 'The Seeds of Doom', both featuring, apart from the obvious plant menace, a villainous chauffeur and a dotty lady botanist. Scenes involving Peterson's house were shot at the BR Centre, The Grove, Watford. Surrey Green is Letchmore Heath.

They Leave: On a haycart.

90
'Two's a Crowd'
18 December 1965
Filmed: May 1965
US Transmission: 9 May 1966
Steed is single minded - Emma sees double
Writer: Philip Levene
Director: Roy Baker
Guest Cast: Warren Mitchell (Brodny),
Maria Machado (Alicia Elena),
Alec Mango (Shvedloff), Wolfe Morris (Pudeshkin),
Julian Glover (Vogel), John Bluthal (Ivenko),
Eric Lander (Major Carson).

Colonel Psev, a mysterious and unseen foreign spy with a toy fixation, arrives in London to infiltrate a defence conference. His four aides bully Brodny, the ambassador, until he comes up with a cunning ruse: Gordon Webster, rakish male model, is Steed's double!

Wit: ☆☆☆ Steed to Major Carson: 'Do you always squeeze the toothpaste in the middle?'
'I didn't until I got married.'

Kinkiness Factor: ☆☆ Emma as a shopgirl with glasses is bound and carried away.

Fights: ☆ Emma pulls Carson down to the carpet by his fingers.

60s Concerns: Superspies.

Eccentrics: Erm, no. Real spies, albeit with an interest in model aircraft.

149

Notes: Patrick Macnee's wonderful portrayal of Webster proves that he's not just playing himself. Webster *looks* different, even when he's pretending to be Steed. He models a 'champagne-resistant jacket', with 'shirt proof against lipstick'. Steed's umbrella has a transmitter in it, and his height is stated as 6'2". Webster aspires to class, but actually used to be a cashier. He calls everyone 'ducky'. Note for *Doctor Who* fans: complaining about Webster's messy buttonhole, the spies mutter, 'Why don't you put a stick of celery in there as well?' *The Avengers'* satire on actual spy trickery is very funny and very clever. Foreign embassy footage was filmed at Edge Grove School, Aldenham; lake footage at Tyke's Water Lake, Elstree.

They Leave: On a pair of horses.

91
'Too Many Christmas Trees'
25 December 1965
Filmed: February/March 1965
US Transmission: 11 August 1966
Steed hangs up his stocking – Emma asks for more
Writer: Tony Williamson
Director: Roy Ward Baker
Guest Cast: Mervyn Johns (Brandon Storey),
Edwin Richfield (Dr Felix Teasel),
Jeanette Sterke (Janice Crane),
Alex Scott (Martin Trasker), Robert James (Jenkins),
Barry Warren (Jeremy Wade).

Christmas. Steed is having bad, seemingly prophetic, dreams, involving festive themes and a dead agent. Can he find solace at a fancy-dress party in the country home of a Dickens enthusiast? Of course not.

Wit: ✩✩✩ Em on attire: 'I've always rather fancied myself in one of these.'
   Steed: 'So have I.'
   Steed on there being no Santa Claus: 'Oh dear. Isn't there?'

Champagne: None, despite the fact that Emma offers to cheer Steed up with a bottle.

Fights: ✩✩✩ Versus psychic aggressors in a hall of mirrors. Plus, Steed shoots Santa.

60s Concerns: Telepathy.

Strangeness: 'It's funny how Freddy came into my dream last night.' Prophetic..?

Eccentrics: Storey, the jolly host and huge Dickens fan.

Notes: Cathy Gale sends Steed a Christmas card from Fort Knox (Honor Blackman was starring in *Goldfinger*). He also gets one from 'Bouffums', the postmistress at Ongar. Steed feels comfortable chatting up women in front of Emma, but not so comfortable about her male friends. His present to her: a teargas-firing pen. The design, script and atmosphere produce a lovely seasonal feeling, if based around a rather half-hearted telepathy plot. This episode also exists with an alternative title sequence. Brandon Storey's house was Hilfield Castle, Elstree.

They Leave: On a horse and trap, Steed producing some mistletoe which Emma only raises an eyebrow at.

French Title: 'Faites de Beaux Reres'.

92

'Silent Dust'

1 January 1966
Working Title: 'Strictly for the Worms'
Filmed: June 1965
US Transmission: not networked
Steed watches birds – Emma goes hunting
Writer: Roger Marshall
Director: Roy Baker
Guest Cast: Jack Watson (Juggins),
Conrad Phillips (Mellors),
Norman Bird (Croft), Hilary Wontner (Minister),
Joanna Wake (Miss Snow),
Isobel Black (Clare Prendergast),
Aubrey Morris (Quince), Robert Dorning (Harvard).

The lack of martens in a pleasant stretch of English countryside alerts Steed to the possible release of a fertiliser that has failed, reducing a landscape to a wasteland. But why is the local farming community so aggressive?

Wit: ☆

Kinkiness Factor: ☆☆ Emma is hunted from horseback, and is threatened with a whip.

Fights: ☆☆ Steed fights a villain with a scythe in a stableyard. Em knocks out the gamekeeper and a farmer, only to be rescued by a horseriding Steed (no stunt double was used) brandishing a hunt saboteur's placard.

60s Concerns: Isolated areas destroyed by biological weapons.

Strangeness: Steed has a bizarre *Prisoner* esque dream sequence that briefly reformats the story as a Western.

Eccentrics: Quince, a myopic birdwatcher; Juggins, a blood-thirsty cider-sipping farmhand with a Yorkshire accent. 'You should have heard that sow, t'were like music!'

With a Young . . . : William Franklyn (Omrod), Charles Lloyd Pack (Sir Manfred Fellows).

Notes: Steed takes shoe size 9 and is in his Edwardian outfit. The gamekeeper is called Mellors, and the devastated area is Manderley. The farmer villain is asked if the government will pay his ransom. 'They will . . . After we destroy Dorset!' Well End Lodge doubled for the Stirrup Cup Inn. The punting scene was shot on (you guessed it) Tyke's Water Lake, Elstree.

They Leave: In a balloon.

French Title: 'La Poussiere Qui Tue'.

93
'Room Without a View'
8 January 1966
Filmed: April 1965
US Transmission: 27 June 1966
Steed becomes a gourmet – Emma awakes in Manchuria
Writer: Roger Marshall
Director: Roy Baker
Guest Cast: Paul Whitsun-Jones (Chessman),
Peter Jeffrey (Varnals), Richard Bebb (Dr Cullen),
Philip Latham (Carter), Peter Arne (Pascold),

153

Vernon Dobtcheff (Pushkin),
Peter Madden (Dr Wadkin),
Jeanne Roland (Anna Wadkin).

A brilliant scientist reappears at the house of his wife. Has he escaped from notorious Manchurian prison camp Ni-San? And why have so many missing people stayed at the Chessman Hotel? Steed and Emma book in.

Wit: ☆

Kinkiness Factor: ☆ Em is stroked with a swagger stick.

Fights: ☆☆ Emma knees a laundryman in the groin. Steed fights two men with rifles using a broom; Emma rescues him, punching one over the table.

Eccentrics: Max Chessman, the chess-fixated gourmet hotel owner on a crash diet (a vaguely Maxwellian figure).

Notes: Room 621, gas kidnappings to distant parts, Chessman Hotel . . . All very *Prisoner* esque. Good to see Chinese people without stupid accents, and Steed helps Emma deal with a very sexist agent. Odd to hear of Chinese and Russian villainy amongst the usual 'foreign powers'. A rather dull episode, but notable for the possibility that Kenneth Williams turned down a part in it. In his diaries, he mentions declining a 'lousy little part, could have been played by anyone' in this season, but doesn't say which part. However, he, Joe Orton and Ken Halliwell sat down to watch this particular episode when it was screened, rating it as 'puerile'. If this is the declined episode, it's tempting to speculate on the part. Not Chessman, since he's obese, but Varnals, or more likely Carter, would have suited the Williams touch.

They Leave: By Steed pulling a rickshaw with Emma in it.

French Title: 'Avec Vue Imprenable'.

94
'Small Game for Big Hunters'
15 January 1966
Filmed: September 1965
US Transmission: 4 April 1966
Steed joins the natives – Emma gets the evil eye
Writer: Philip Levene
Director: Gerry O'Hara
Guest Cast: Bill Fraser (Col. Rawlings),
James Villiers (Simon Trent),
Liam Redmond (Prof. Swain),
A.J. Brown (Dr Gibson), Peter Burton (Fleming),
Paul Danquah (Razafi), Tom Gill (Tropical Outfitter),
Esther Anderson (Lala), Peter Thomas (Kendrick).

When a man is found under Shirenzai, the trance-like Kalayan voodoo, in the heart of Hertfordshire, Steed finds himself amidst the horror of the last days of empire. Are bandits loose in the English countryside?

Wit: ☆ 'Take 'em some coloured beads, always seems to help.'

Fights: ☆☆ Steed and Emma (in native dress) vs villains with knives and spears. Steed swings in like Tarzan: 'Me Steed.', 'Me Emma.'

60s Concerns: Tse-tse flies and sleeping sickness.

Eccentrics: Colonel Rawlings, who lives in a replica of Kalayan jungle in Britain, and can't accept leaving the country to the Kalayans.

Notes: Steed carries a swordstick. Good to see British imperialists as villains, and to meet Steed's Kalayan opposite number (a real black man in an *Avengers* story!). In Steed's car, we see a file marked 'Pzev', as in 'Two's a Crowd'. Unfortunately, the episode is very dull indeed. Gibson's house scenes were filmed at Starracres, Radlett.

They Leave: Paddling a canoe.

95
'The Girl from Auntie'
21 January 1966
Filmed: October 1965
US Transmission: 6 June 1966
Steed almost outbids himself – Emma is a bird in a gilded cage
Writer: Roger Marshall
Director: Roy Baker
Guest Cast: Liz Fraser (Georgie Price-Jones),
Alfred Burke (Gregorio Auntie),
David Bauer (Ivanov), Mary Merrall (Old Lady),
Sylvia Coleridge (Aunt Hetty),
Yolande Turner (Receptionist),
Roy Martine (Taxi Driver),
Maurice Browning (Russian),
John Rutland (Fred Jacques).

Steed returns from holiday to find that a quite different Mrs Peel is inhabiting his old friend's flat. With the aid of actress Georgie Price-Jones, he discovers that Art Incorporated and the Arkwright Knitting Circle are doing more together than just sharing needles.

Wit: ☆☆☆ 'Six bodies in an hour and twenty minutes, what do you call that?'

'A good first act?'

Steed's advice on umbrella-swinging: 'Eager is untrustworthy, almost the next worst thing to enthusiastic.' And Lady Bracknell is reminded not to forget her handbag in a script nearly as sparkling as Marshall's 'Dial a Deadly Number'.

Kinkiness Factor: ☆☆ Em, trapped in a swinging cage wearing a feather bikini, is auctioned for £200,000.

Fights: ☆☆☆ Steed vs Ivanov while paying taxi fare (he only forgets the tip). Georgie uses Ray Austin's book entitled *Self Defence* to knock out an assailant.

Strangeness: Obviously a holiday episode for Diana Rigg, but Georgie is actually a reasonable substitute. Oddly enough, her involvement is rather like that of the innocents tangled in a *Man from UNCLE* episode.

Eccentrics: Arkwright, who conducts his knitting circle like a square dance.

With a Young . . . : Bernard Cribbins (Arkwright).

Notes: Steed knocks Auntie out by breaking the real Mona Lisa over his head. Steed takes 9¾ size socks. Unfortunately, Georgie, who's meant to look like Emma, doesn't. The Bates and Marshall advertising agency presumably belonged to Roger

Marshall and Story Editor Richard Bates (or Diana Rigg's fashion designer John Bates?). Another vivacious Marshall script, but where on earth is West London Air Terminal? Still, it was the beginning of the end as far as Marshall was concerned, as he did not like this episode and was concerned at the direction Clemens was taking the show. He would leave the show during the scripting of the next season, going on to be involved in the creation of *Public Eye* and *Adam Adamant Lives!*. Mrs Peel's kidnap was filmed at Dyrham Park Golf Club, Dancer's Hill.

They Leave: In a bubblecar, overtaking Georgie riding in Steed's Bentley.

96
'The Thirteenth Hole'
29 January 1966
Filmed: September 1965
US Transmission: 18 August 1966
Steed finds a bogey – Emma gets a birdie
Writer: Tony Williamson
Director: Roy Baker
Guest Cast: Patrick Allen (Reed),
Hugh Manning (Col. Watson),
Victor Maddern (Jackson),
Norman Wynne (Prof. Minley),
Donald Hewlett (Waversham).

An agent is shot on the thirteenth hole of the Craigleigh golf club, so Steed and Emma join the club. Steed puts his limited skills to use in a murderous tournament, but Emma helps him get a hole in one.

Wit: ☆

Kinkiness Factor: ☆☆ Em handcuffed to a chair.

Champagne: ☆

Fights: ☆☆☆ Emma vs the club professional in a bunker, Steed and Emma face the villains with a club and the aforementioned chair (which Emma snarls through the bars of), while foreign scientists watch and wince on a TV monitor. Steed stops the final villain with a precise shot down the fairway.

60s Concerns: Communications satellites.

Eccentrics: None, but Professor Minley looks a bit like Patrick Moore.

With a Young . . . : Peter Jones (Adams), Francis Matthews (Collins), Richard Marner (Man on TV screen).

Notes: Steed is in his Edwardian gear. His golf trilby is chainmail-lined. This episode was the first episode of the second recording block. The golf course is mainly an optically-printed background to close-up shots (it was planned to shoot all the exteriors at the Mill Hill Golf Course). Vostick 2 is, it seems, a Soviet satellite. Steed tries to draw his swordstick, but finds he's carrying a golf club.

They Leave: On a golf cart, sipping champers.

French Title: 'Le Jeu S'Arrele Au 13'.

97
'Quick-Quick Slow Death'
5 February 1966
Filmed: October/November 1965
US Transmission: Not networked
Steed has two left feet – Emma dances with danger
Writer: Robert Banks Stewart
Director: James Hill
Guest Cast: Eunice Gayson (Lucille Banks),
Maurice Kaufmann (Ivor Bracewell),
Carole Gray (Nicki), Larry Cross (Chester Read),
James Bellchamber (Peever),
John Woodnutt (Capt. Noble),
Alan Gerrard (Fruity), David Kernan (Piedi),
Colin Ellis (Bernard), Graham Armitage (Huggins),
Charles Hodgson (Syder),
Ronald Govey (Bank Manager),
Michael Peake (Willi Fehr).

An agent is run over disposing of the body of a man in a dinner suit, while he was pushing him along in a pram. This all has something to do with Terpsichorean Training Techniques, a dance school where Emma teaches and Steed enrols.

Wit: ☆☆ Tailor: 'Without us, Ascot race week would look like a nudist convention.'

On an agent found with his head encased: 'Bernard got himself plastered.'

Kinkiness Factor: ☆☆☆☆ Italian foot-fetishist shoemaker Piedi actually offers Emma 'Wellington boots in the kinkiest black leather?'

Fights: ☆☆☆ Versus dance instructors using dummies and shoes, finishing with Steed spinning the villain over his head.

60s Concerns: Infiltration.

Strangeness: The drunken band leader leads a band comprising of a tape recorder and photo cut-outs of him playing various instruments.

Eccentrics: The Yorkshire tattooist, who wants to put 'pretty pink rosebuds, one on each' or 'this view of Sydney I've always wanted to do' on Emma, and leaves a final message on a garlic sausage.

Notes: Steed demonstrates his lonely bachelor act, and refers to himself as Jonathan. ('Steed' came over with the Vikings.) He opens a door in a high-rise, and finds that the office he wanted has vanished, nearly falling. Fehr manages to make a phone call after being shot through the side point-blank, and there's a really odd ending, Emma summarising the episode's contents. Altogether, a bit unfocused and sagging around the edges. The busy high street scenes were filmed on Shenley Road, Borehamwood, just outside the studios.

They Leave: By dancing into a superimposed sunset.

French Title: 'La Danse Macabre'.

98
'The Danger Makers'
12 February 1966
Filmed: November 1965

US Transmission: 4 July 1966
Steed joins a secret society - Emma walks the plank
Writer: Roger Marshall
Director: Charles Crichton
Guest Cast: Douglas Wilmer (Dr Lang),
Fabia Drake (Col. Adams), Moray Watson (Peters),
Adrian Ropes (Stanhope),
Richard Coleman (RAF Officer),
John Gatrell (Lomble).

Several military figures have been killed in dangerous games of daring. Emma and Steed follow the trail to a secret society of military men with very dangerous aims.

Wit: ☆☆ Steed on how Emma is to greet an amateur phrenologist: 'Show him your bumps.'

Em on escaping using knotted sheets: 'Originality didn't seem important at the time.'

Kinkiness Factor: ☆☆☆ In the very masochistic society of The Danger Makers, Steed is handcuffed and Emma is chained to electrified cables in a game straight out of an S&M version of *The Crystal Maze*.

Fights: ☆☆☆ Emma throws herself at a table of military men, and multiple fencing ensues.

Strangeness: 'That's the Adams' family crest.'

Eccentrics: A whole society of danger junkies, notably Major Robertson, who's interested in Napoleon's bumps and plays 'The Last Post' for victims. Female Colonel Adams, last of a great military line: 'She's recreating the Indian Mutiny in the potting shed.'

162

With a Young . . . : Nigel Davenport (Robertson).

Notes: Steed swaps his bowler for a steel helmet, and visits RAF Hamelin (obviously before 'The Hour That Never Was'), though nobody there seems to know him. He also beats the honourable secret society at its own game . . . by cheating! Mention is made of 'Beatniks' doing 'chicken runs'. Steed rather too carefully 'defuses' the chocolates that Robertson has sent Emma. 'Don't touch the wrapped ones.'

'Why?'

' 'Cos I like 'em.'

Great design on Emma's initiation game, again she's subjected to a male test only to rise above it. Odd ending though, Emma quickly running through the plot again. Manton House scenes were filmed at the BR Centre, the Grove, Watford.

They Leave: On two go-karts.

German Title: 'Club der Schwarzen Rose'.

French Title: 'Les Chevaliers de la Mort'.

99
'A Touch of Brimstone'
19 February 1966
Working Title: 'The Hellfire Club'
Filmed: c.December 1965
US Transmission: Not networked
Steed joins the Hellfire Club – Emma becomes Queen of Sin
Writer: Brian Clemens
Director: James Hill

Guest Cast: Peter Wyngarde (Cartney),
Robert Cawdron (Horace),
Michael Latimer (Roger Winthrop),
Jeremy Young (Willy Frant), Bill Wallis (Tubby Burn),
Steve Plytas (Kartovski), Art Thomas (Pierre),
Alf Joint (Big Man), Bill Reed (Huge Man).

Silly tricks are being played on various VIPs in diplomatic situations. All the clues point to the beautifully wasted John Cleverly Cartney, but would even a rake like that stoop to murder by electrified opening ribbon? Of course he would . . . It's Peter Wyngarde and his Hellfire Club!

Wit: ☆☆ A raid on the House of Lords: 'Whoopee cushion under the woolsack . . . Some of them took it as a vote of sanction.'

Kinkiness Factor: ☆☆☆☆☆ We've got Cartney, in riding boots, being fed grapes on a lounger by a woman with an anklet, then kicking her aside. We've got orgies on a budget.
   (Emma: 'On the surface it's innocent enough . . . '
   Steed: 'When can I join?').
   We've got Emma done up as the Queen of Sin ('Do with her what you will'), with snake, boots and spiked collar, a role she doesn't actually object to until Cartney attacks her with a whip, muttering 'Now what are you like with the big boys?' And they expected the American networks to show this??

Champagne: Erm, astonishingly, none . . .

Fights: ☆☆☆ Steed fights a duel with Willie, the digitally challenged fencing master (his choice of weapons, overruled, is 'feather dusters at 400 yards') and the Queen of Sin deals with little Pierre, the bearded kickboxer, with much panache and rather too much enthusiasm.

60s Concerns: What the neighbours are getting up to in the caves.

Strangeness: Lord Cardigan, one of the lords named, doesn't seem to have sued.

With a Young . . . : Colin Jeavons (Darcy), Carol Cleveland (Sara).

Notes: Some of the scenes with the whip were cut by nervous ITV bosses in some areas (the edited print was repeated by Channel 4; the original print is on the video release). It was originally submitted early in the season but ABC weren't keen on it. The *Evening Standard* on the day of broadcast carried a publicity still of Diana Rigg with a whip and the headline 'What You *Won't* See on *The Avengers* Tonight!' (In America the episode was, inevitably, banned, although legends persist of US TV middle-management gathering in hotel rooms to watch pirate copies of this episode.) Steed joins the club by chugging a quart of ale and then asking for more, and then cheating on another test. Cartney's first word to Emma is 'Mrs?' She is genuinely flattered by him – 'We got on rather well' – but frowns at his description of women as 'mere vessels of pleasure'. This episode achieved the series' highest-ever vewing figures (8.4 million) and fifth place in the weekly charts. This figure is all the more remarkable when it is remembered that the episode wasn't properly networked. Then again, with the advance publicity this episode got *nothing* is surprising. This is actually the height of the series, as camp as coffee and chicory and with the magnificent OTT grandeur of Wyngarde. One laughs at the sheer verve of it.

They Leave: In a coach and horses.

French Title: 'Le Club de L'Enfer'.

100
'What the Butler Saw'
26 February 1966
Filmed: c.December 1965/January 1966
US Transmission: 28 July 1966
Steed becomes a gentleman's gentleman – Emma faces a fate worse than death
Writer: Brian Clemens
Director: Bill Bain
Guest Cast: Thorley Walters (Hemming),
John Le Mesurier (Benson),
Denis Quilley (Group Captain Miles),
Kynaston Reeve (Maj.-Gen. Goddard),
Howard Marion Crawford (Brig. Goddard),
Humphrey Lestocq (Vice-Admiral Willows),
Ewan Cooper (Sgt Moran),
Leon Sinden (Squadron Leader Hogg),
David Swift (Barber), Norman Scace (Reeves),
Peter Hughes (Walters).

According to Steed's double-agent barber, one of three military men is a traitor. But which? To find out, Steed becomes a butler, and Emma starts Operation Fascination to trap the woman-hungry Group Captain Miles.

Wit: ☆☆ Miles: 'You like my etchings?'
Emma: 'You actually have some.'
Steed: 'Don't do anything I would do.'

Kinkiness Factor: None, but quite a lot of old-fashioned seduction though.

Champagne: ☆☆ Part of Miles's amorous arsenal.

Fights: ☆☆ Em slumps into Miles's embrace and throws him over the sofa. Steed vs butler with knife-wielding tea trolley. Emma finishes off a fellow unarmed-combat expert.

Strangeness: Three military men seal themselves into a giant plastic sack to avoid hidden microphones.

Eccentrics: Eccentric admiralty, soldiery, and RAF, all full of stereotypes, right down to appropriate facial hair. Steed matches them all in his disguises.

Notes: Rather a Tara episode, crossing that fine line between silly and stupid. Clemens sets up one of his formal approaches, Steed visiting each military man in suitable disguise and with a suitable name. It's a typical timewasting technique when there's not a lot in the episode beyond set pieces. It's nice that Miles is finally charmed by Emma's insistence that he doesn't have to seduce her, and they play Ludo. And there's fun with the training of butlers ('Obsequious, man, obsequious!'), as well as a genuinely unexpected hidden villain. Overall though, a bit ordinary.

They Leave: In a helicopter, Emma commenting that 'the butler did it'.

French Title: 'Les Espians Font le Service'.

101
'The House that Jack Built'
5 March 1966
Filmed: c.January 1966
US Transmission: 16 May 1966
Steed takes a wrong turning – Emma holds the key to all
Writer: Brian Clemens
Director: Don Leaver
Guest Cast: Michael Goodliffe (Prof. Keller),
Griffith Davies (Burton), Michael Wynne (Withers),
Keith Pyott (Pennington).

Emma inherits some property from her deceased Uncle Jack. The property is a very bizarre house, and when Emma goes to inspect it, she finds herself trapped in a labyrinth of psychological torture.

Kinkiness Factor: The whole situation is a vaguely Hitchcockian power fantasy, but it's not that much fun.

60s Concerns: Electronic brains.

Strangeness: The key given to Emma is, in effect, magical, seeming to be not only electronic, but radioactive too, its image fogging photo negatives.

Eccentrics: Frederic 'Pongo' Withers, an undercover agent dressed as a scoutmaster.

Notes: A holiday episode for Macnee. Emma's maiden name was Knight, which is what Steed is compared to when he rescues her at the end. He used to cycle in the area, and they leave on a tandem. The story's fast and cruel, but too damn serious and rather horrible in the drooling department. And the house itself is nowhere near as well designed as people will tell you it is. Mrs Peel meets Withers at Ivinghoe Beacon; the house exteriors were filmed at Shenley Lodge, Shenley.

They Leave: On a tandem.

102
'A Sense of History'
12 March 1966
Filmed: c.January/February 1966
US Transmission: 20 June 1966
Steed dons a gown – Emma becomes a don
Writer: Martin Woodhouse
Director: Peter Graham Scott
Guest Cast: Nigel Stock (Richard Carlyon),
John Barron (Henge), John Glyn-Jones (Grindley),
John Ringham (Prof. Acheson),
Robin Philips (John Pettit),
Peter Blythe (Millerson), Peter Bourne (Allen).

A death by archery sends Steed and Emma undercover at St Bodes Academy, where the arguments between staff and hip students, and between different theories of history, seem to have taken on a murderous edge.

Wit: ✪ Groping for a weapon: 'What do you want, historical memoirs or encyclopedia of erotica?'
   'The memoirs, they're heavier.'

Kinkiness Factor: ✪✪ Emma's Robin Hood costume. Oh dear. Not very politically correct at all.

169

Fights: ☆☆ Robin Hood battle with a bendy sword.

60s Concerns: New economics. Drop-outs.

Eccentrics: Professor Acheson, into isometric exercise? Not very.

With a Young . . . : Patrick Mower (Duboys), Jacqueline Pearce (Marianne).

Notes: A potentially deep illustration of conflict between Marxist and Fascist views of history – the latter fought for by Duboys's hip student rebels, dangerous because of their intellect rather than their violence – is rather obscured by Emma's Robin Hood costume. Steed gets to be rather dangerous and threatening, too. All a bit serious and thoughtful, really.

Woodhouse's second submission for this season: previously he had submitted a script entitled 'Rip Van Winkle', about a scientist experimenting with suspended animation.

They Leave: On a motorcycle-and-sidecar combination.

French Title: 'L'Econome et le Sens De L'Histoire'.

103
'How to Succeed . . . at Murder'
19 March 1966
Working Title: 'How to Succeed at Murder . . . Without Really Trying'
Filmed: February 1966
US Transmission: 13 June 1966
Steed becomes a perfect boss – Emma goes seeking charm

Writer: Brian Clemens
Director: Don Leaver
Guest Cast: Sarah Lawson (Mary),
Angela Browne (Sara), Anna Cunningham (Gladys),
Zeph Gladstone (Liz), Artro Morris (Henry),
Jerome Willis (Joshua Rudge),
Christopher Benjamin (Hooter),
Kevin Brenon (Sir George Morton),
David Garth (Barton), Robert Dean (Finlay),
Sidonie Band (Annie).

When several top executives die, their secretaries take over their firms. Is it mere chance, or are women trying to take over the world? Steed employs a deadly secretary, and Emma finds sorority down at the gym.

Wit: ☆☆

Kinkiness Factor: ☆☆☆ Steed puts a Sarah Cracknell lookalike (who's strangled a man with a stocking and shot another with her charm bracelet) over his knee and tickles her into telling all.

Fights: ☆☆☆ Emma fights off five secretarial assassins.

60s Concerns: The 'frightening reality' behind Women's Lib.

Strangeness: The secretaries want to rule the business world, 'bring men to heel and put women at the pinnacle of power' and have a slogan: 'Ruination to all men'. Did we fall asleep and watch some other series by mistake?

Eccentrics: J.J. Hooter, perfume manufacturer who bandages his nose to preserve his membranes. 'I smell a great deal,' he

171

confesses, before recognising his own creation 'Leap into My Fervid Arms'.

Notes: Emma paints a cubist Steed. Nice secretarial fantasies at the start: a secretary blowing up her boss after putting on a helmet, etc. Pity it turns into such sexist gittery. The leader of the rad-fem women is a ventriloquist's dummy with a brow-beaten male assistant. Can you guess who's really in charge? Tosh tosh tosh. Mary Merryweather's offices were actually the studio exterior.

They Leave: In the back of a caravan, Steed reading *The Ventriloquist*, Emma reading *Advanced Ventriloquism*.

French Title: 'Abus de Confiance'.

104
'Honey for the Prince'
26 March 1966
Filmed: February/March 1966
US Transmission: Not networked
Steed becomes a genie – Emma joins a harem
Writer: Brian Clemens
Director: James Hill
Guest Cast: Ron Moody (Hopkirk),
George Pastell (Arkadi), Roland Curram (Vincent),
Bruno Barnabe (Grand Vizier), Ken Parry (B. Bumble),
Jon Laurimore (Ronny Westcott),
Roy Pritchard (Postman), Peter Diamond (Bernie),
Carmen Dene (Eurasian Girl),
Richard Graydon (George Reed).

Steed and Emma return from a party to find a dying agent in Steed's flat. What is the connection between honey, a firm which makes fantasies to order and the oil deal promised by a visiting Baravian prince?

Wit: ☆☆☆ Villain cuts notes in half. 'Half now . . . '

Steed's proposed fantasy: 'A secret agent, pitting your wits against a diabolical mastermind.'

'It would certainly make a change.'

Kinkiness Factor: ☆☆☆ Em does a rather clodhopping dance of the six veils.

Fights: ☆☆☆ Steed throws East out of the window, Emma duels him with cutlasses.

Eccentrics: B. Bumble, honey-maker in striped pullover. 'One of them has a bad knee at the moment, I may have to operate.' Crown Prince Ali, cricket-loving potentate who keeps up Arab clichés for the sake of his Vizier.

With a Young . . . : Zia Mohyeddin (Prince Ali).

Notes: Steed has a great conversation about the bodies that keep appearing in his flat. 'It's very untidy.' There's the cool blonde 60s killer, Vincent East, and some lovely scenes of Steed and Emma arriving home from a party across countryside. Also a wonderfully toadying vizier, and we also get a black man, but he's just there to bang a gong. At least Ali gets some respect (could it be that *The Avengers* is only anti-black when they live in Britain?). Bridge scenes filmed at Tyke's Water Lake, Elstree. A test mini-episode, 'The Case of the Missing Corpse', was made in colour on the set of this story. It lasted approximately twenty minutes, and was intended exclusively for the American market as a trailer for the next season.

They Leave: On a magic carpet . . . on the back of a van.

Fifth Season

Introduction

The Avengers In Colour: A caption slide appears of a carnation stuck in a revolver (very 60s. . .). Then the title sequence, that marvellous choppy jazz tune, as Steed and Emma walk towards each other. The title comes up, and the tune becomes jauntier. We see swordsticks, karate moves and very red carnations. A stylistic summary of the series. Then a teaser sequence, usually showing how the body our heroes are going to investigate came to get where it is. The title, and a little description: Steed Does This, While Emma Does That. After that, unknown to viewers of the Channel 4 repeats, there's always an incredibly swift little scene where Steed tells Emma: 'Mrs Peel, we're needed.'

From that surprised first caption onwards, the show luxuriates in its newfound colourfulness. Colour first came to *The Avengers* camp in the form of a trailer, 'The Strange Case of the Missing Corpse'. This was filmed on the set of 'Honey for the Prince', and broadcast in America as a prelude to the new fifteen-part series (one episode not being transmitted in the original run). After the transmission of most of the black-and-white Rigg episodes, it was clear that a British series was becoming increasingly popular on primetime network TV in the States. Why? Because 1966 was the year when Davy Jones was the most popular of the Monkees, when the Beach Boys were going weirdo and the Beatles had seen it, done it and smoked it. In short, 1967 was going to be a good year to be British, a good year to be young, and a good year to be psychedelic. And since the previous year's big hit had been *Batman*, it might be a good idea to adopt a tongue-into-cheek posture.

The relationship between Emma and Steed is by now well established, and is seldom referred to. They no longer seem to have history, such is the confidence of this season. In America, there was no longer that embarrassing explanatory voice of last season, booming out our heroes' mission in life, one they never saw fit to explain in Britain. In this season, Steed simply shows up on Emma's doorstep and they're off, without backgrounds, motives or organisations to hinder them, and only an unspoken agreement holding them together. What sleight of hand that something so simple conquered America!

Wit: It must be said that with colour came a slight decline in the subtlety one had come to expect of the series. Some of these episodes have, dare one say it, their dull moments. However, there is humour to be had from the actual situations on occasion, with 'A Funny Thing Happened on the Way to the Station' and 'Who's Who???' being riotous in themselves: the cool lines are an added bonus.

Kinkiness Factor: Emma has stopped being tied to things on such a regular basis, but Steed's eyebrow has heightened an inch or two with some of the knowing exchanges between them.

Champagne: Still not the all-encompassing cultural weapon that it was later to become. Champagne appears in only five of the episodes, and we hear that Basil and Lola have finished it off in a sixth. However, it is now part of the title sequence.

Fights: These had now become outrageous production numbers. It's obvious from 'The Winged Avenger' that the production team had taken note of the development of this artform in *Batman*.

The Writers: Philip Levene writes exactly half the season, including the first four episodes to be transmitted, and does a very good job. It's his *Avengers*land that people remember, with one foot firmly in the real world and the other. . . not. Verbal wit is an important part of what he does, but so is the complete interrogation of a concept. For example, in 'The Hidden Tiger', we get every possible take on killer cats, every possible pussy line, etc. Brian Clemens, on the other hand, is a very direct writer, who tends to present the central problem, the 'twenty four words or less' of American screenwriting fame, straight away, and then simply do variations on it. He contributes six scripts. These range from the wonderful 'The Bird Who Knew Too Much' through to the patchwork 'The Living Dead' (a cut-and-paste job from an Anthony Marriott story that bears the signs of swift rewriting and steals hugely from 'The Town of No Return') to the horrid 'Epic'. Just what makes 'Epic' so awful is worth considering. It seems to be an attempt to do an iconic *Avengers* episode, one that Clemens could point to and say: now that's how it should be done. Everything that one expects in an episode is in it. Perhaps as a direct result of this it is completely vacuous and soulless, without heart or individuality. This was to be the problem in later years, *The Avengers* trying too hard to be itself, and, like some neurotic impersonator, losing all confidence in the process. Richard Harris contributes the very nice 'The Winged Avenger'. One of the best scripts of the season is actually a rewrite: 'A Funny Thing Happened on the Way to the Station' started off as a Roger Marshall script, but he and Clemens clashed over the direction the series was taking (Marshall objecting, very farsightedly, to some of Clemens's excesses), and he walked out on the series, refusing to have anything to do with the final draft. The pseudonym Bryan Sherriff is Brian doing the Marshall's job. Whether the quality of the end product is the result of a typically good Marshall script or of Clemens's forceful moulding of the series into its own image is hard to decide. We prefer to think

177

of it as typical *Avengers* serendipity, a happy accident of the kind that was soon to prove impossible to reproduce deliberately.

Top Five Episodes: 'The Hidden Tiger'
                                     'Escape in Time'
                                     'Who's Who???'
                                     'A Funny Thing Happened on the Way to the Station'
                                     'From Venus with Love'

Transmission Details

Broadcast details are as ABC. The season was partially networked. Associated Rediffusion transmitted the episodes one day earlier in London and affiliated regions.

16 colour episodes (60 mins)
ABC Television

Producers: Albert Fennell and Brian Clemens
Executive Producer: Julian Wintle

Music: Laurie Johnson

Regular Cast: Patrick Macnee (John Steed),
Diana Rigg (Emma Peel).

105
'From Venus with L♥ve'
14 January 1967, time not known
Working Title: 'The Light Fantastic'
Filmed: October/November 1966
US Transmission: 20 January 1967
Steed is shot full of holes – Emma sees stars
Writer: Philip Levene
Director: Robert Day
Guest Cast: Barbara Shelley (Venus),
Philip Locke (Primble), Jon Pertwee (Brig. Whitehead),
Derek Newark (Crawford), Adrian Ropes (Jennings),
Arthur Cox (Clarke), Paul Gillard (Cosgrove),
Michael Lynch (Hadley), Kenneth Benda (Mansford).

The strange deaths of several astronomers, left bleached white, pose a problem. Whilst Steed joins the stargazers, Emma chases a bright light, and finds herself in the hot seat.

Wit: ☆ ☆ ☆ Steed applies for membership of the British Venus Society.

'We're a very small, select group.'

'Good, I abhor overcrowding.'

Emma tries to describe the sphere to a disbelieving Steed: 'A thing!'

'From outer space?' he asks.

Kinkiness Factor: ☆ ☆ ☆ ☆ Emma is strapped into an optician's chair and menaced by a laser.

Fights: ☆ Emma (in a catsuit) fights Martin, a silver-suited henchman.

60s Concerns: Astronomy. Laser power.

Strangeness: Emma chases a glowing sphere down a country lane in her car. The sphere torches a scarecrow before disappearing. You *can't* get much stranger than this! Steed's eye-test with Primble consists of him looking at several rows of hats and naming them.

Eccentrics: Bert Smith, chimney sweep (actually Bertram Fortescue Wyndthrope-Smythe, an upper-class twit who is also into astronomy: 'In my position, sweeping chimneys, I do a lot of looking at the sky!'). Venus Brown, secretary of the BVS, wants to launch a satellite to Venus. Brigadier Whitehead (Jon Pertwee at his most manic), a mad ex-soldier who dictates his memoirs accompanied by sound effects from several gramophones simultaneously.

With a Young. . . : Jeremy Lloyd (as Bertram Smith).

Notes: 'Excellent!'
   'Not from where I'm sitting!'
   Pure 60s fantasy, with an eye-rolling SF 'mad scientist' in horn-rimmed spectacles (we wonder if *The Goodies'* Graeme Garden watched this episode). There are memorable scenes (notably Steed pursued through a graveyard by the sphere in true Hammer style), and a witty script. For the second season running our first sight of Emma is of her practising fencing in her flat when Steed arrives. (Although it appears on-screen as 'From Venus with L♥ve', this episode is referred to as 'From Venus With Love' elsewhere in the book.) Some footage was shot at Stanmore Hall, Stanmore.

Trivia: Emma says 'We've got to the moon' when the first moon landings were not for another two years.

106
'The Fear Merchants'
21 January 1967
Filmed: September 1966
US Transmission: 27 January 1967
Steed puts out a light – Emma takes fright
Writer: Philip Levene
Director: Gordon Flemyng
Guest Cast: Patrick Cargill (Pemberton),
Brian Wilde (Raven), Annette Carell (Dr Voss),
Garfield Morgan (Gilbert), Andrew Keir (Crawley),
Jeremy Burnham (Gordon White),
Edward Burnham (Meadows), Bernard Horsfall (Fox),
Ruth Trouncer (Dr Hill), Declan Mulholland (Saunders),
Philip Ross (Hospital Attendant).

Four men involved in the production of ceramics suffer nervous breakdowns in everyday situations. All have recently turned down the opportunity to merge with the British Porcelain Company. Steed and Emma investigate the world of fear, with terrifying consequences.

Wit: ☆☆ Raven: 'If I've bagged most of the market, it's merely the fruits of enterprise.'
    Steed: 'Which seems to have ripened pretty quickly.'

Kinkiness Factor: ☆☆☆☆ A lingering shot of Mrs Peel's bottom as she bends over the bonnet of a car to look at the engine (nobody said anything about 'subtle kinkiness'). At the end of the episode Emma wears a legendary black leather number with holes everywhere and is (as usual) tied in a chair and menaced by various lethal-looking bits of medical equipment.

Fights: ☆☆ Steed is trapped in a sand quarry by a bulldozer and has a very energetic fight with Gilbert before the man is killed when the bulldozer topples over the edge and crushes him.

60s Concerns: Phobias. Executive stress.

Strangeness: A man wakes up in his pyjamas in the middle of a deserted Wembley stadium. The noise of a nonexistent crowd sends him into hysterics. The episode's car chase for once has a specific plot point – Crawley suffers from speed-phobia. The tattoo of a spider on the arm of a hospital orderly aggravates Raven's arachnophobia.

Eccentrics: Pemberton, leader of the Business Efficiency Bureau, who makes businesses more efficient by eliminating the opposition. He has a chair that is really a lie detector and wears dark glasses because he is afraid of light. Jeremy Raven (motto 'creation by automation') wants a monopolised control over the ceramics industry.

Notes: Emma is, according to Pemberton, 'a woman without fear'. The episode is a bit sadistic and lacking in the usual quick-fire wit one associates with Philip Levene. It was largely filmed at Pinewood. (Jeremy Burnham, who played White, would go on to write for the show in the seventh season.)

Trivia: Possibly the first use of a telephone answering machine on (fictional) television. Steed has such a 'recording device' (obviously one of the perks of the job).

German title: 'Schock Frei Haus'.

107
'Escape in Time'
Filmed: September 1966
US Transmission: 17 July 1968
Steed visits the barber - Emma has a close shave
Writer: Philip Levene
Director: John Krish
Guest Cast: Peter Bowles (Thyssen),
Geoffrey Bayldon (Clapham), Judy Parfitt (Vesta),
Imogen Hassall (Anjali), Edward Caddick (Sweeney),
Nicholas Smith (Parker), Roger Booth (Tubby Vincent),
Richard Montez (Jusino), Clifford Earl (Paxton),
Rocky Taylor (Mitchell).

Several notorious criminals have vanished into thin air. A whisper has been received that the escape chain starts in London, but, when agent Paxton follows it, he winds up dead in the Thames with a 300-year-old bullet in him. 'Mrs Peel, we're needed!'

Wit: ☆☆☆☆☆ Steed is surprised to find that Emma can sew. 'Our relationship hasn't been exactly domestic,' she says.
Thyssen shows Steed film of the 1904 Derby:
'A little before my time. . .'
'Not necessarily!'
Thyssen suggests sending Mrs Peel back to 1760, an era where women 'were appreciated. You need to be appreciated, Mrs Peel.'
'I appreciate your appreciation!'
When apparently in the 1560s with the evil Matthew Thyssen: 'These strange clothes you wear. The devil's work! Designed to inflame a man's passion!' 'You should see me in 400 years' time!' And many, many more. Another flawless script from Philip Levene.

Kinkiness factor: ✩✩✩✩ Emma is sent to the horror of Matthew Thyssen's Elizabethan inquisition, complete with hooded executioner. She is placed in foot-stocks and threatened with a red-hot poker. Very Edward II. 'I can think of a few names to call you,' she tells Matthew, 'Short, up-to-date, highly descriptive names!' Steed, meanwhile, fights Vesta and handcuffs her to a pillar. When he and Emma 'return to the 1960s', Emma sees the handcuffed woman and asks, 'Didn't we get the vote?'

Champagne: ✩ Steed pours three glasses whilst he and Emma await the arrival of Tubby Vincent.

Fights: ✩✩✩✩ Emma fights a Steed lookalike in a railway siding. At the episode's climax Emma tackles Thyssen while Steed takes on his henchman. She finishes first and sits fanning herself as Steed carries on.

60s Concerns: Escape (in all its forms), equality, you name it . . .

Strangeness: On opening the morgue slab containing Paxton, Steed shows Mrs Peel his feet rather than his face. Steed and Emma follow Jusino, a criminal, in a brilliant silent sequence involving the passing to different couriers of various stuffed animals. Emma is then pursued by a man in full hunting uniform on a motorcycle! She falls into what appears to be the same sand quarry Steed fell into in 'The Fear Merchants'.

Eccentrics: Waldo Thyssen, a stuttering genius with an interesting past.

Notes: This is another great episode, a dialogue triumph. Peter Bowles is magnificent playing four parts (but one part really). Again, as with other Levene scripts, it's the little things that are

The Avengers

Steed (Partrick Macnee) and Cathy Gale (Honor Blackman) hide in the shrubbery from 'The Undertakers'.

Mit Schrim, Charme und Melone, as they say in Germany. Steed in the fourth season title sequence.

Enter television's first great feminist superhero. Emma Peel (Diana Rigg) from the season four credits.

Steed and Emma survive a car crash in green-belt Hertfordshire during "The Hour That Never Was."

Thwack! It's the Cybernauts.

The iconic,

voyeuristic

games of

'The House That

Jack Built'.

Patrick Macnee on the

set that Jack built.

Ooo, kinky.

The Queue of Sin at Peter Wyngarde's

Hellfire Club – Mrs Peel in 'A Touch of

Brimstone.'

A nice white girl – is she

for sale? Mrs Peel in

'Honey for the Prince'.

They enjoyed their champagne, and still caught the Diabolical Masterminds. From the fifth season title sequence.

'The Superlative Seven', with a young . . . Charlotte Rampling.

The end of an era. The beginning of the end? Mrs Peel hands over to Tara (Linda Thorson) in 'The Forget-Me-Knot'.

A year too late for 'The Hidden Tiger', Tara's pussy fetish finds an outlet in 'Whoever Shot Poor George/XR40?'

We've run out of jokes.

Tara with a sword.

A man's best friend is h Mother (Patrick Newell).

The Avengers

impressive. The 'Time Machine' is a wonderfully tacky slot machine. The barber is called 'T. Sweeney' ('Shaving a speciality!'). There is also an interesting (and none-too-patronising) stab at Indian religious culture. Much of the story was filmed at Pinewood, with Starracres, Radlett, doubling as Thyssen's house. Both this tag scene and that of the next two stories were filmed at Beaulieu in Hampshire.

Trivia: Steed is said to be 6' 2", 170 pounds and always carries his umbrella in his right hand (except when he doesn't, of course).

German Title: 'Fahrkarin in die Vergangenheit'.

108
'The See-Through Man'
4 February 1967
Filmed: November 1966
US Transmission: 3 February 1967
Steed makes a bomb – Emma is put to sleep
Writer: Philip Levene
Director: Robert Asher
Guest Cast: Moira Lister (Elena),
Warren Mitchell (Brodny), Roy Kinnear (Quilby),
Jonathan Elsom (Ackroyd),
John Nettleton (Sir Andrew Ford),
Harvey Hall (Ulric), David Glover (Wilton).

The Ministry has been broken into by, it seems, an invisible man. A trail leads via inventor Quilby to the Eastern Drug Company, a front organisation run by Soviet intelligence. Meanwhile, the crack spies Elena and Alexandre Vazin are in town. But nobody has seen anything of Alexandre . . .

Wit: ☆☆☆ 'The self-propelled bayonet?'
'That left a deep impression!'
Steed explains to Emma the benefits of invisibility: 'You take a tablespoon at night and in the morning your troubles have vanished. And so have you!'

Kinkiness Factor: ☆ Elena keeps her gun in her garter.

Champagne: No, vodka.

Fights: ☆☆ Brodny tries to put Emma in a hammerlock. She breaks it with the 'Emma Peel pushoff!' Emma and Elena fight like a pair of angry cats throwing each other around the room with gay abandon.

Strangeness: Emma follows Elena in her MG through the Hertfordshire backroads accompanied by a swinging mod soundtrack.

Eccentrics: Ernest Quilby, a mad inventor. He has sent an invention a week to the MoD for the last twenty years.

Notes: 'Transparency's all the rage this year!' *The Invisible Man* reworked (and with a twist). An interesting portrayal of the MoD as a real civil service department, drowning in paper and bureaucracy. Warren Mitchell makes his second appearance as Ambassador Brodny (the first was in 'Two's a Crowd'). This is the only episode of *The Avengers* in which the Beatles are mentioned (Brodny has tickets for 'their next concert' – unlikely as they'd given up touring by 1967). Quilby's house is Shenley Lodge, Shenley. Edge Grove School, Aldenham, doubles for the foreign embassy, and once more the BR Centre at the Grove, Watford, is pressed into service, this time as Daviot Hall.

109
'The Bird Who Knew Too Much'
11 February 1967
Filmed: October 1966
US Transmission: 10 March 1967
Steed fancies pigeons – Emma gets the bird
Writer: Brian Clemens
(Based on a story by Alan Pattillo)
Director: Roy Rossotti
Guest Cast: Ron Moody (Jordan),
Ilona Rogers (Samantha Slade),
Michael Coles (Verret), John Wood (Twitter),
Clive Colin-Bowler (Robin), John Lee (Mark Pearson).

Emma and Steed investigate the mystery of how top secret things are being photographed from the air. Could it have something to do with the groovy world of fashion photography and a parrot called Captain Crusoe? Probably.

Wit: ☆ 'Now he's a polly gone.' Yes, that bad.

Kinkiness Factor: ☆☆☆ Emma is gagged and tied to a chair. Also, she locks a chap between her ankles.

Champagne: ☆☆ And caviar.

Fights: ☆☆☆☆ On top of a diving board to cool organ music; also, in a hansom cab, oddly placed in the back of the bird exhibition.

60s Concerns: The absurdities of fashion (Emma cuts a dash as Britannia at a photo shoot).

Strangeness: There is a penny-farthing in the bird exhibition (*Prisoner*esque).

Eccentrics: Edgar J. Twitter, curator of the bird exhibition, is straighter than his name. However, Jordan, headmaster of a school for birds, with a bird atop his mortarboard, has an ordinary name. Weird.

With a Young. . . : Kenneth Cope (Tom Savage), Anthony Valentine (Cunliffe).

Notes: The narrative moves really fast, with great style. Steed gets a grenade put in his umbrella. Good episode to show off to non-fans. Jordan's house footage was shot at Shenley Hall, Shenley.

110
'The Winged Avenger'
18 February 1967
Filmed: December 1966
US Transmission: 17 February 1967
Steed goes birdwatching – Emma does a comic strip
Writer: Richard Harris
Directors: Gordon Flemyng and Peter Duffell
Guest Cast: Nigel Green (Sir Lexius Cray),
Jack MacGowan (Prof. Poole),
Neil Hallett (Arnie Packer), Colin Jeavons (Stanton),
Roy Patrick (Julian), John Gorrie (Tay-Ling),
Donald Pickering (Peter Roberts),

William Fox (Simon Roberts), A.J. Brown (Dawson), Hilary Wontner (Damayn), John Crocker (Fothers), Ann Sydney (Gerda).

Is a creature that can walk up walls clawing to death ruthless and powerful men? Does it have anything to do with Professor Poole's invention of boots that let you walk on the ceiling, or with cartoon superhero the Winged Avenger?

Wit: ☆☆☆ Emma Peel on walking on the ceiling: 'It'll ruin the carpet trade.'

Kinkiness Factor: ☆ At the studio there are, as Emma notes, 'a number of girls in various states of exposure'.
   'Ah yes,' says a fondly remembering Steed.

Fights: ☆☆☆☆ On the ceiling with sticky silver wellies, and with *Batman*like music as the villain is hit with 'Zap!' panels of artwork.

60s Concerns: Comic strips.

Strangeness: Tay Ling, an odd butler in a T-shirt and suit jacket, is meant to be a Sherpa, but is obviously non-oriental.

Eccentrics: Sir Lexius Cray, a mountaineer who climbs everywhere, even downstairs; Professor Poole, an inventor who sleeps hanging from the ceiling.

Notes: Original director Peter Duffell was replaced by Gordon Flemyng. 'It wasn't anything to do with him being a bad director,' said Clemens, 'he just wasn't an *Avengers* director.' Sir Lexius Cray's House is High Commons, Well End; Professor Poole's residence was filmed at Stanmore Hall. On the ceiling, Emma's collar carefully hangs down, but the villain's cape doesn't. Artist Frank Bellamy did the strip frames used to illustrate the action, but did he appreciate the bizarre idea of comic artists using studios and models? The episode is an obvious spoof of *Batman*: pure pop art. 'Ee-urp!'

111
'The Living Dead'
25 February 1967
Filmed: December 1966/January 1967
US Transmission: 3 March 1967
Steed finds a mine of information – Emma goes underground
Writer: Brian Clemens
(based on a story by Anthony Marriott)
Director: John Krish
Guest Cast: Julian Glover (Masgard),
Pamela Ann Davy (Mandy),
Howard Marion Crawford (Geoffrey),
Jack Woolgar (Kermit), Jack Watson (Hopper),
Edward Underdown (Rupert), John Cater (Oliphont),
Vernon Dobtcheff (Spencer), Alister Williamson (Tom).

Strange apparitions rise from the graveyard on the estate of the sixteenth Duke of Benedict. Did the mine disaster of five years previously really kill his predecessor and thirty men? When Emma is taken underground, Steed ventures into the giant secret that hides under the village.

Wit: ☆☆ 'What's in season now?'
   'Me!'

Kinkiness Factor: ☆ Emma fights with Mandy. Not very politically correct.

Fights: ☆☆ Emma's karate duel with Mandy, and she gets to shoot a whole firing squad with an SMG.

60s Concerns: Psychic investigators. Ideal communities.

Strangeness: The foreign firing squad is led by a very British sergeant-major.

Eccentrics: Kermit the hermit; Mandy from FOG (Friends Of Ghosts) and Spencer from SMOG (Scientific Measurement Of Ghosts).

Notes: Steed wears a miner's lamp on his bowler. The stock footage mine is on the edge of the studio graveyard. Emma and Steed share a peck on the cheek after she's saved him from certain death.

112
'The Hidden Tiger'
4 March 1967
Filmed: January 1967
US Transmission: 17 March 1967
Steed hunts a big cat – Emma is badly scratched
Writer: Philip Levene
Director: Sidney Hayers
Guest Cast: Ronnie Barker (Cheshire),
Lyndon Brook (Dr Manx), John Phillips (Nesbit),
Michael Forrest (Peters), Stanley Meadows (Erskine),
Jack Gwillim (Sir David Harper),

**Frederick Treves (Dawson),
Brian Haines (Samuel Jones), John Moore (Williams),
Reg Pritchard (Bellamy).**

The mauling to death of several members of the committee of PURRR (the Philanthropic Union for the Rescue, Relief and Recuperation of Cats) exposes Steed and Emma to a diabolical scheme to take over the entire country.

Wit: ☆☆☆☆ Steed on finding Emma has a pile of books about milk: 'You mean you've waded through these?'

'I believe the word is skimmed!'

Cheshire asks the name of Steed's 'faithful pussy': 'Emma!'

'What a joy it must be for you when she's curled up in your lap?'

'I've never really thought of it that way.'

The best line, however, is when Emma sees Steed trapped in a room full of maddened cats. 'Pussies galore!'

Kinkiness Factor: ☆☆☆☆ Diana Rigg and Gabrielle Drake in one episode. Me-owww! Steed calls Emma a 'beautiful, bronzed tabby', to which she makes a purring noise. Rather uniquely, Steed is tied to a chair in mortal peril and Emma has to rescue him.

Champagne: ☆ Steed enjoys a glass whilst Emma listens in on her walkie-talkie. 'Cheers,' she says before asking if they can establish radio silence. Emma tells Cheshire her cat (John) is very bad-tempered in the morning until he's had his first glass of champagne.

60s Concerns: Killer pussies (very big in the 60s. . .).

Strangeness: Emma enters a laboratory chasing Erskine's

192

killer. As she opens the door, a milk churn rolls towards her: 'Grade 1 Pasturised'. Steed arrives at PURRR in the midst of a cat funeral (complete with harmonium and undertakers).

Eccentrics: Major Nesbitt, a big game hunter whose aid Steed enlists. Mr Cheshire, head of PURRR. Dr Manx and Angora, his assistants who plan to turn Britain's moggies into an unholy army of the night. And you thought this was a serious story?

With a Young. . . : Gabrielle Drake (Angora).

Notes: 'Inside every cat there's a hidden tiger.' A classic example of Philip Levene's *Avengers*: wonderfully mad, and complete with a set of dangerous lunatics whose names reflect their obsession. The dialogue is sparkling (Cheshire tells Emma one of the cats in his care was a mental wreck on arrival. 'Persecution complex. Thought it was being pursued by a poodle!'). If ever an episode defined what *The Avengers* was all about, it's this one. A masterpiece. PURRR scenes were filmed at North Mymms Park, Welham Green.

German Title: 'Vorsicht Raubkatzen'.

113
'The Correct Way To Kill'
11 March 1967
Filmed: January/February 1967
US Transmission: 24 March 1967
Steed changes partner – Emma joins the enemy
Writer: Brian Clemens
Director: Charles Crichton
Guest Cast: Anna Quayle (Olga),

**Michael Gough (Nutski), Philip Madoc (Ivan),
Terence Alexander (Ponsonby),
Peter Barkworth (Percy), Graham Armitage (Algy),
Timothy Bateson (Merryweather),
Joanna Jones (Helga), Edwin Apps (Winters),
John G. Heller (Grotski).**

Foreign agents are being killed, but not by British agents. Steed thinks it terribly unfair, and so does his opposite number, Nutski. They make an arrangement, and Steed and Emma find themselves with Soviet partners in an investigation of a group of very British killers.

Wit: ☆☆☆ 'My cheek is going to be nowhere near his jowel.'

Kinkiness Factor: ☆ Steed's new partner Olga is tied up with old school ties. 'And the bonds of the old school tie are well-nigh impossible to break.'

Fights: ☆☆☆ Steed takes on a swordsman with umbrella and rapier, while Emma fences with two opponents, until Olga pitches in.

60s Concerns: Them and us, again explored as something rather silly.

Eccentrics: Nutski, antique-shop owning boss of foreign powers in Britain; J. Nathan Winters, umbrella maker who tries his new lines in the shower; Tarquin Ponsonby-Fry, boss of SNOB ('Sociability, Nobility, Omnipotence, Breeding, Inc.'), who trains young bowler-hatted gentlemen, and is overjoyed with Steed's style even as he threatens him with a gun. There's also a chiropodist involved, but he's not an eccentric, and how many can one episode stand?

Notes: This story is a reworking of the third season script 'The Charmers'. All SNOBs have swordstick umbrellas like Steed. One of the murdered Soviet agents is identified as poor old Arkadi from 'Honey for the Prince'. Emma finds a photo of Steed labelled 'Dangerous, handle with care', and then one of her labelled 'Very dangerous, do not handle at all'. Olga is a fun creation, and just as dangerous as Emma. The whole thing lopes along merrily, especially when the villains bicker about whose job it is to chloroform Olga.

German Title: 'Kennen sie 'Snob'?'.

French Title: 'Meurtres Distingues'.

114
'Never, Never Say Die'
18 March 1967
Filmed: February 1967
US Transmission: 31 March 1967
Steed meets a dead man – Emma fights a corpse
Writer: Philip Levene
Director: Robert Day
Guest Cast: Christopher Lee (Prof. Stone),
Jeremy Young (Dr Penrose),
Patricia English (Dr James), David Kernan (Eccles),
Christopher Benjamin (Whittle),
John Junkin (Sergeant), Peter Dennis (Private),
Geoffrey Reed (Carter), Alan Chuntz (Selby),
Arnold Ridley (Elderly Gent),
David Gregory (Young Man), Karen Ford (Nurse).

An unfortunate motorist keeps knocking down and killing the same man: a man who's rampaging through the countryside, bulletproof and intent on destruction. A man who just happens to be identical to the urbane Professor Frank N. Stone.

Wit: ☆ Emma, on her condition after being locked in cell full of robot duplicates: 'Untouched by human hands.'

Fights: ☆ Emma and Steed fight the androids and are saved by a nurse.

60s Concerns: Brainwave reading, distrust of establishment.

Eccentrics: George Eccles. He plays chess by radio with foreign nationals, not in different languages, but in English with different accents.

Notes: An interesting teaser scene: Emma is sitting at home watching television which is showing a scene from 'The Cybernauts' when Steed appears with his inevitable 'Mrs Peel, we're needed'. Lee gets to play characters with hints of both Dracula and Frankenstein's Monster in an incredibly dull location runaround with one odd hint of political reality to it: since Stone has mended his first batch of malfunctioning killer robots, Steed won't trouble him about the murders they committed. Cybernauts in human form, but all teeth-grindingly tedious. Arnold Ridley gets to play with a remote-controlled boat, though. Hospital scenes shot at Haberdasher Aske's School, Elstree.

French Title: 'Interferences'.

115

'Epic'
1 April 1967
Filmed: February 1967
US Transmission: 14 April 1967
Steed catches a falling star – Emma makes a movie
Writer: Brian Clemens
Director: James Hill
Guest Cast: Peter Wyngarde (Stewart Kirby),
Isa Miranda (Damita Syn),
Kenneth J. Warren (Z.Z. von Schnerk),
David Lodge (Policeman), Anthony Dawes (Actor).

Three Hollywood veterans, led by an insane director, decide
that Emma would be perfect for their latest movie, so they
kidnap her and film some surreal and deadly footage. (Yes, it
really is as simple as that.)

Wit: ☆ Emma roars in the Schnerk company's movie logo.

Kinkiness Factor: ☆☆ Emma is tied to an upright chair and
menaced by both buzzsaw and pendulum. Schnerk's drooling
makes it all rather unpleasant but at least Emma gets to say:
'Gloat all you like, but just remember I'm the star of this
picture!'

Fights: ☆☆ Emma vs Kirby three times, on two of which he
puts aside his sword first. Emma gets conked twice by Kirby's
'Mum'.

60s Concerns: The prison of fictionality (cf. *The Prisoner*).

Strangeness: A very expressionist storm of confetti in Emma's wedding/funeral scene. Hmm, wedding = funeral? Do we detect Freudian overtones?

Eccentrics: The three movie clichés.

Notes: Emma is kidnapped from her mews flat, gassed, and wakes up in a replica of it (very *Prisoner*). A rather horrid episode, just a series of witless clichés put to groovy music, the viewer emerging feeling dirtied rather than entertained. Oh, and there's an actor playing a policeman. Whatever next, an actor playing a black character?

German Title: 'Filmstar Emma Peel'.

French Title: 'Camera Meutre'.

116
'The Superlative Seven'
8 April 1967
Filmed: February/March 1967
US Transmission: 21 April 1967
Steed flies to nowhere – Emma does her party piece
Writer: Brian Clemens
Director: Sidney Hayers
Guest Cast: Brian Blessed (Mark Dayton),
James Maxwell (Jason Wade),
Hugh Manning (Max Hardy),
Leon Greene (Freddy Richards),
Gary Hope (Joe Smith), John Hollis (Kanwitch),
Margaret Neale (Stewardess),
Terry Plummer (Toy Sung).

Steed is invited to a party, and finds himself trapped in a remote-controlled aircraft, with six fancy-dressed specialists in various combat styles, en route to a distant island. There, they are pitted against each other in a deadly test.

Wit: ☆ ☆ ☆ ☆ Steed on hearing that a bullfighter had killed 400 bulls: 'That is quite a lot of. . . That's a very impressive record.'

Fights: ☆ Around a table with sword and spear a couple of times. Dull, with much use of doubles.

60s Concerns: Remote control.

Strangeness: The world's strongest man is very camp and plays the piano. And why not?

Eccentrics: Jessel, the hippy eastern spy-trainer. Not very.

With a Young. . . : Charlotte Rampling (Hana), Donald Sutherland (Jessel).

Notes: This episode is loosely based on the third-season script 'Dressed to Kill'. (Brian Clemens commented that 'not having taken the Blackman episodes, the Americans hadn't had the chance to see these, and they were so good we thought we'd do them again.') A 'Diana Rigg takes a week off' episode. It's very *New Avengers*, from the comic strip prologue (a lot of karate experts killing each other) to the *New Avengers* option of Mrs Hana Wilde, an expert shot with the show-off traits required. (Steed's partner in the *Avengers* stage play was called Hannah Wild.) Steed has the skills of all the other participants, straightening a poker bent by the strongman. Some quite clever playing with expectations, and good studio use of the aircraft. Altogether, rather subtle and wonderful.

117

'A Funny Thing Happened on the Way' to the Station

15 April 1967
Filmed: March 1967
US Transmission: 28 April 1967
Steed goes off the rails – Emma finds her station in life
Writer: Bryan Sherriff (see Notes)
Director: John Kirsch
Guest Cast: James Hayter (Ticket Collector),
John Laurie (Crewe), Drewe Henley (Groom),
Isla Blair (Bride), Tim Barrett (Salt),
Richard Caldicott (Admiral), Dyson Lovell (Warren),
Peter J. Elliott (Attendant), Michael Nightingale (Lucas),
Noel Davis (Secretary).

When Lucas, an agent investigating something subversive, gets off his train at the wrong station he is murdered. Has the crime got anything to do with a mole at the admiralty, a train ticket and a fiendish plot to kill the Prime Minister? (Indeed.)

Wit: ✩✩✩✩ Emma on finding a corpse in Steed's flat: 'You really must have a word with that cleaning lady of yours.'

Steed on the villain's threat to kill the Prime Minister: 'How do you know which way I voted?'

Kinkiness Factor: ✩ Steed is cuffed to an overhead rail.

Champagne: ✩ Only with the married couple.

Fights: ✩✩✩✩✩ Emma vs woman in compartment (she leaves her on the luggage rack and explains: 'A slight difference of opinion.') Emma vs the groom out of the train door.

Everybody vs everybody in a steam-filled compartment.

60s Concerns: Post-Beeching derelict stations.

Strangeness: The name of the Prime Minister is obscured by a passing train. (Jokes in the tag scene make it clear that the Prime Minister is Harold Wilson.)

Eccentrics: Crewe, a railway fanatic who lives in a semi-detached signal box. There are also assassins disguised as the bride and groom, the groom whistling 'Here Comes the Bride' and using a *Bonnie and Clyde* tommy gun. The ticket collector supervillain has a with full-scale control room on the train and wears a little eyeshade hat. What more do you need?

Notes: Real trains used to good effect. There is a tape recorder in Steed's umbrella handle. And, yes, a real uniformed policeman! But still no black characters. Still, this one's just what people think the show is always like. Smashing! (Bryan Sheriff is a pseudonym for a Brian Clemens rewrite of a Roger Marshall script, who left the show suddenly. Apart from 'The £50,000 Breakfast' (a remake which Marshall had little to do with), Marshall never wrote for the programme again.)

French Title: 'Une Petite Gare Desaffectee'.

118
'Something Nasty in the Nursery'
22 April 1967
Filmed: March/April 1967
US Transmission: 5 May 1967
Steed acquires a nanny – Emma shops for toys!

Writer: Philip Levene
Director: James Hill
Guest Cast: Dudley Foster (Mr Goat),
Paul Eddington (Beaumont), Paul Hardwick (Webster),
Patrick Newell (Sir George Collins),
Geoffrey Sumner (General Wilmot),
Clive Dunn (Martin), George Merritt (James),
Enid Lorimer (Nanny Roberts),
Louise Ramsay (Nanny Smith)
Penelope Keith (Nanny Brown),
Dennis Chinnery (Dobson).

Secrets known only to a small group of trusted men have leaked, and the men are having strange dreams of their childhood, featuring their nannies and a bouncing ball. Emma checks out the toyshop, Steed explores a school for nannies.

Wit: ☆☆ 'Haven't you noticed, as soon as we discover someone who can supply the answer–'
   'Someone always gets to them first.'

Kinkiness Factor: Zero, surprisingly.

Champagne: ☆ On ice at Steed's place, but nobody drinks it.

Fights: ☆ A series of brief tussles, including Emma memorably attacking a Mini as it tries to run her over.

60s Concerns: Brainwashing, psychedelics, regression therapy.

Strangeness: Sir George Collins seemingly lives at Park Mansions, a very downmarket block of flats.

Eccentrics: Martin, the toyshop owner, who does toys for the aristocracy. Goat, senior nanny tutor, but actually a cross-dressing, pretend-disabled Communist. How PC.

With a Young. . . : Yootha Joyce (Miss Lister), Trevor Bannister (Gordon).

Notes: Emma has a 'shush' that silences babies. A bomb that's a black sphere with 'bomb' written on it is thrown into Steed's flat, and we see a nanny with a tommy gun and a pistol-firing jack-in-the-box. Great! Location filming at North Mymms, Welham Green and Starracres, Radlett.

119
'The Joker'
29 April 1967
Filmed: April 1967
US Transmission: 12 May 1967
Steed trumps an ace – Emma plays a lone hand
Writer: Brian Clemens
Director: Sidney Hayers
Guest Cast: Sally Nesbitt (Ola),
Ronald Lacey (Strange young man),
John Stone (Major George Fancy).

Invited for the weekend to the home of a fellow Bridge expert, Emma finds herself trapped in a house designed to send her mad. Her tormentor is Max Prendergast, a man she befriended and then betrayed in Berlin some time before. Then Steed came to the rescue but now he's at home nursing a sprained ankle.

Wit: ☆☆ The 'strange young man' asks Emma if she'd like him to tuck her up in bed. 'How'd you like me to break your

203

arm?' she replies. Steed, driving along a road in a real pea-soup of a fog passes a sign offering 'a splendid view of four counties'.

Kinkiness factor: ☆ Emma is seen in a bra and spied on throughout the episode through various peep-holes in the walls.

Fights: Emma takes on Prendergast and Ola (both armed) on a staircase and beats them both without the help of Steed who's still stuck in the fog. He arrives in time to bonk Prendergast with an oversized playing card.

Strangeness: Doors disguised as playing cards. The card motif runs throughout the episode on things like rings, clock-faces, etc. All of the records in the house are the same: *Mein Liebling, Mein Rose*.

Eccentrics: Ola Chamberlain, obsessed with her teeth and interesting-sounding words. A right weirdo.

With a Young. . . : Peter Jeffrey (Prendergast).

Notes: 'It's the end of the world here so nobody stays very long.' 'Don't Look Behind You' re-done with Hammer overtones. You get the impression that Emma is not so much frightened by the spooky goings-on as irritated by them.

Trivia: Emma's article in the June issue of *Bridge Players* is called 'Better Bridge Playing with Applied Mathematics'. Whilst in the house, Emma begins to read a book called *Trump Hand*.

120
'Who's Who???'
6 May 1967
Filmed: April 1967
US Transmission: 19 May 1967
Steed goes out of his mind - Emma is beside herself
Writer: Philip Levene
Director: John Moxey
Guest Cast: Patricia Haines (Lola),
Freddie Jones (Basil), Campbell Singer (Major 'B'),
Peter Reynolds (Tulip), Arnold Diamond (Krelmar),
Philip Levene (Daffodil), Malcolm Taylor (Hooper).

When one of the Floral Network of agents is found dead atop a pair of stilts, Steed and Emma's interest is piqued. That's the idea, because foreign agents Basil and Lola have a trap prepared for them: a machine that swaps their minds into the pair's bodies!

Wit: ☆☆☆ 'Do you take me for a perfect idiot?'
'Nobody's perfect.'

Kinkiness Factor: ☆☆☆☆ Steed and Emma, in their new bodies, are handcuffed together while Basil and Lola are having serious snogging fun in their old ones, having fancied them in a very creepy wife-swapping kind of way beforehand.

Champagne: None: Basil and Lola have drunk the last of Steed's '47. And not even chilled!

Fights: ☆☆ Battles with doubles using a psychiatrist's couch.

60s Concerns: Mind transfers and so on (*The Prisoner* again).

Strangeness: A practising GP has invented a mind-transfer device.

Notes: After every ad break, a seriously British announcer explains to us just what's happened to Steed and Emma, not, he says, that he quite understands it either. Basil and Lola are a wonderful couple, giving Macnee and Rigg the chance to have fun, boogie and kiss (Macnee convincing us that there's another mind in there, in much the same way as he did in Levene's 'Two's a Crowd'), and Jones and Haines get the chance to do wonderful impersonations of the leads, complete with mannerisms. Basil puts Brylcreem on Steed's hair! Writer Philip Levene gets a cameo role in this story, and he's excellent as well.

French Title: 'Qui-Suis-Je?'.

Sixth Season

Introduction

Following a six-week break after the completion of 'Who's Who???' in April 1967, the production team returned to Borehamwood to complete a further ten episodes. Along with the sixteen from the fifth season these were intended to be sold as a 26-episode package to the American networks.

In the end, it didn't turn out that way. The schedule was tight – the first episode was due to go out as part of the ITV autumn package in September 1967, at which point the team would still be filming the later episodes – and if anything went wrong, the consequences could be disastrous.

When something did go wrong, it came in the formidable shape of Diana Rigg. The popular perception of the mid-60s was of an *Avengers* episode being completed and then Steed and Emma popping into town in the Bentley to enjoy an evening at the discotheque with the Beatles. In fact, according to Rigg, 'It *was* great fun to do but everyone thinks it was party, party, party. In fact it was work, work, work. You had to get to the studio at Elstree for 6.30 every morning, and you'd be working until eight o'clock every night.' She claimed that she was 'earning less than the cameraman', and issued an ultimatum to ABC, describing her working conditions as 'the life of a mole'. She got her pay rise but indicated that this would be her final batch of episodes. Having already earned more than five million dollars from US syndication rights (according to an article in *The Times* in March 1967), the production team could afford to be generous to its biggest asset.

Aesthetically, the stories from the fifth and sixth seasons are very similar, although the 'Mrs Peel, we're needed' sequences disappeared in the sixth season. However, something seems to have changed in the writers' bible during the summer of 1967. The new batch of episodes were much more serious than those of the previous few months (a trend that would continue into the next season). Philip Levene provided four of the scripts, whilst Brian Clemens worked on three, and between them they began to draw Steed and Emma back from the brink of science fiction and (vaguely) into the real world.

Ultimately, only eight episodes were completed (the season ending, somewhat prematurely, with the broadcast of 'Mission . . . Highly Improbable' on 18 November 1967). The episode 'The Forget-Me-Knot', begun in September, was abandoned before completion due to the hierarchical changes taking place behind the camera. The point at which season six becomes season seven is actually very difficult to establish. However, by 30 October 1967 – when *The Times* announced that Linda Thorson ('who is 20 and rather disarmingly admits that she has dyed her hair blonde') was 'stepping into the shoes, or boots, of two famous predecessors' and that filming had started on 'Invitation to a Killing' – the sixth season had, effectively, been put to bed. What happened to the mysterious tenth episode is lost in the mists of time.

So, of the eight episodes broadcast, we have a sequel for the series' most popular foes, a rewrite of a Cathy Gale episode, a story about nightmares, a location travelogue, two 'plot device' episodes, an Emma solo adventure and a parody of SF non-sense. Filmed in the three months that included the release of *Sgt Peppers'*, the Six-Day War and the devaluation of sterling, Steed's suave charm and Emma's acid Chelsea wit were probably just what the country needed. Certainly the episodes were as popular as ever, both critically and in terms of viewing figures.

We are solemnly informed by the end credits that 'the principle items of Mr Macnee's wardrobe [are] designed by Pierre Cardin', whilst Diana Rigg managed to get out of the leather suits and into Alan Hughes's brilliantly designed Crimplene catsuits (dubbed 'Emmapeelers' by their creator). For Rigg herself, this was a moment of personal satisfaction. 'It meant I could move – we are talking about three-quarters of an hour to go to the lavatory, because they were so tight!'

As Diana Rigg has noted, 'I was *always* getting tied to dentists' chairs with my legs in the air!' However, by this stage much of the inherent kinkiness had been diverted into dialogue. A case of too much talk and not enough action, perhaps? Conversely, these are possibly the best bunch of episodes for fisticuffs since Honor Blackman left the show: the sight of Mrs Peel dancing the kung-fu seven years before Carl Douglas is still an awesome one.

Critique: By this stage critics were divided on the series' progression into the fantastic. Carole Millington wrote: 'The programme has always suffered from a surfeit of fantasy, and in that lies much of its charm. Steed and Mrs Peel can cope placidly with the most outrageously improbable situations and introduce a touch of extravagant myth into the run-of-the-mill adventure series.' This contrasts sharply with another critic, Lesley Blake, who considered that the series was not what it once had been, and reckoned that the rot set in with Emma's pants: 'This was a cracker of a series until Mrs Peel's leather trouser suit became a fashion craze ... My heart sank when the current series began and all we seem to hear is what everyone would wear, who would design them and what the clothes were going to cost. Dianna [sic] Rigg, poor girl, hasn't half the character of Honor Blackman, anyway.' Blake concluded: 'It's just conceivable that if they spent less on all these expensive fashion trimmings they might still be able to make a programme that was, simply, a good programme.'

A fine article in *The Viewer* coincided with the beginning of the season. Rupert Butler described in detail his visit to the set of 'You Have Just Been Murdered'. Diana Rigg told Butler 'I had to do a deep sea fight with a sinewy villain'. It sounded, the reporter thought, 'intriguing in a kinky sort of way. I can reveal that, with mounting visions of swelling insurance premiums, the girl just dived in and got on with it. In a masterpiece of understatement that might have come straight from an *Avengers* script, Diana breathed: "It was a welcome cooler on a hot day!"'

Perhaps the last word on this season should go to Steed and Mrs Peel themselves, from the tag sequence at the end of 'The Positive Negative Man'. Magnetised by all of that 'messing around with electricity', they find themselves stuck to Steed's Bentley. 'Don't fight it, Mrs Peel,' notes Steed, 'We're inseparable.' Not for much longer, they weren't, but for that beautiful, mad summer of 1967 they were.

Top five episodes: 'Death's Door'
                                          'Dead Man's Treasure'
                                          'The £50,000 Breakfast'
                                          'Return of the Cybernauts'
                                          'Mission . . . Highly Improbable'

Broadcast Details

Broadcast details are as ABC. The season was partially networked. Associated Rediffusion transmitted the episodes two days earlier in London and affiliated regions.

8 colour episodes (60 mins)
ABC Television
Producers: Albert Fennell and Brian Clemens
Executive Producer: Julian Wintle

Music: Laurie Johnson

Regular Cast: Patrick Macnee (John Steed),
Diana Rigg (Emma Peel).

121
'Return of the Cybernauts'
30 September 1967, time not known
Filmed: June 1967
US Transmission: 21 February 1968
Steed pulls some strings – Emma becomes a puppet
Writer: Philip Levene
Director: Robert Day
Guest Cast: Peter Cushing (Paul Beresford),
Frederick Jaeger (Benson),Charles Tingwell (Dr Neville),
Roger Hammond (Dr Russell),
Anthony Dutton (Dr Garnett),Noel Coleman (Conroy),
Aimi MacDonald (Rosie),Redmond Philips (Hunt),
Terry Richards (Cybernaut).

The brother of the late Clement Armstrong sets a deadly trap for Steed and Mrs Peel, whom he blames for his brother's death at the hands of his murderous creations, the Cybernauts.

Wit: ☆☆ Beresford: 'Surely Steed could handle this alone?'
   Emma: 'He could, but I mustn't let *him* find out!'
   Later, Beresford explains that he is controlling Emma via her watch: 'No ordinary watch, Mr Steed. It controls the will . . .'
   'But does it keep good time?'

Kinkiness Factor: Not a trace.

211

Champagne: None, but lots of wine ('the '29'). After Steed has been laid out by a Cybernaut Emma asks where he wants the ice placed. 'In a large whisky!'

Fights: ☆☆☆ Both Steed and Emma (unsuccessfully) take on the automatons. The epic climax involves a *huge* tussle featuring six characters, a Cybernaut and a gun.

60s Concerns: Cybernetics (again!).

Strangeness: Emma discusses Beresford's self-sculpture in bronze in very pretentious 'arty' terms. The dichotomy of the Cybernauts wandering around the English countryside is, as ever, very surreal. It is never explained why Armstrong's brother is called Beresford.

Eccentrics: Rosie, a bimbo secretary-dolly-bird who owns a tiny bikini ('I've nearly been arrested twice wearing it'), and takes a shine to both Steed and one of the Cybernauts. A rather obvious stereotyped brainless female; not very liberated.

With a Young . . . : Fulton Mackay (Professor Chadwick, an immoral scientist).

Notes: Some clever continuity with the first Cybernauts story, including some footage featuring Michael Gough and the return of Benson. A good adventure tale, with a chilling performance from Peter Cushing. Very sombre, however, with few laughs to the pound. On the other hand, the tag sequence with Steed putting Emma's toaster in orbit is a delight. The kidnap of Neville was filmed at Haberdasher Aske's School, Elstree; with Woolmers Park, Letty Green providing the exteriors for Beresford's house.

German Title: 'Und Noch Einmal Roboter'.

122
'Death's Door'
7 October 1967
Filmed: May/June 1967
US Transmission: 31 January 1968
Steed relives a nightmare – Emma sees daylight
Writer: Philip Levene
Director: Sidney Hayers
Guest Cast: Clifford Evans (Boyd),
William Lucas (Stapley),
Allan Cutherbertson (Lord Melford),
Marne Maitland (Becker), Paul Dawkins (Dr Evans),
Michael Faure (Pavret), Peter Thomas (Saunders),
William Lyon Brown (Dalby), Terry Yorke (Haynes),
Terry Maidment (Jepson).

A European peace conference comes under the threat of sabotage when the British delegates begin to suffer from premonitions and nightmares. After Sir Andrew Boyd, who has witnessed his death in a dream, is killed, Steed and Emma must keep his replacement, Lord Melford, sane (and alive).

Wit: ☆☆ Emma and Steed discuss premonitions: 'There was that horoscope of mine. Told me I'd run into a tall dark stranger.'
    'And?'
    'I bumped into your car!'

Kinkiness Factor: ☆☆ Steed describes one of his dreams thus: 'I was in a sultan's harem, stifled with incense, bound in silken cords. I was being beaten mercilessly with a large bunch of black grapes . . .' Little overt kinkiness, but one incredible moment as Emma is given a walkie-talkie by Steed. 'You know my wave-length?' she asks.

Champagne: No: Steed asks Emma if she would prefer coffee or orange juice for breakfast after a night's surveillance. 'Both,' she replies.

Fights: ☆☆☆ Steed, trapped on Becker's shooting range, ingeniously kills the agent with a bullet and a stone, accompanied by a groovy Hammond organ soundtrack. Emma has two fights with henchmen, whilst Steed is at his most energetic, sliding along a table to tackle Stapley.

Strangeness: Lord Melford's dream is Dali on acid, with much use of giant-sized props, faceless men and strange camera angles. The scenes of Emma wandering around the warehouse where Melford's dreams were created are very spooky indeed.

Notes: 'Welcome to Nightmare alley.' Surrealism and phobias finally explained via a fiendish plot that throws up many disturbing images. A very serious episode, and a genuinely great one. Conference Centre scenes shot at the International University, Bushey.

123
'The £50,000 Breakfast'
14 October 1967
Filmed: June 1967
US Transmission: 28 February 1968
Steed dabbles in Tycoonery – Emma in Chicanery
Writer: Roger Marshall (Based on a story by
Roger Marshall and Jeremy Scott)
Director: Robert Day

Guest Cast: Cecil Parker (Glover),
Yolande Turner (Miss Pegrum),
David Langton (Sir James Arnall),
Pauline Delaney (Mrs Rhodes), Anneke Wills (Judy),
Cardew Robinson (Minister),
Eric Woolfe (1st Accountant),
Philippe Monnet (2nd Accountant),
Richard Curnock (Rhodes),
Jon Laurimore (Security Man),
Richard Owens (Mechanic),
Michael Rothwell (Kennel Man),
Yole Marinetti (Jerezina),
Christopher Greatorex (1st Doctor),
Nigel Lambert (2nd Doctor).

The accidental death of a ventriloquist reveals that he had been carrying a fortune in gems inside his stomach. Steed stoops to blackmail and Emma goes shopping for ties in the search through the business community for a rich Borzoi.

Wit: ☆☆☆ 'High in carat, low in protein.'

'He likes rich food.'

Steed on why the room is spinning: 'It must have been the Worcester sauce and tomato juice.'

Tie for 'Old Anonians, the school of hard knocks.' Another of Marshall's witty ones.

Kinkiness Factor: ☆☆ Steed and Emma are handcuffed to bedposts.

Fights: ☆☆ Emma shuts one villain in a car boot, and throws another into the road, and fights the villainess across a four-poster.

Strangeness: 'Can I give you one?'
'Not before sundown.' Hmm . . .

Eccentrics: The vicar in charge of Happy Valley pet cemetery. Judy, the tie-seller wearing a kipper tie.

Notes: There's a whole steel band of black men. 'Why the jungle music?' asks Steed, rather shaking our faith in him. Marshall's traits reappear: informed, witty script with greater use of women (particularly as villains) and more scenes not involving Steed and Emma than the usual. The butler villain is great. The script is a rewrite of 'Death of a Great Dane'. The hospital exteriors were actually those of the studios.

French Title: 'Un Petit Dejeuner Trop Lourd'.

124
'Dead Man's Treasure'
21 October 1967
Filmed: June/July 1967
US Transmission: 13 March 1968
Steed rallies around – Emma drives for her life
Writer: Michael Winder
Director: Sidney Hayers
Guest Cast: Valerie Van Ost (Penny),
Edwin Richfield (Alex), Neil McCarthy (Carl),
Arthur Lowe (Benstead), Ivor Dean (Bates),
Rio Fanning (Danvers), Penny Bird (Miss Peabody),
Gerry Crampton (1st Guest), Peter J. Elliott (2nd Guest).

The search for a small despatch box containing secret information hidden by a dying agent leads Steed and Emma into a race (quite literally) for the 'treasure'. In the process they must face foreign agents, new partners and a car simulator that electrifies its guests. Shocking!

Wit: ☆☆ Steed (referring to the car simulator): 'Marvellous chassis.'

Benstead (referring to Mrs Peel): 'I'll say!'

Emma (to Penny): 'You must tell me about your clutch control.' These make up for several (dreadful) 'shocking' puns used throughout.

Kinkiness Factor: ☆☆ Emma is chained to the simulator with the voltage on full. She still doesn't lose her cool.

Champagne: ☆☆☆ Yes, in the first scene! Emma asks if she's intruding when she turns up on Steed's doorstep at 3am. 'You're not intruding,' says Steed when he sees the bottle in her hand. Another bottle is used at the climax in celebration of Emma's Grand Prix-style performance.

Fights: ☆☆ Emma and Carl fight in a room full of car horns. Honk! Honk!

60s Concerns: The 'toys' of the idle rich.

Strangeness: One of the villages on the race-route is called 'Swingingdale'. It would be, wouldn't it?

Eccentrics: Sir George Benstead, a racing nut who has a Brands Hatch simulator. He also owns several car prints that he 'picked up cheap in a shop in Prestatyn'. Penny Plain, Steed's partner in the race, is a 'kooky' chick whose boyfriends have an unfortunate habit of dying on her. Not very eccentric, but outrageously 'London'.

217

With a Young...: Norman Bowler (Mike, the suave double-agent).

Notes: Lots of shots of Bentleys and Jaguars speeding around the Hertfordshire backroads. (The footage was shot at Aldbury Ridge and Letchmore Heath, with Shenley Hall doubling for Benstead's house.) Great fun, and rather like an extended episode of *The Wacky Races* (with the bumbling villains Carl and Alex in the roles of Dastardly and Mutley, perhaps).

125
'You Have Just Been Murdered'
28 October 1967
Filmed: July/August 1967
US Transmission: 24 January 1968
Steed chases a million – Emma walks off with it
Writer: Philip Levene
Director: Robert Asher
Guest Cast: Barrie Ingham (Unwin),
Robert Flemyng (Lord Maxted),
George Muncell (Needle), Leslie French (Rathbone),
Geoffrey Chater (Jarvis), Clifford Cox (Chalmers),
John Baker (Hallam), Les Crawford (Morgan),
Frank Maher (Nicholls), Peter J. Elliott (Williams).

Various millionaires are withdrawing large sums of money from the bank. Steed suspects blackmail but none of the men is willing to talk. Then he gets a call from Gilbert Jarvis, who tells Steed he has just been murdered. Again.

Wit: ☆☆☆ Steed tells Emma about a recent party with millionaire George Unwin. 'There were three topics of conver-

218

sation: money, how to get it, and how to hold on to it. Very dull unless one's income was in the seven-figure bracket!'

Steed and Emma speculate on the collective noun for millionaires. Emma suggests 'a multi' but Steed prefers 'a tycoonery'.

Champagne: ☆☆☆☆☆ A party full of it. And 'a very old, very rare sherry'.

Fights: ☆☆☆☆☆ Emma is attacked by Nicholls wielding a scythe in a very brutal sequence (the swishes of the blade coming ever-closer to Emma's head really make the viewer wince). Then she nearly drowns Morgan in an underwater knife fight ('take me to your leader, or lead me to your taker, which ever you prefer!').

60s Concerns: Blackmail.

Strangeness: Needle persuades Unwin to tune his TV into 'Channel B' at 10pm , where the 'programme' turns out to be details of where to deliver the £1 million 'ransom'. Needle's HQ is a disguised haystack (as in 'Needle in a haystack' . . . Groan).

Eccentrics: The millionaires are all pretty strange. Money does this to people, apparently.

With a Young . . . : Simon Oates (later to play Steed on stage) as Skelton.

Notes: 'Murder is a shocking crime.' A great villain, Needle (so called because he is 'so hard to find'), who uses television techniques to extort money from his victims. The episode is a little formulaic (especially the seemingly endless country-lane car chases). Steed seems to tape-record his phone calls. Paranoid, or what?

French Title: 'Meutres à Episodes'.

126
'The Positive Negative Man'
4 November 1967
Filmed: August 1967
US Transmission: 17 January 1968
Steed makes the sparks fly – Emma gets switched on
Writer: Tony Williamson
Director: Robert Day
Guest Cast: Michael Latimer (Haworth),
Caroline Blakiston (Cynthia Wentworth-Howe),
Peter Blythe (Mankin), Sandor Elés (Maurice Jubert),
Joanne Dainton (Miss Clarke),Bill Wallis (Charles Grey),
Ann Hamilton (Receptionist).

When a scientist is found embedded in a wall, Steed and Emma pursue a man in make-up and wellies, whose appearance is terribly shocking.

Wit: ☆ As Emma says: 'It was a corny situation, calling for corny measures.'

Kinkiness Factor: ☆☆ Emma is tied to a couch and wrapped in silver foil. 'As you can see, I'm all tied up.'
   But she does get to ask Steed: 'What are you, AC or DC?'
   'I've never had occasion to find out.'

Fights: ☆☆ Em, with one rubber boot, vs electrified villain, while Steed knocks his partner out of the window. Then they both manage to fire the Positive Negative Man through the roof.

60s Concerns: The projection of electrical power, *à la* Tesla.

Eccentrics: Cynthia, the secret secretary, who keeps keys in her stockings ('Don't forget to return the key,' Emma tells Steed), and angles on her 'day orf'.

With a Young . . . : Ray McAnally (Creswell).

Notes: The monster in a Morris Minor van, obviously an attempt to do a Cybernauts again, fails to impress. It's odd to see Steed (possessor of the Red Card that allows him to read all military files) up against bureaucracy. What with the presence of a Terribly English Hyphenate, also an eccentric, in the intelligence services, and an obvious lack of wit, it all adds up to the starting point of Tara-ism. This time, the BR Centre in Watford doubles for Risley Dale.

127
'Murdersville'
11 November 1967
Filmed: August/September 1967
US Transmission: 7 February 1968
Emma marries Steed – Steed becomes a father
Writer: Brian Clemens
Director: Robert Asher
Guest Cast: John Ronane (Hubert),
Ronald Hines (Dr Haynes), John Sharp (Prewitt),
Sheila Fearn (Jenny), Eric Flynn (Croft),
Norman Chappell (Forbes), Robert Cawdren (Banks),

Marika Mann (Miss Avril), Irene Bradshaw (Maggie), Joseph Greig (Higgins), Geoffrey Colville (Jeremy Purser), Loughton Jones (Chapman), Tony Caunter (Miller), John Chandos (Morgan), Andrew Lawrence (Williams).

Emma's old friend, Paul Croft, returns from abroad to retire to Little Storping-in-the-Swurf. Unfortunately, the village seems to be run along very strange lines. Threatened by yokels, Emma finds herself outnumbered.

Wit: ☆ On seeing a 'silence' sign in library, the assassin adds a silencer to his gun.

Kinkiness Factor: ☆☆ Em is secured to a wall by a chastity belt and ducked on a ducking stool.

Champagne: ☆☆☆ Three glasses in Steed's flat at start ('27 rather than '26), and sipped through a helmet at end.

Fights: ☆☆ Emma fells the doctor when she sees Paul's body, and stops herself killing him (real sentiment! Goodness!); then takes on the whole village before helping Steed to finish the baddies off with ancient weapons (a huge spear straight through the doctor), books and cream cakes.

With a Young . . . : Colin Blakeley (Mickle).

Notes: Eric Flynn looks rather like Errol. Could he be . . . ? This is obviously a holiday story for Macnee, Emma being solo most of the time. There's a uniformed policeman (albeit a bogus one). 'Get the helicopter!' yell the yokels at one point: the one they get is very *Prisoner*esque, and shows off the huge location budget. The Iron Maiden from 'Castle De'ath' is in the village

222

museum. Pretending to be his wife on the phone, Em tells Steed to 'kiss little Albert for me, and Julian, and baby Brian.' Presumably Fennell, Wintle and Clemens, but who's the Gordon that Steed adds to the list? Perhaps Gordon L.T. Scott? A fun episode, albeit one that takes a bit of time to show off its location filming (largely at Aldbury, with Stocks Hotel being Croft's house).

French Title: 'Le Village de la Mort'.

128
'Mission . . . Highly Improbable'
18 November 1967
Working Title: 'The Disappearance of Admiral Nelson'
Filmed: September 1967
US Transmission: 10 January 1968
Steed falls into enemy hands – Emma is cut down to size
Writer: Philip Levene
Director: Robert Day
Guest Cast: Ronald Radd (Shaffer),
Jane Merrow (Susan), Noel Howlett (Prof. Rushton),
Francis Matthews (Chivers), Richard Leech (Col. Drew),
Stefan Gryff (Josef), Nicholas Courtney (Gifford),
Kevin Stoney (Sir Gerald Bancroft),
Peter Clay (Sergeant), Nigel Rideout (Corp. Johnson),
Cynthia Bizeray (Blonde), Nicole Shelby (Brunette),
Nosher Powell (Kenrik), Denny Powell (Karl).

When Sir Gerald Bancroft and his Rolls-Royce vanish whilst being escorted at a military base, Steed is called upon to solve the puzzle. But before he can he experiences that old shrinking feeling . . .

Wit: ☆☆ After a miniaturised Steed has stabbed the villain Emma is fighting in the foot with the nib of a giant fountain pen: 'The pen is mightier than the sword, Mrs Peel.'
'Between us we've written them off.'

Kinkiness Factor: ☆ Steed and Emma discuss things they would like to see reduced, inevitably ending with bermuda shorts and mini skirts.

Champagne: None: astonishingly, Steed passes up the opportunity to attend a gathering for drinks after the military show to continue his investigations. A first, surely?!

Fights: ☆☆

Strangeness: Dr Chivers first appears with a butterfly net, chasing (and catching) a miniaturised Bancroft. This is another story with huge Dali-esque props (notably a giant telephone).

Notes: Francis Matthews and Ronald Radd have a wonderful double act as the scheming spies. The miniaturisation effects are breathtaking although the story itself is a little dull. The forced surrealism of the scenes in which first Steed and then Mrs Peel are reduced is apparent. 'The Disappearance of Admiral Nelson' was originally proposed for a black and white film episode in 1964. One interesting note: Nicholas Courtney's character is almost a dry run for the actor's long-running performance of Brigadier Lethbridge-Stewart in *Doctor Who*. Shaffer's house scenes filmed at Rabley Park, Ridge.

German Title: 'Haben sie's Nicht ein Bißchen Kleiner?'.

Seventh Season

Introduction

The roots of the seventh season of *The Avengers* actually go back to the end of the sixth, which was originally planned for ten episodes but was abandoned with eight completed during the production of a ninth, 'The Forget-Me-Knot', in September 1967.

At this point things become a little confusing. Either as a result of influence from the American backers, or due to the insistence of Thames Television, Brian Clemens and Albert Fennell left the production team (Clemens moving to work on *The Champions* with Dennis Spooner). The reasons given for this extraordinary decision are many (and highly apocryphal), the most frequently cited being that the company thought *The Avengers* was becoming too 'way out', and wanted a return to the style of the early seasons. To this end, John Bryce, the producer of the later Cathy Gale era, was reappointed.

One of Bryce's first problems was finding a replacement for Diana Rigg. After 'screen-testing half of London', including Mary Peach and Tracey Reed (see 'The Curious Case of the Countless Clues'), six actresses were short-listed. Among them were Gabrielle Drake, Jane Merrow and Valerie Van Ost, all of whom had appeared in colour Rigg stories.

In the end, however, 20-year-old Canadian actress Linda Thorson, who had no previous television experience (and was, according to Brian Clemens, 'fresh out of drama school'), was chosen. Thorson developed Steed's new companion's name: Tara being the place where Scarlet lived in *Gone With the Wind,* her favourite film, and King being shortened from the English attitude to 'King and Country'.

Having sent her to a health-farm to lose weight, and taken the decision to have the character as a blonde (which Clemens describes as 'making her look like Harpo Marx'), production for the seventh season began in October 1967 with a 90-minute Donald James episode entitled 'Invitation to a Killing'.

However, after two episodes ('Invitation to a Killing' and 'Invasion of the Earthmen') it became very clear that the new style of the series wasn't working. Clemens and Fennell were rushed back onto the project in December 1967, during the filming of 'The Great Great Britain Crime'. Of the three episodes, 'Invasion of the Earthmen' was the easiest to salvage, with just a few short scenes inserted to explain Tara's use of a blonde wig. (In reality, the dyeing of Linda's hair had proved a disaster, especially for the actress whose hair rebelled and began to break off at the roots. She looked much better as a brunette anyway.) 'Invitation to a Killing' was almost completely refilmed as 'Have Guns – Will Haggle', whilst 'The Great Great Britain Crime' was left in the vaults for some considerable time, before being remounted as a 'flashback' episode.

Clemens and Fennell then completed work on 'The Forget-Me-Knot', which they thought would be a useful bridge into the new era (they even persuaded Diana Rigg to come back and film a final crossover scene with Tara, which was done on 19 January 1968), before throwing themselves into saving the seemingly doomed season.

By March 1968, with the first seven episodes (including the refilmed 'Have Guns – Will Haggle') completed, they were broadcast in America (forming, with the last eight Rigg episodes, a 15-week season). 'The Forget-Me-Knot' was first shown in the States on 20 March 1968 (a full six months before it would debut in Britain). American reaction was positive, especially to the character of Mother (Steed's crippled boss played by Patrick Newell). It was suggested that the character should become a recurring one and so, starting with 'You'll Catch Your Death' (filmed in April), Newell appeared in most of the remaining episodes. The American run also had a different title sequence (Tara chased by a hovering rifle-sight being protected by Steed's bowler). The British title sequence, meanwhile, maintained the high standard of the classic fifth and sixth season titles with Steed and Tara in a field full of knights in armour, and with a mad jazz trumpet solo added to the theme music.

Production continued through 1968 and on into 1969 ('The Great Great Britain Crime' was finally remounted in January 1969, 15 months after filming had begun), ending with 'Bizarre', which was completed in early March. By this stage the series had begun transmission, 'The Forget-Me-Knot' going out on 25 September 1968.

It is believed that Clemens and Levene clashed over the show's style soon after the former's return: Levene wanted gritty, 'old-fashioned' episodes, whilst Clemens wanted fantasy. Of the Bryce-commissioned scripts, only Nation's 'Invasion of the Earthmen' impressed Clemens, and so Nation was asked to step into Levene's shoes as script supervisor. (Levene was recalled by ITC after this season to form part of a team, with Julian Wintle and Laurie Johnson, to produce two pilots. One was *Mr Jericho*, starring Patrick Macnee as a con man; the other was *The Firechasers*, with American Chad Everett, based on a Levene radio series about insurance investigators.)

This season includes possibly the second most ridiculous piece of aggrandisement on an end credit when stating 'Patrick Macnee's costumes designed by himself'. For connoisseurs, the *most* ridiculous occurs on *The Persuaders!* ('Lord Brett Sinclair's suit designed by Roger Moore. Gowns by 'The Total Look of Debenhams''!)

Another semi-regular member of the cast was Rhonda, Mother's assistant, played by Australian actress Rhonda Parker.

Rhonda doesn't speak in any episode in which she appears.

For one episode ('Killer'), when Linda Thorson was on holiday, the character of Lady Diana Forbes-Blakeney was created (played charmingly by Jennifer Croxton). Jennifer had appeared in 'Invitation to a Killing', but had been lost on the cutting-room floor when it was refilmed.

Despite the fact that in Europe the season was a major success, in America, where it was placed in a time-slot opposite the massively popular comedy show *Rowan and Martin's Laugh-in*, the season stiffed. It has been claimed since that the increased violence in the series was a factor in the decision to cancel it, but this is dismissed by the production team.

Critique: TV critic Max Wilkinson wrote of his pleasure at the series in 1969. 'One wonders idly whether the ritual violence and studied kinkiness of *The Avengers* are corrupting. For if they are not, why is the series so enjoyable? I enjoy it anyway, in spite of the repetitive gimmicks, stereotyped stories and rather silly characters. The series still has a certain class no doubt largely because of Steed's simple technique of failing to register emotion (it's so attractive). And I like the girl too, especially when she is spread-eagled waiting to be shot. But I know it is naughty; presumably it takes a lot of other viewers the same way.'

Brian Clemens still regards the scripting on the Tara episodes as 'the best of all. Much more variety, ingenuity, originality.'

Top five episodes: 'Game'
     'Look - (stop me if you've heard this one) But There Were These Two Fellers . . . '
     'False Witness'
     'The Rotters'
     'Super-Secret Cypher Snatch'

Transmission Details

The transmission details are as Thames (i.e. what remained after the ABC/Associated-Rediffusion merger). The season was partially networked until December 1968, and there are extremely divergent transmission orders across the country. 'My Wildest Dream' was only broadcast in late-night slots (hence being shown late on 7 April 1969 rather than prime-time 9 April).

33 colour episodes (60 mins)
ABC Television

Producers: Albert Fennell and Brian Clemens
Producer (uncredited): John Bryce
(episode 144 and parts of 140, 154)
Executive in charge of production:
Gordon L.T. Scott
Consultant to the series: Julian Wintle
(episodes 129, 132–134, 139, 140, 144, 147, 156, 160)

Story Consultant: Philip Levene
(episodes 129–134, 136, 139, 140, 144, 147, 156, 160)
Script Editor: Terry Nation
(episodes 135, 137, 138, 141–143, 145, 146, 148–155, 157–159, 161)

Music: Laurie Johnson
(episodes 129, 133–135, 137, 139–141, 143–150, 152, 154–161)
Music Supervisor: Laurie Johnson
(episodes 130, 131, 136, 138, 142, 151, 153)
Score: Howard Blake

(episodes 130, 131, 136, 138, 142, 151, 153)
Additional Music: Howard Blake (episodes 148, 156)

Regular Cast: Patrick Macnee (John Steed),
Linda Thorson (Tara King),
Patrick Newell (Mother,
episodes 129, 131, 132, 135, 136, 138, 141, 142,
143, 145, 148–154, 157, 159, 161),
Rhonda Parker (uncredited, Rhonda,
episodes 135, 136, 138, 143, 149, 152, 154, 157),
Diana Rigg (Emma Peel, episode 129)

129
'The Forget-Me-Knot'
25 September 1968, time not known
Originally filmed: September 1967
Refilmed: December 1967/January 1968
US Transmission: 20 March 1968
Writer: Brian Clemens
Director: James Hill
Guest Cast: Patrick Kavanagh (Sean),
Jeremy Burnham (Simon Filson),
Jeremy Young (George Burton), Alan Lake (Karl),
Douglas Sheldon (Brad), John Lee (Dr Soames),
Beth Owen (Sally), Lean Lissek (Taxi Driver),
Tony Thawnton (Jenkins), Edward Higgins (Gardener).

Steed's friend Sean Mortimer arrives at Steed's flat in a state of
confusion. He cannot remember how he has got there or even
who he is. He only nows that there is a traitor in the organisation. While Mortimer and Emma are captured by a pair of
motorcycle villains, Steed seeks help from his Mother, meets

Agent 69, and becomes the centre of suspicion himself.

Wit: ☆☆ Tara: 'You want my address and phone number? I've read your file and it tells everything. Even your Achilles heel.'
   Steed: 'Rubber-soled shoes?'
   Tara: 'The opposite sex. I would have written it in invisible ink, but I couldn't find any!'
   There are numerous 'Mother' puns (e.g. 'Mother knows best', 'Mother sent me'). The first few are funny, then the joke wears a bit thin.

Kinkiness factor: Zero. The tag-scene is touching and the long-awaited kiss between Emma and John alone is worth the licence fee.

Champagne: No. Mother gives Steed a whisky and soda.

Fights: ☆☆☆ Emma and Mortimer are attacked by the motorcycle boys with dart guns in Steed's flat. Later, Steed and Emma take on the same pair, with the same result. Emma has one last wonderful fight, taking on both of her captors. A fitting finale.

Strangeness: Mother's HQ is a strangely designed mixture of geometric shapes, step ladders and ceiling grips. (Mother can 'walk' in this episode.) There's also a drug-induced psychedelic dream sequence for Steed, but by 60s standards, it's pretty normal.

With a Young ... : Linda Thorson.

Notes: 'Even the biggest idols can have feet of clay.' A fine episode, especially considering the production problems. The episode has the standard Rigg title sequence, but a new set of end titles which, though similar to the American 'third season' titles, was only ever used in the UK on this episode. (Tara sticks her finger through a bullet hole in Steed's bowler, and fires a revolver whilst applying some lipstick. Very kinky.) Interestingly, this title sequence crops up on episodes transmitted in Germany (as *Mit Schirm, Charme und Melone*).

Trivia: Tara ('ra-boom-de-aye!') has the trainee number 69 (really, Brian . . .). She is aware of Steed ('the star pupil of the spies' academy'), and has always been taught to do things the way Steed would. Steed takes three lumps of sugar in his tea and, according to Emma, likes it stirred anti-clockwise. Steed's address is 3 Stable Mews. Emma's husband is called Peter and is an 'air ace' whose plane crashed in the Amazon jungle. When he returns at the episode's end, he dresses *exactly* like Steed.

German Title: 'Auf Wiedersehen, Emma'.

French Title: 'Ne M'Oubliez Pas!'.

130
'Game'
2 October 1968
Filmed: June 1968
US Transmission: 23 September 1968
Writer: Richard Harris
Director: Robert Fuest
Guest Cast: Peter Jeffrey (Bristow),
Garfield Morgan (Manservant),
Aubrey Richards (Professor Witney),
Anthony Newlands (Brigadier Wishforth-Brown),
Alex Scott (Averman),

Desmond Walter-Ellis (Manager),
Geoffrey Russell (Dexter), Achilles Georgiou (Student),
Brian Badcoe (Gibson).

The sudden deaths of several of Steed's former army colleagues are revealed to be part of an elaborate engine of destruction, devised by a man court-martialled by them all. And now he is playing a deadly game . . .

Wit: ☆☆ Bristow, referring to the game of 'Super Secret Agent' that he makes Steed play: 'Embodied in the game is that traditional element of all spy sagas, the damsel in distress . . . '

Kinkiness Factor: ☆☆☆☆ The first signs of Steed's spanking fetish – slapping Tara to wake her up for a dawn appointment – emerge. If he'd tried that with Mrs Peel we speculate she'd have rammed his umbrella down his windpipe. Tara displays disturbing neo-schoolgirl tendencies, asking Steed if she should wear a gymslip when visiting Professor Witney. All very worrying indeed.

Champagne: No champagne, but just about everything else. Steed drinks brandy, and tea and biscuits are served in the Brigadier's trench.

Fights: ☆☆ Tara takes on Bristow's manservant and is somewhat easily overcome with chloroform. Steed, meanwhile, tackles a gang of 'dicemen' and a 'fiendish Japanese wrestler' as part of the game.

60s Concerns: Revenge by plot device!

Strangeness: A real-life game of Snakes and Ladders. The bodies of Bristow's victims are left in a children's playground in Merton for Steed and Tara to find. The bomb that Steed must defuse in his game of 'Super Secret Agent' is clearly marked as such, with the word 'BOMB' painted on the side.

Eccentrics: Brigadier Wishforth-Brown, Steed's ex-commander. Monty Bristow, 'the game king', formerly Sgt Daniel Edwards, court-martialled by Steed for profiteering in 1946. A 'Bondian' super-villain with a plethora of devices at his disposal.

Notes: 'Someone's playing a game with you.' This is one of the great episodes, a mini-Bond movie with a superb Richard Harris script, which gives equal priority to genuine wit, action and some astonishing set-pieces. It's an example of the Steed/Tara relationship at its best and most mature, although the rather contrived tag-scene (where Steed invents his own game 'Steedopoly', making up the rules as he goes along) lets it down. For the only time, Tara appears in spectacles in one (brief) scene, and more of Steed's military career is revealed. Bristow's house scenes filmed at Grim's Dyke Hotel, Harrow Weald.

German Title: 'Puzzlespiel'.

131
'Super-Secret Cypher Snatch'
9 October 1968
Working Title: 'Whatever Happened to Yesterday?'
Filmed: June 1968
US Transmission: 30 September 1968
Writer: Tony Williamson
Director: John Hough

Guest Cast: Allan Cuthbertson (Webster),
Ivor Dean (Ferret), Angela Scouler (Myra),
Simon Oates (Maskin), John Carlisle (Peters),
Nicholas Smith (Lather), Alec Ross (1st Guard),
Lionel Wheeler (2nd Guard), Anne Rutter (Betty),
Clifford Earle (Jarret), Anthony Bradshaw (Davis),
David Quiller (Wilson).

Problems of a secret leakage from Cypher HQ and the disappearance of agent Jarret are first handed to rival Department MI12, and then to Mother's group. But why does everybody at Cypher HQ claim never to have seen Jarret and state that the only thing worthy of note that happened yesterday was that it rained?

Wit: ☆☆☆☆ Telling Steed that the matter of the missing cyphers has been placed in the hands of MI12, Mother asks if he can drop Steed anywhere. 'The employment exchange.'

Kinkiness: Not a trace.

Fights: ☆☆☆ Steed chokes one window cleaner with his umbrella hook, and has a great fist-fight with another in a leafy hollow to cool jazz. Tara throws a villain through a window and, dramatically, leaps through after him.

60s Concerns: Cyphers.

Strangeness: Great pre-title sequence as an agent on a motor-cycle fights with a cypher thief dressed as an old lady whilst a helicopter hovers above. It's got nothing to do with the plot but it's real James Bond stuff. Steed and Tara play chess as they discuss the twists and turns of the plot.

Eccentrics: Peters the MI12 photographer, who has watched *Blow Up* several times too often, wants to be David Bailey. He snaps Tara 'for the collection'. Camp as Butlins. The cypher thieves, undercover as a window cleaning company (Classy Glass Cleaning), are a right bunch of weirdos, led by Mr Lather.

With a Young . . . : Donald Gee (Vickers).

Notes: Despite the lack of both kinkiness *and* champagne, a super Tony Williamson script ensures that this episode, which could have been dull as ditchwater, works very well. It works because of the little things, like the discussion between Maskin and Vickers (who has brought his sandwiches with him whilst they are snatching the cyphers) as to whether his superior would like one. When Maskin finds out they are ham and chutney he makes a face and declines the offer. The episode takes place on 2 April 1968 (the calendar page for the day before is found in a concealed compartment in Jarret's pen). The MI12 agent has lots of cool gadgets (microphones in tie-clips, cigarette-case guns) but still gets killed. As Mother says, 'Gimmicks will never replace men.' 'Or women,' adds Steed helpfully. Tara goes undercover as a secretary and gets into trouble for making personal phone calls to Steed. The title is given on-screen as 'Sepct Sucpre Cncehl Sypare' (a fiendish cypher) before changing to 'Super-Secret Cypher Snatch'. Cypher HQ scenes filmed at Brookmans Park Transmitting Station.

German Title: 'Das Glaspflegeinstitut'.

French Title: 'Le Document Disparu'.

132
'You'll Catch Your Death'
16 October 1968
Working Title: 'Atishoo, Atishoo, All Fall Down'
Filmed: May 1968
US Transmission: 7 October 1968
Writer: Jeremy Burnham
Director: Paul Dickson
Guest Cast: Ronald Culver (Col. Timothy),
Valentine Dyall (Butler), Fulton Mackay (Glover),
Sylvia Kay (Matron), Peter Bourne (Preece),
Charles Lloyd Pack (Dr Fawcett),
Henry McGee (Maidwell), Hamilton Dyce (Camrose),
Bruno Barnabe (Farrar), Fiona Hartford (Janice),
Geoffrey Chater (Seaton), Jennifer Clulow (Georgina),
Emma Cochrane (Melanie), Willoughby Gray (Padley),
Andrew Laurence (Herrick),
Douglas Blackwell (Postman).

Ear, nose and throat specialists are sneezing themselves to death, each after receiving a mysterious empty envelope. When Tara is kidnapped, Steed takes great care over his morning mail.

Wit: ✩✩

Kinkiness Factor: ✩✩✩ Tara is manacled to a bar and straitjacketed. Plus, Steed in a gasmask, anyone?

Fights: ✩✩ Tara has a go at the villains while hanging from her bar.

60s Concerns: Germ warfare.

Eccentrics: Colonel Timothy, owner of a research institute devoted to the common cold, terrified of disease, and Dr Glover, who has rather the opposite point of view.

With a Young...: Dudley Sutton (Dexter).

Notes: Mother eats an ice-cream cornet while talking to 'Grandma' on the phone. The cold laboratory contains a large nose. First episode of the second shooting block.

133
'Split!'
23 October 1968
Filmed: Jan/February 1968
US Transmission: 10 April 1968
Writer: Brian Clemens
(and Dennis Spooner, uncredited)
Director: Roy Baker
Guest Cast: Nigel Davenport (Lord Barnes),
Julian Glover (Peter Rooke),
Bernard Archard (Dr Constantine),
John G. Heller (Hinnell), Jayne Sofiano (Petra),
Steven Scott (Kartovski), Maurice Good (Harry Mercer),
Iain Anders (Frank Compton), John Kidd (The Butler).

When an agent at the Ministry of Top-Secret Information is murdered, Steed and Tara have little difficulty in locating the man responsible. But when a handwriting test indicates that he is Boris Kartovski, someone Steed thought he had killed in Berlin five years before, our heroes find themselves drawn into the dangerous experiments of Dr Constantine.

Wit: ☆ Steed releasing Tara from operating table-bondage: 'I can't promise you'll play the violin again . . . '

Kinkiness Factor: ☆☆☆☆ Apart from Tara being tied to an operating table for a mind-swap, Steed displays a very ungentlemanly manner (and further evidence of a spanking fetish), locking Petra the nurse in a cupboard with a hefty slap on the bottom.

Champagne: ☆☆ Dr Constantine and Himel discuss 'cracking open a bottle' to celebrate Tara's capture. Later, Tara wants a bizarre cocktail (ingredients too numerous to list); Steed doesn't have this, but does have two bottles of champagne 'second drawer down'.

Fights: ☆ Tara disables two thugs with a metal chair and a post tray.

60s Concerns: Schizophrenia, mind transfer.

Strangeness: Lord Barnes is playing classical piano when he receives the phone call that changes his personality.

Eccentrics: Swindin, the graphologist.

With a Young . . . : Christopher Benjamin (Swindin).

Notes: A rather grim tale, with few lighter moments, 'Split!' was originally a script for Rigg. It was rewritten by Clemens and Spooner on the weekend of their return to the show. The location filming at Barnes' stately home (with its bizarre purple interior design) is beautiful. Haberdasher Aske's School, Elstree, makes another appearance in the show, this time as Nullington Hospital. The character of Boris Kartovski (previously mentioned in 'A Touch of Brimstone') turns up, albeit as a living corpse.

French Title: 'Double Personalité'.

134
'Whoever Shot Poor George Oblique Stroke XR40?'

30 October 1968
Filmed: April 1968
US Transmission: 9 December 1968
Writer: Tony Williamson
Director: Cyril Frankel
Guest Cast: Dennis Price (Jason),
Clifford Evans (Pelley), Judy Parfitt (Loris),
Anthony Nicholls (Dr Ardmore),
Frank Windsor (Tobin), Adrian Ropes (Baines),
Arthur Cox (Anaesthetist), Tony Wright (Keller),
John Porter-Davison (Jacobs), Jacky Allouis (Jill).

Somebody is out to get super-computer George/XR40. He is shot, given false data, attacked with acid, and nearly gets his power supply cut. But until George works properly the name and nature of the culprits cannot be established.

Wit: ☆ 'I don't like right-angled girls, although I do like girls with the right angles!'

Kinkiness Factor: ☆ Tara is in a pussy outfit on her way to a fancy-dress ball.

Champagne: ☆ Yes, and George/XR40 creates the recipe for a 'lethal cocktail'.

Fights: ☆

60s Concerns: Super-computers. Drugs that turn brilliant scientists into apathetic morons.

Strangeness: There's the very silly idea of operating on a computer. Tara goes undercover as Pelley's niece (with a very good American accent), and the earrings she wears have to be seen to be believed.

Eccentrics: George himself is fairly groovy.

With a Young . . . : Valerie Leon (Betty).

Notes: Tara's girlish nature comes to the fore when she slides down a long bannister to greet Steed. The final episode of the first filming block.

Trivia: George's previous incarnation was the more prosaic Fred Mk III.

French Title: 'George et Fred'.

135
'False Witness'
6 November 1968
Working Title: 'Lies'
Filmed: June/July 1968
US Transmission: 25 November 1968
Steed comes home with the milk – Tara gets up to her

neck in butter
Writer: Jeremy Burnham
Director: Charles Crichton
Guest Cast: John Bennett (Sykes),
Barry Warren (Melville), Tony Steedman (Sir Joseph),
William Job (Lord Edgefield), Dan Meaden (Sloman),
Michael Lees (Plummer), Simon Lack (Nesbitt),
Arthur Pentelow (Dr Grant), Peter Jesson (Penman),
Rio Fanning (Lane), John Atkinson (Brayshaw),
Larry Burns (Gould), Jimmy Gardner (Little Man),
Terry Eliot (Amanda).

Trusted agent Melville has lost three partners in quick succession, and seems to be lying at every opportunity. Is he really the man to partner Steed in an attempt to convict Lord Edgefield, noted blackmailer? And what is the odd connection between this whole affair and daily milk deliveries?

Wit: ☆☆ 'I've devised a rather unusual death for you . . . '
'Thank you.'
And some inspired lying.

Kinkiness Factor: ☆ Tara trapped in a giant butter pat. *Batman*esque!

Champagne: ☆☆☆ Steed discovers 'something that shouldn't be there' in an apparently burgled fridge: a bottle that's 'plucky, but from the wrong side of the hill'. Also, the villains toast their success, with very successful results. Not.

Fights: ☆☆ Tara attacks villains with a milk bottle and a milk-stirring paddle, and ends up in the milk vat, as Steed does when he has a go with the crates. The dairy-related violence pales in comparison to Steed's taking of Melville into a forest to thump him for his 'services not rendered'.

60s Concerns: Mind control.

Eccentrics: Sykes, owner of DreemyKreem Dairies, with ideas way above his station.

Notes: A very well-directed episode. Tara is rather sidelined, but quite impressive when she does do things, albeit in an impulsive, non-useful sort of way, all whilst wearing horrid purple shorts. Mother has set up his HQ on a bus, and Steed puts out a portable stop to catch it. Here we have an early example of a *New Avengers* cliché, a dying agent crashing into Steed's flat. The vaguely Holmesian blackmail plot gives it a Cathy Gale feel, but this swiftly dissolves into milky fun. Surprisingly good stuff, this almost gives one the illusion that the new format might just work.

136
'All Done with Mirrors'
13 November 1968
Filmed: May/June 1968
US Transmission: 2 December 1968
Writer: Leigh Vance
Director: Ray Austin
Guest Cast: Edwin Richfield (Barlow),
Peter Copley (Sparshott), Joanna Jones (Pandora),
Michael Trubshaw (Col. Withers),
Tenniel Evans (Carswell), Nor Nicholson (Miss Emily),
Liane Aukin (Miss Tiddiman),
Anthony Dalton (Seligman),
Peter Thomas (Kettridge), Graham Ashley (Markin),

**Michael Nightingale (Real Colonel),
Robert Sidaway (Real Barlow),
Desmond Jordan (Guthrie), David Grey (Williams),
Peter Elliott (Arkin), John Brown (Roger).**

The leaking of secrets at Carmadoc Research Establishment throws suspicion on to Steed, who must suffer the torment of house arrest while Tara goes in with a new partner.

Wit: ☆ Colonel Withers, after he has heard the sound of Tara and Kettridge fighting via the radio telescope: 'I'm taking the rest of the day off!' Tara counts the number of steps Kettridge falls down in the lighthouse. It's 366. She decides the lighthouse must have been built in a leap year.

Kinkiness Factor: ☆ Nice shots of lots of girls in swimwear. Not a lot else.

Champagne: ☆☆☆ Steed drinks tons of the stuff while under arrest.

Fights: ☆☆ Tara takes on the huge bearded Gozzo and leaves him impaled on a garden rake (not a scythe as stated in other *Avengers* books) after a lengthy and extremely violent sequence.

60s Concerns: Solar power.

Strangeness: Steed under house arrest is forced to spend most of the episode beside a swimming pool with a bevy of beauties. Mother sits in the middle of the pool surrounded by floating telephones. In the tag-scene, Steed and Tara dine in the middle of a field. Very civilised.

Eccentrics: Watney, Tara's new partner ('you'll find me fair but completely dedicated') is a bumbling fool who Tara gets rid of at every opportunity but who proves useful at the end.

With a Young . . . : Dinsdale Landen (Watney).

Notes: 'She's female and she's vulnerable,' says Steed when told Tara is going on a mission without him. Very rad fem, John. Beautiful location filming (Rabley Park, Ridge; the army barracks, Stanmore; Beachy Head, East Sussex; and Start Point Lighthouse, Devon) and some nice stunts (especially when Tara is knocked over a cliff edge by a motorbike, apparently to her death). The first episode where Thorson didn't wear a wig and the first to feature Rhonda (who was apparently Newell's idea).

Trivia: The tag sequence appears to have been filmed in the same field (and possibly at the same time) as the title sequence.

German Title: 'Spieglein, Spieglein in der Hand'.

French Title: 'Miroirs'.

137
'Legacy of Death'
20 November 1968
Working Title: 'Falcon'
Filmed: July/August 1968
US Transmission: 4 November 1968
Steed inherits a dagger – Tara undergoes the feather torture
Writer: Terry Nation

Director: Don Chaffey
Guest Cast: Stratford Johns (Sidney),
Ronald Lacey (Humbert),
Ferdy Mayne (Baron Von Orlak),
Kynaston Reeves (Dickens),
Richard Hurndall (Farrer), John Hollis (Zoltan),
Leon Thau (Ho Lung), Tutte Lemkow (Gorky),
Peter Swanwick (Oppenheimer), Vic Wise (Slattery),
Teddy Kiss (Winkler), Michael Bilton (Dr Winter).

Anticipating the arrival of his enemies to kill him, millionaire Henley Farrer sets a deadly trap for them involving an Oriental dagger and, inevitably, Steed and Tara.

Wit: ☆☆ Steed is playing with a model aeroplane. 'Aren't you a little old for that?' asks Tara.
'It's for my nephew's tenth birthday,' he replies.
'When's that?'
'Three years ago!'
Later Steed looks sadly around his flat, littered with bodies, and exclaims: 'I've a feeling it's going to be one of those days.'
During an excellent chase sequence involving several cars and a motorbike Tara tells Steed that they are being followed.
'By whom?'
'Just about everyone!'

Kinkiness factor: ☆☆☆ Tara is captured, strapped down, and subjected to Chinese water torture by the sadistic, one-armed German Von Orlak. Very disturbing.

Champagne: ☆☆☆ Tara ('between parties') arrives at Steed's flat with a bottle. Steed also shares several glasses with Gorky (who smashes them in Cossack style, much to the chagrin of his host).

Fights: ☆☆ Tara and Gregor fight in her apartment over the dagger, which Gregor falls on to. The climax is a huge fight involving all of the protagonists.

Strangeness: A Chinese curio shop is owned by Ho Lung, who is obviously non-oriental. Slattery, a gangster, incompetently attempts to flip peanuts into his mouth.

Eccentrics: In a story full of weirdos, we have 'Old' Gorky, a mad Russian agent, Dickens the solicitor (of the firm Dickens, Dickens, Dickens, Dickens and Dickens – the other four are all deceased – Steed commenting 'He knows a dickens of a lot of Dickens'). All of the 'dagger fanciers' are decidedly odd, too.

Notes: A barely disguised parody of *The Maltese Falcon* with Johns and Lacey in the Sidney Greenstreet/Peter Lorre roles. Very funny, if a little insane, with lots of good comedy lines. *The Prisoner*'s Peter Swanwick makes a cameo appearance.

French Title: 'Le Legs'.

138
'Noon Doomsday'
27 November 1968
Filmed: July 1968
US Transmission: 28 October 1968
Tara hits the hay – Steed faces a gunfight at high noon . . .
Writer: Terry Nation
Director: Peter Sykes
Guest Cast: Ray Brooks (Barrington),
T.P. McKenna (Grant), Griffith Jones (Baines),
Lyndon Brook (Lyall), Peter Bromilow (Kafka),

**Peter Halliday (Perrier), Anthony Ainley (Sunley),
John Glynn-Jones (Dr Hyde), David Glover (Carson),
Lawrence James (Cornwall),
Alfred Maron (Taxi Driver).**

Tara visits Steed in a special hospital following an injury to his leg. This is just the backdrop needed by Gerald Kafka, ex-head of Murder International, as he plans his revenge against Steed, who sent him to prison exactly seven years ago. At noon, Steed will die.

Wit: ☆ Steed explains his broken leg: 'It happened crossing the wall.'
   'Berlin?'
   'No, the garden!'

Kinkiness Factor: A gun in a crutch? Bit clever and Freudian, that. Steed tries to 'protect' Tara by locking her in a cupboard, but thankfully she smacks him over the head and heads off for the Wild West-style showdown on her own. Atta girl!

Champagne: ☆☆☆☆ Tara smuggles a bottle of 'extra-special vintage' champers in to the recuperating Steed. She also hits Steed with a bottle. At the end Steed's plaster-cast contains various presents, including another bottle.

Fights: ☆☆☆☆ A rather *New Avengers*-like leaning towards violence.

Strangeness: The 'hospital for spies' in the middle of nowhere which seems to contain French, pacifist and battle-fatigued agents. Mother has a suitcase full of different-coloured telephones.

Eccentrics: Perrier, a one-eyed Frenchman.

Notes: 'Is Steed there?'

'No, he's gone to Department S.'

A spoof Western (based on *High Noon*, of course), heavily re-written by Clemens and mostly shot at the farm which was at that point owned by him, Park Farm, Ampthill. The railway station footage was shot at Stanbridgeford station, Bucks. There are a couple of references to *Department S*, including a mention of Monty (Berman, the show's producer).

Trivia: Steed's injuries were caused by stepping on to a cucumber frame. Allegedly. The events take place on 19 June.

German Title: 'Wenn ex Zwölf uhr Sehläght'.

French Title: 'Je Vous Tuerci á Midi'.

139
'Look – (stop me if you've heard this one) But There Were These Two Fellers...'
4 December 1968
Filmed: March 1968
US Transmission: 8 May 1968
Writer: Dennis Spooner
Director: James Hill
Guest Cast: Jimmy Jewell (Maxie Martin),
Julian Chagrin (Jennings),
Bernard Cribbins (Bradley Marler),
John Cleese (Marcus Rugman),

William Kendall (Lord Dessington),
John Woodvine (Seagrave),
Garry Marsh (Brig. Wiltshire),
Gaby Vagas (Miss Charles), Bill Shire (Cleghorn),
Richard Young (Sir Jeremy Broadfoot),
Robert James (Merlin),
Talfryn Thomas (Fiery Frederick),
Jay Denver (Tenor), Johnny Vyvyan (Escapologist),
Lew Belmont (Ventriloquist).

The directors of the Capital Land and Development Company are being murdered and the only clues Steed and Tara have are a massive footprint and a red nose. (Those Comic Relief people will do anything for charity.)

Wit: ☆☆☆☆☆ 'Clowns don't lay eggs.'
  'Bad ones do!'
  'Bradley Marler?'
  'If I'm not I've been havin' a great time with his wife!'
  'As you know, vaudeville is dead.'
  'Vaudeville might just have decided to fight back!' – and many, many more.

Kinkiness Factor: ☆ Tara wears a leotard in one scene for no adequately explained reason. Later, she is bound and gagged in the lotus position.

Fights: ☆☆☆ Steed and Tara dress as a pantomime horse and knock out most of the vaudevillians with joke truncheons. Steed then knocks seven costume changes out of Maxie.

60s Concerns: Corrupt property developers.

Strangeness: For starters, you've got clowns killing property developers, a metamorphosing walking stick, a man killed on a duck hunt by a 'bopper', John Cleese playing . . . well John Cleese really, Bernard Cribbins as a hack-comedy writer buried in rejected jokes (autobiographical, Dennis?), a man tumbling out of a tower block after the carpet is pulled from under him . . . This is *madness*!

Eccentrics: The inmates of Vauda Villa, a rest home for retired variety artists, include Merry Maxie Martin and Jennings his mute sidekick, plus a deadly Punch and Judy man, both ends of a pantomime horse, an escapologist, and Fiery Frederick, a failed magician whose act is to burn, rather than saw, a woman in half. As we said, *madness* . . .

Notes: 'Very theatrical . . . ' Dennis Spooner's tribute to vaudeville – originally written for one of the Rigg seasons – is the height of *The Avengers* as a pure comedy series. Maybe this should be called (given John Cleese's involvement) 'The Ministry of Silly Super Heroes'. Mind you, there is much subtlety amongst the slapstick, Steed telling Marler he isn't in the entertainment business. 'Oh, television,' replies the writer.

Trivia: Maxie disguises himself as a (uniformed) policeman to kidnap Tara. The episode takes place 230 shopping days before Christmas. Steed goes undercover as 'Gentleman Jack – a song, a smile and an umbrella'. We learn Tara was in north Alaska as a two-year-old. This is the only *Avengers* episode to feature the word 'antidisestablishmentarianism'. Tara's interests include 'skiing, motor sport, fashion and classical music'.

French Title: 'Clowneries'.

140
'Have Guns – Will Haggle'
11 December 1968
Working Title: 'Invitation to a Killing'
Originally Filmed: October 1967
Refilmed: February 1968
US Transmission: 1 May 1968
Writer: Donald James
Director: Ray Austin
Guest Cast: Johnny Sekka (Col. Nsonga),
Nicola Pagett (Lady Adriana Beardsley),
Jonathan Burn (Conrad Beardsley),
Timothy Bateson (Spencer), Michael Turner (Crayford),
Roy Stewart (Giles), Peter J. Elliott (Brace).

The spectacular theft of 3,000 top-secret FF70 rifles from a Government establishment brings Steed and Tara. Steed meets an old 'friend' and is invited to an auction. Tara has other reasons for being there.

Wit: ☆☆ Colonel Nsonga: 'I didn't know you were still in touch with the President.'
   Steed: 'I've never missed a Christmas card yet!'
   The auction between Steed and Nsonga descends into the pair checking in their wallets for loose change, and offering to throw in their watches.

Kinkiness factor: ☆ Tara practises on a trampoline in a very revealing body stocking. Cor . . . (We're told that much of this was filmed with a stuntperson/body-double. Boo . . .)

Champagne: No. Steed and Tara share a glass of brandy.

Fights: ☆☆ Tara (easily) fights off two thugs who pursue her in a Rolls-Royce. Once again, Tara is attacked in her flat whilst changing (into a rather fetching little tartan number with white leather boots). The poor girl must be developing a complex about this.

60s Concerns: Arms smuggling to Third World dictatorships.

Strangeness: Mask-wearing criminals use a trampoline to infiltrate a top security installation. Colonel Nsonga's state-of-the-art radiogram plays African tribal rhythms. 'I see you're playing our tune,' says Steed. The arms are to be sold at an auction while tea on the terrace is taken. How delightfully English.

Eccentrics: Lady Adriana Beardsley, a debby arms dealer.

With a Young . . . : Robert Gillespie (Lift Attendant).

Notes: Originally the first filmed Tara episode, 'Invitation to a Killing', later largely reshot (location footage contains scenes filmed in both autumn and summer: what a giveaway!). A bit of a mess, hardly surprising given the horrors of production. Again, two lengthy (and disruptive) 'wig' scenes were inserted to explain Tara's blonde hair. We have a black actor in evidence (hurrah!), but he's the villain (boo!).

Trivia: 'Loyalty, amongst other things, was one of the things they impressed upon us at Eton,' notes Steed when he is offered the 'lucrative post' of Minister of Information after Nsonga's coup d'état. Steed knows Nsonga from a previously foiled coup during which Steed aided the country's president. During training, Steed's record for opening handcuffs was 32 seconds. He breaks it to save Tara.

141
'They Keep Killing Steed'
18 December 1968
Filmed: August 1968
US Transmission: 11 November 1968
Writer: Brian Clemens
Director: Robert Fuest
Guest Cast: Ian Ogilvy (Baron Von Curt),
Ray McAnally (Arcos), Norman Jones (Zerson),
Bernard Horsfall (Capt. Smythe).
With: William Ellis, Hal Galili, Nicole Shelby,
Rosemary Donnelly, Gloria Connell,
Michael Corcoran, Ross Hutchinson, Reg Whitehead,
Anthony Sheppard, George Ghent.

To infiltrate a peace conference, Arcos, a brilliant plastic surgeon, uses a new moulding technique to transform an agent into a duplicate Steed. But when the transformation proves to be unstable, Arcos decides they need the real Steed.

Wit: ☆☆☆ A bound Steed questions Zerson's loyalty to Arcos: 'Dedicated idealist or altruistic opportunist?'

Mother asks Tara if she had any trouble finding his submarine base: '... straight downstream, turn left at the salmon nets.'

Steed attempts to convince Tara that he is the real Steed: 'Remember that time in Tibet? We rescued that little lama, a friend of the Dalai's... Oh my goodness, it wasn't you at all!'

Kinkiness Factor: ☆ Baron Von Curt is chased along a hotel corridor in the best *Carry On* style by two scantily clad girls.

Champagne: ☆☆☆ The peace conference is full of the stuff.

Fights: ☆☆☆☆ The duplicate Steeds first start to wipe each other out; then Steed fights one of them in a car with the line 'I've just seen somebody I know'. In the quarry, with bodies littered everywhere, Curt sword-fences a thug with a metal bar and Tara tackles a knifeman with no more protection than a silk hanky.

60s Concerns: Plastic surgery.

Strangeness: Mother's HQ is underwater. We first see him and Rhonda (in a wet-suit) in a rowing boat complete with a telephone (so what's it attached to?) sinking slowly into the river. Tara later visits them, diving into the river from a bridge.

Eccentrics: Arcos, the plastics expert. He plays chess with Steed and notes that John relies on his knights. 'You can tell a great deal of a man's character from the way he plays chess.' Steed agrees and notes that Arcos relies on his pawns.

With a Young . . . : Angharad Rees.

Notes: 'That's not my face!' *The Avengers* returns to one of its conceptual homes, Little England (the village green by the church that hides foreign spies). An interesting example of the Clemens/Fuest seventh-season *Avengers*: high action, bizarre locale (a quarry hiding an underground bunker), a somewhat frantic runaround in fact. The ending is very downbeat, though. Tara has a nice double-act with Curt, a romantic, dashing younger version of Steed. The final line, 'That's Steed, who else would smile at a time like this?', sums up the episode very well. The bridge at Tyke's Water Lake, Elstree, is pressed into service again. The car chases were filmed at Burnham Beeches, and the conference-centre footage was shot at Caldecote Towers, Bushey and Ye Olde Sun Hotel in Northaw.

French Title: 'Mais Qui Est Steed?'.

142
'The Interrogators'
1 January 1969
Filmed: October 1968
US Transmission: 20 January 1969
Writers: Richard Harris and Brian Clemens
Director: Charles Crichton
Guest Cast: Christopher Lee (Col. Mannering),
David Sumner (Minnow), Philip Bond (Caspar),
Glynn Edwards (Blackie), Neil McCarthy (Rasker),
Neil Stacy (Mallard), Neil Wilson (Norton),
Cardew Robinson (Mr Puffin), Cecil Cheng (Capt. Soo),
Mark Elwes (Naval Officer),
David Richards (RAF Officer).

When agents find themselves in Colonel Mannering's interrogation centre, they think it's a test of their abilities, and relax with drinks when the sessions are over. But who's fooling who? Steed plays catch the pigeon.

Wit: ☆☆

Champagne: Dry Martini and various other relaxants.

Fights: ☆☆☆ Rather wonderful climactic fight in the old style.

60s Concerns: The interrogations are clearly designed to train one against capture by the Chinese.

Eccentrics: Izzy Pound ('and his pound-of-sound'), the one man marching band, and Mr Puffin, balloon seller.

Notes: Mother's flat, filled with flowers (from secret admirers?), is accessible through a telephone box. The interrogation centre footage was shot at Brocket Hall, Lemsford.

143
'The Rotters'
8 January 1969
Filmed: September/October 1968
US Transmission: 16 December 1968
Writer: Dave Freeman
Director: Robert Fuest
Guest Cast: Gerald Sim (Kenneth),
Jerome Willis (George), Eric Barker (Pym),
John Nettleton (Palmer), Frank Middlemas (Sawbow).
With: Dervis Ward, Harold Innocent, Tony Gilpin,
Amy Dalby, John Stone, Charles Morgan,
Harry Hutchinson, Noel Davis, John Scott.

Members of the Institute of Timber Technology are being killed by a pair of caddish assassins, their advantage being an ability to destroy wood in seconds. (Great title, eh?)

Wit: ☆☆ 'You don't really believe all this rot, do you?'
   'We plant trees. When they've grown, we cut them down.'
   'What a full, rich life you must lead.'
   'He's got a plan to release dry rot and destroy the world!'

'Haven't we all?'

Kinkiness Factor: ☆☆ Tara manacled to a wall and then tied to a chair.

Fights: ☆☆ Tara pursued by an axeman in the woods. Steed fights the rotters over a nice tea.

60s Concerns: Giant mushrooms and the misuse of fungi in general.

Eccentrics: Kenneth and George, identically dressed upper-class cads ('I do so despise the lower classes. Ever strangled anybody, old chap?') with a wood-rotting pistol: reps for Wormdoom Ltd. Professor Palmer, who camps out on a newly planted hillside to protect his seedlings and shoot at sparrows. Reggie Pym, the world's foremost authority on timber decay, who can tell timbers by their smell. Merlyn Sawbow, antique restorer who uses a blunderbuss to simulate woodworm. Wainwright, who plans to rot Europe with his pillar box fungus sprays. Mrs Forsythe, cultivator of plastic flowers.

Add to them a man from the BBC ('British Burial Caskets') and it becomes obvious that somebody is Trying Too Hard.

Notes: This has the feel of an Emma Peel script written by a fan, and is thus slightly too self-conscious to be really good. (Dave Freeman is a comedy writer with several *Carry On* films and scripts for *Bless This House* to his credit.) It's still quite satisfying though, with all aspects of wood decay being thoroughly explored in the same way that the Peel scripts used to treat their central theme. Mother lives in an inflatable room. Tara is particularly ineffectual, Thorson managing to fumble every witty line, shouting some of them so as to be initially inaudible. The villains, however, are great. Wainwright (Harold

258

Innocent) particularly goes for it with his cry of 'The whole of Europe will rot! Rot! ROT!!' The church is St Andrews, Little Berkamstead, and Wainwright Timber Industries footage was shot at Hatfield Country Club, Essendon.

French Title: 'Du Bois Vermoulu'.

144
'Invasion of the Earthmen'
15 January 1969
Filmed: November 1967
US Transmission: 27 March 1968
Writer: Terry Nation
Director: Don Sharp
Guest Cast: William Lucas (Brett),
Christian Roberts (Huxton),
Christopher Chittell (Bassin), Wendy Allnutt (Sarah),
George Roubicek (Grant).

The death of agent Bernard Grant, while investigating the strange goings-on at the Alpha Academy where teenagers are being prepared for inter-planetary conquest, leads Steed and Tara into the generation war.

Wit: ☆☆ 'Colonel Steed' after boasting of his military career to Brigadier Brett. 'I'm afraid I'm in the civil service now.'
  'It happens.'

Kinkiness factor: ☆☆ The yellow/black storm trooper uniforms of the teenagers are quite striking (the girls are in miniskirts, of course).

Champagne: No: most of the protagonists are too young to drink.

Fights: ✩✩ Tara defeats two of the teenagers with a fire bucket full of sand.

60s Concerns: Inter-generational tension (killer teenagers). Space exploration.

Strangeness: The Academy commander's office is electrified and features a model of the solar system. A humpty-dumpty shaped astronaut features prominently.

With a Young . . . : Lucy Fleming (Emily), Warren Clarke (Trump).

Notes: The second Tara story to be filmed (hence the blonde wig). Terry Nation clearly hadn't quite got the series' style, scripting a wildly clashing mixture of SF and *The Midwich Cuckoos*. Steed also refers to Tara as 'Miss King' throughout. Much use of Nazi imagery (a common Nation trait, cf. *Blake's 7*). Quite funny in places, but production problems and forced 'explanation' scenes detract from the action. Alpha Academy footage shot at Knebworth House, Stevenage. It was originally planned that Steed should drive an AC Cobra throughout this season, but he only actually does so in this episode. (The rest of the time it's the more vintage Bentleys and Rollers.)

145
'Killer'
22 January 1969
Filmed: September 1968

US Transmission: 30 December 1968
Writer: Tony Williamson
Director: Cliff Owen
Guest Cast:
Jennifer Croxton (Lady Diana Forbes-Blakeney),
Grant Taylor (Merridon), William Franklyn (Brinstead),
Richard Wattis (Clarke), Harry Towb (Paxton),
Anthony Valentine (Calvin).
With: John Bailey, Michael Ward, James Bree,
Michael McStay, Charles Houston, Jonathan Elsom,
Clive Graham, Oliver MacGreevy.

Remak is a killer, one the department are desperate to find. But a succession of agents on the trail of Remak are turning up dead, wrapped in polythene. And with Tara on holiday, Steed must go into this case with a new partner.

Wit: ☆ 'Why kill somebody in so many ways?'
'Practice!'

Kinkiness Factor: ☆ Steed sweats under Remak's sonic attack but maintains his dignity despite having his umbrella chopped in half (how phallic).

Champagne: ☆ Steed and Tara share a glass before she leaves on holiday.

Fights: ☆☆☆ There's a magnificently staged one as Trouncer tries to escape from Remak's factory HQ.

Strangeness: Agent Gillers meets his contact Paxton on a disused film set. He's then directed to a pub, the Pirate, near to Remak's factory, but it's all a trap. In the pub, Steed orders 'two tomato juices with everything'.

Eccentrics: Freddie Frills, a camp ribbon salesman.

Notes: 'Programmed for Murder!' Without Tara (off on leave with a 'pink and purple pass'), Steed's new partner is Lady Diana, who's just spent eighteen months in the Orient. She's a very promising character, whom Steed calls 'Forbes'. She gets solo scenes, a good fight sequence with Brinstead and develops a sardonic relationship with Steed. (The script was originally written for Tara but Linda Thorson was on holiday.) Anthony Valentine plays a rather twitty agent.

Trivia: Remak notes that Steed is 6' 1" and weighs 175 pounds. This means he's gained five pounds and lost one inch since 'Escape in Time'! Remak, incidentally, is a computer (the initials stand for Remote Electro-Matic Agent Killer). Remak sequences filmed at Haberdasher Aske's School, Elstree.

French Title: 'Meutre au Programme'.

146
'The Morning After'
29 January 1969
Filmed: October/November 1968
US Transmission: 27 January 1969
Writer: Brian Clemens
Director: John Hough
Guest Cast: Peter Barkworth (Merlin),
Penelope Horner (Jenny),
Joss Ackland (Brigadier Hansing),
Brian Blessed (Sgt Hern),
Donald Douglas (Major Parsons), Philip Dunbar (Yates),
Jonathan Scott (Cartney).

Steed, attempting to capture super-spy Merlin, is knocked out by a sleeping capsule, and wakes to find London deserted and under martial law. Firing squads are at large, and a nuclear bomb is holding the government to ransom.

Wit: ☆ Merlin tries to offer Steed a bribe of £20,000. Steed turns it down. 'Sorry, I only deal in guineas.'

Kinkiness Factor: ☆ Tara wears a very slinky dress in the tag sequence.

Fights: ☆☆☆☆

60s Concerns: Blackmail via nuclear bombs. Computers taking over people's jobs.

Strangeness: The exterior scenes in a very deserted London are strange and almost too grim for this season. (They were actually filmed in St Albans, Watford and Old Hatford.) For some reason, all of Tara's scenes feature a teddy bear.

Eccentrics: Jimmy Merlin is a lovely character, and spends much of the episode handcuffed to Steed.

Notes: Linda Thorson was on holiday, so Tara sleeps through most of this story, with journalist Jenny Firston partly assuming her role. Steed, rather sportingly, lets Merlin go at the end.

147
'The Curious Case of the Countless Clues'

5 February 1969
Working Title: 'The Murderous Connection'
Filmed: January 1968
US Transmission: 3 April 1968
Writer: Philip Levene
Director: Don Sharp
Guest Cast: Anthony Bate (Earle),
Kenneth Cope (Gardiner), Tracy Reed (Janice),
Edward de Souza (Flanders),
George A. Cooper (Burgess), Reginald Jessup (Dawson).

Rich men are being blackmailed by two crime experts who plant clues to them all over the scenes of the crimes that they themselves commit. However, when they try to allege that Steed would murder Tara . . . they gain a measure of viewer sympathy, actually.

Wit: ☆

Champagne: ☆ Steed delivers a bottle of 1957 to Tara, which is later used to set him up.

Fights: ☆☆☆ Steed chokes a villain on a cigar, and traps a mechanic under a car bonnet. Tara fights off her assailants from a comfy chair, having sprained her ankle on the slopes and been in a wheelchair all episode, and has a genuinely exciting fight scene, doing in villains with a hot water bottle, bowler, umbrella, ski pole, basket of fruit, palette and, finally, gun.

Eccentrics: Sir Arthur Doyle, Holmesian sleuth in deerstalker and cape. However, despite what other books may tell you, there's no sign of a Watson, female or otherwise.

With a Young...: Tony Selby (Stanley), Peter Jones (Doyle).

Notes: Thorson's style of playing still seems to vary as often as her hairdo, but then this was a very early story. Tracy Reed was almost Tara, so it's interesting to compare the two. It is intimated that Steed has had an affair with the horsey Janice, and they have a small kiss. There's some real tension in this rather old-fashioned script with its blackmail plot and hard Steed, especially when Tara's trapped in her flat towards the end. And the fireman's pole in there gets used. Unfortunately, Patrick Macnee's own designs for Steed now include a series of fluffy 60s shirts for use in the tag scenes. The Elstree studios car park was pressed into service in this story, with the Edgwarebury Hotel in Elstree appearing as the Burgess's house.

French Title: 'Trop D'Indices'.

148
'Wish You Were Here'
12 February 1969
Working Title: 'The Prisoner' (*Prisoner*esque!)
Filmed: August/September 1968
US Transmission: 18 November 1968
Writer: Tony Williamson
Director: Don Chaffey
Guest Cast: Liam Redmond (Charles Merrydale),
Robert Urquhart (Maxwell), Brook Williams (Basil),
Dudley Foster (Parker), Gary Watson (Kendrick),
Richard Caldcott (Mellor), Derek Newark (Vickers),

**David Garth (Brevitt), Louise Pajo (Miss Craven),
John Cazabon (Mr Maple),
Sandra Fehr (Attractive Girl).**

Tara's uncle is being held against his will in a country hotel. So Tara books in, and finds herself equally discouraged from leaving. Could the place also be home to the agent that Mother is missing?

Wit: None: some slapstick attempts to leave the hotel instead.

Kinkiness Factor: ☆ Tara dresses as a maid. Sorry, we're clutching at straws.

Fights: ☆☆ Short slapstick encounters.

60s Concerns: Industrial espionage.

Strangeness: Table footballers seem to be a visual motif. Steed's neighbours give him a baby in a box.

Eccentrics: Basil Crighton-Latimer, a silly young agent who calls Mother 'Uncle'.

Notes: Very *Prisoner*esque! Chaffey uses bannister-like bars in front of Tara's face, the hotel is an 'open' prison, and Mother uses a bizarre rotating photo contraption reminiscent of that series' technology. A Macnee holiday episode, with some filming again done at the Edgwarebury Hotel, Elstree. Tara can recognise Steed's car by the sound of its engine. Inventive, but dull.

French Title: 'Etrange Hotel'.

149
'L♥ve All'
19 February 1969
Filmed: November 1968
US Transmission: 3 February 1969
Steed falls down a manhole – Tara falls in love
Writer: Jeremy Burnham
Director: Peter Sykes
Guest Cast: Veronica Strong (Martha),
Terence Alexander (Bromfield),
Robert Harris (Sir Rodney), Patsy Rowlands (Thelma).
With: Brian Oulton, Frank Gatliff, Ann Rye,
Zulema Dene, Peter Stephens, Norman Pitt,
John Cobner, Robin Tolhurst, Larry Taylor,
David Baron.

Security lapses seem to point to top civil servants suddenly falling in love and giving secrets to an enemy agent disguised as a char lady. Steed investigates, but first has to save Tara from killing herself out of unrequited love.

Wit: ☆☆ 'Three shots. Very civil. You even shoot people in triplicate.'

Kinkiness Factor: ☆ Martha removes her clothes in Sir Rodney's car. Actually not as kinky as it sounds.

Fights: ☆

Strangeness: Steed purposefully falls down an open manhole in the street for his briefing with Mother, who is playing cricket with Rhonda. There's also a rather good scene with Tait declaring his eternal love to the policewoman who has just

267

given him a parking ticket.

Eccentrics: Sir Rodney Kellogg. What a fine name.

Notes: An interestingly silly plot, very well done. A particularly good performance from Veronica Strong. Tara instantly recognises Martha's perfume: it's called 'Reckless Abandon'. Steed approves. Episode title is 'L♥ve All' on screen (cf. 'From Venus With Love'); referred to as 'Love All' elsewhere in this book.

150
'Stay Tuned'
26 February 1969
Filmed: November/December 1968
US Transmission: 24 February 1969
Writer: Tony Williamson
Director: Don Chaffey
Guest Cast: Gary Bond (Proctor),
Iris Russell (Father), Duncan Lamont (Wilks),
Howard Marion-Crawford (Collins),
Denise Buckley (Sally), Roger Delgado (Kreer),
Harold Kasket (Dr Meitner), Ewan Roberts (Travers),
Patrick Westwood (Taxi Driver).

Steed, packing for a holiday, is knocked unconscious. When he wakes, he continues to pack but is confused when Tara arrives and tells him that he has been away for three weeks. Could it have anything to do with the mysterious man following him, whom everybody else but Steed can see?

Wit: ☆☆☆ Steed (to Father, after he's lost his memory): 'You shouldn't touch me. You never know where I might have been.'

There is a great scene in which Sally Unstrutter arrives at Steed's flat and apologises for scraping his car the previous week. This confirms to Steed that he hasn't been out of the country as everyone believes and he kisses the girl and promises to buy her lunch. Sally has the best line of the episode when, on leaving his flat, she says to herself 'So honesty really is the best policy after all!'

Kinkiness factor: ✰✰✰✰ Tara is tied up and gagged (so what else is new?). She then has a real 'handbags-at-ten-paces' fight with Kate O'Mara's character. It's a question of which of them will burst into tears first. Tara has a brass 'kinky boot' hanging on the back of her door.

Champagne: No.

Fights: ✰✰ Tara has a brilliantly staged fight with Kreer which ends with him falling on his own sword stick.

60s Concerns: Conditioning.

Strangeness: Steed, packing for his holiday, digs out an aqualung. Travers, the forensics expert, dresses as a doctor (with surgical mask and stethoscope) whilst examining Steed's car. Steed and Tara also wear surgical masks.

Eccentrics: Dr Meitner, the departmental psychologist whose office is an immense dark room filled with Roman columns.

With a Young . . . : Kate O'Mara (Lisa).

Notes: Tony Williamson confirms his ability for weird comedy – cf. *Randall and Hopkirk (Deceased)* – with a bizarre plot which has a resemblance to the *déjà vu* sequence in *Monty Python's Flying Circus*.

Trivia: When Mother is on holiday, his place is taken by Father (a blind woman). She tells Steed that he is still using the same tailor and remembers that he doesn't like dimly lit rooms.

French Title: 'Le Visage'.

151
'Take Me to Your Leader'
5 March 1969
Filmed: November 1968
US Transmission: 10 February 1969
Writer: Terry Nation
Director: Robert Fuest
Guest Cast: Patrick Barr (Stonehouse),
John Ronane (Captain Tim), Michael Robbins (Cavell),
Henry Stamper (Major Glasgow).
With: Penelope Keith, Hugh Cross,
Elizabeth Robillard, Michael Hawkins,
Sheila Hammond, Bryan Kendrick, Raymond Adamson,
Matthew Long, Cliff Diggins, Wilfred Boyle.

The discovery of a talking attaché case passed from courier to courier until it finally reaches 'Mr Big' takes Steed and Tara on a dazzling and surreal romp around London.

Wit: ☆☆ Sally Graham (a precocious schoolgirl-spy): 'Are you trying to bribe me?'
 Steed: 'In a word, yes.'
 'Good, my susceptibility to bribes is one of my few weak-

nesses. So let's talk money instead of lollipops!'

Kinkiness Factor: No time for any of that.

Champagne: ☆☆ The case which is about to emit a poisonous gas and kill Tara also contains a gift to make her final moments 'more comfortable'. Two bottles of champagne.

Fights: ☆☆☆☆ Tara spends the entire episode getting in and out of them. Steed and Tara conspire to run across a karate school while following the attaché case.

60s Concerns: Chasing around London with a talking suitcase. (Honest, guv.)

Strangeness: A thief breaking into an apartment picks up an attaché case which says 'Stop! Thief!' The apartment's owner then attacks the thief with a clarinet which turns into a bayonet. The case is passed, first, by Fang the Wonder Dog to a biker, then to, amongst others, a worldwise schoolgirl, a man who keeps his key to the case under his wig, a karate expert (whom Tara beats with Steed's help), and finally to a crypt where it threatens to self-destruct. Somebody's been watching too many *Mission Impossible*s.

Notes: 'Ala Kazam, Kazam!' Terry Nation's best *Avengers* script. A witty, surreal but very silly travelogue through London chasing an audible attaché case. A fun episode: no 'big issues' here, just good, old-fashioned Keystone Kops-style action. The two cases talk to each other at the end. Mother sends a memo to 'Grandma' (see 'You'll Catch Your Death'). Andrews is perhaps the first stumble towards Gambit as one of many strategies the production team adopted in an attempt to de-emphasise Tara.

Trivia: It's not Macnee as Steed in the bubblecar at the beginning (he was unavailable for filming).

French Title: 'L'Homme au Sommet'.

152
'Fog'
12 March 1969
Working Title: 'The Gaslight Ghoul'
Filmed: December 1968
US Transmission: 17 February 1969
Steed rides a hansom cab – Tara meets the Gaslight Ghoul
Writer: Jeremy Burnham
Director: John Hough
Guest Cast: Nigel Green (The President),
Guy Rolfe (Travers), Terence Brady (Carstairs),
Paul Whitsun-Jones (Sanders),
David Lodge (Maskell), Norman Chappell (Fowler).
With: David Bird, Patsy Smart, John Gorrie,
Frederick Peisley, Arnold Diamond, John Barrard,
Frank Sieman, Virginia Clay, Bernard Severn,
Stan Jay, William Lyon Brown.

When a member of the International Disarmament Committee is stabbed with a swordstick on a foggy night, it looks like the Gaslight Ghoul, murderer of the 1890s, has set up in business again. Can Steed and Tara catch him before the committee is severely lacking in personnel?

Wit: ☆ The most witty bit is the tag scene, Steed and Tara lost in the fog.

Champagne: None. Whisky, though.

Fights: ☆☆☆ The villain traps Tara using a fog machine, but Steed arrives to take him on in a rather wonderful sword fight.

60s Concerns: Well, 1890s concerns, actually. Jack the Ripper was on a lot of people's minds at the time, with various programmes concerning the case being screened.

Eccentrics: The members of the Gaslight Ghoul Club, who dress up as the ghoul, complete with false beards, and have the motto 'Never Say Die'. A little tasteless, surely?

Notes: Too much fog, not enough plot. The villain's motive is that he's a multilateralist! You'd think that a British writer, with the British market in mind, wouldn't see London as a fog-filled gothic nightmare, wouldn't you? David Lodge's sword-expert character didn't make it beyond the editing room, but he's still credited on screen.

153
'Who Was That Man I Saw You With?'
19 March 1969
Filmed: January 1969
US Transmission: 3 March 1969
**Tara meets a Field Marshall – Steed puts on boxing
gloves**
Writer: Jeremy Burnham
Director: Don Chaffey
**Guest Cast: William Marlowe (Fairfax),
Ralph Michael (Gen. Hesketh), Alan Browning (Zaroff),**

Alan Wheatley (Dangerfield),
Bryan Marshall (Phillipson),
Aimee Delamain (Miss Culpepper),
Richard Owens (Perowne), Nita Lorraine (Kate),
Ralph Ball (Hamilton), Ken Haward (Powell),
Neville Marten (Pye).

Tara has been employed to test the security on the top-secret war-room computer the Field Marshall. But when a strange foreign man starts sending her flowers, Mother suspects that she's doing her job a bit too efficiently.

Wit: ☆ Steed checks out the villain's body, not for the name of his employer, but for 'something much more important, the name of his tailor'.
Kinkiness Factor: ☆ Tara is tied to a corner of a boxing ring.

Champagne: ☆☆☆ Steed builds a champagne fountain.

Fights: ☆☆☆ Tara knocks out the guard in her apartment, and helps Steed in a choreographed bout in the ring (Steed pauses to compliment the villain on his suit).

60s Concerns: Nuclear defence systems. Double agents.

Eccentrics: Dangerfield, narcissistic villain who lives in a boxing ring.

Notes: Uncannily, this episode forecasts the 'Star Wars' defence system, the Field Marshall being a computer designed to coordinate a missile defence shield. The box has a badge and medal ribbons. ('For protecting London during the rocket attack of 1961.'

'But there wasn't . . . '

'Exactly.') Tara looks dangerous, if still rather clunking, in her blacked-up terrorist actions against the war room. Her banter with Steed is still hideously mistimed, and she spends ten minutes explaining the obvious to him, but Thorson's acting has visibly grown in confidence. It's still stretching a point to expect the audience to think of her as a traitor, though. Steed is unflapped by her secret admirer. Mother is living in a castle (with Rhonda in pageboy's tabard), and gets very angry about Tara's apparent misdeeds. Oh, and Steed's granddad was a 'charming old man', apparently.

French Title: 'Affectueusement Votre . . . '.

154
'Homicide and Old Lace'
26 March 1969
Working Titles: 'The Great Great Britain Crime',
'Tall Story'
Originally filmed: November/December 1967
Extra filming: January 1969
US Transmission: 17 March 1969
Writers: Malcolm Hulke and Terrance Dicks
Director: John Hough (see Notes)
Guest Cast: Joyce Carey (Harriet),
Mary Merrall (Georgina),
Gerald Harper (Colonel Corf), Keith Baxter (Dunbar),
Edward Brayshaw (Fuller).
With: Donald Pickering, Mark London,
Kristopher Kum, Bari Johnson, Stephen Hubay,
Bryan Mosley, Gertan Klauber, Kevork Malikyan,
John Rapley, Anne Ruller.

It's Mother's birthday and he is visiting two of his aunts, Harriet and Georgina. To celebrate he tells them a hair-colour-changing story, 'The Great Great Britain Crime'.

Wit: ☆ Mother referring to the colour of Tara's hair: 'This is my story and if I wish to make Tara sky-blue-pink I will!' Mother informs his aunts that an impasse has been reached. 'What's an impasse?' asks Georgina. 'It's when they run out of plot!' explains Harriet. Intercrime does not, according to Mother, have a 'sense of humour'.

Kinkiness Factor: ☆☆ Tara is interrogated but 'doesn't squeak'. This, according to Mother, is because she 'isn't a mouse'. Tara wears a perfectly scandalous outfit, including knee-length leather boots.

Champagne: No. 'Five fingers of red-eye' instead. And tea . . .

Fights: ☆ Stock footage from various stories, including Steed fighting from 'The Fear Merchants' (in a sandpit) and 'Never Never Say Die' (battling Christopher Lee), are used as a cost-saving device, with only limited success.

Strangeness: Tara's hair. (The experience of the episode, according to Mother, turned her brunette. It should have been grey, really . . .)

Eccentrics: Georgina and Harriet, Mother's spy-story-loving aunts.

Notes: Hulke and Dicks, whose writing credits included *Doctor Who* and *Crossroads*, weren't involved in this rewrite that turned 'The Great Great Britain Crime' into a comedy. Brian Clemens managed this quite successfully, as it happens, writing all of the scenes involving Mother and the aunts. Nevertheless, once the novelty of the episode's format has begun to wear thin, it's not hard to see why the original episode was abandoned. The end music is re-done as a 'silent-movie' style honky-tonk piano solo, partly derived from Izzy Pound and his Incredible Marching Sound from 'The Interrogators'. 'The Great Great Britain Crime' was directed by veteran Vernon Sewell, but John Hough – director of the Mother/aunts segments – receives sole on-screen credit. Intercrime first appeared in the second season-script of the same name. The car-park scenes were filmed in Watford.

German title: 'Mutter's Erzählungen'.

155
'Thingumajig'
2 April 1969
Working Title: 'It'
Filmed: January 1969
US Transmission: 24 March 1969
Writer: Terry Nation
Director: Leslie Norman
Guest Cast: Dora Reisser (Inge),
Jeremy Lloyd (Teddy), Willoughby Goddard (Truman),
Hugh Manning (Major Star),
John Horsley (Dr Grant), Edward Burnham (Brett),
Vernon Dobtcheff (Stenson), Russell Waters (Pike),
Michael McKevitt (Phillips), Neville Hughes (Williams),
John Moore (Greer), Harry Shacklock (Bill).

The Revd Shelley, a wartime pal of Steed's, seeks his help when archaeologists beneath his church are murdered mysteriously.

Do the killings have anything to do with small malevolent mobile metal boxes? No. Oh, all right . . .

Wit: Zilch: really, really serious or clankingly telegraphed.

Champagne: ✰✰✰✰ Tara kills a box with it.

Fights: ✰✰✰ Tara vs metal box in her flat, draining it of power with plug leads. Steed vs an inventor in a spacesuit with an arc welder.

60s Concerns: A vague Hammer parody (very vague).

Strangeness: Steed somehow knows (over the phone) that Tara is icing a cake. She also keeps a penny-farthing bicycle in her flat (*Prisoner*esque).

Eccentrics: A representative of a foreign power who finds England very cold, and an electronics expert who has a permanent cold and keeps sneezing into his snuff box.

With a Young . . . : Iain Cuthbertson (Kruger).

Notes: The early attacks by the box, with the church organ blaring, are really quite scary. The whole thing is done so seriously, with Inge an obvious *Avengers* audition, that suspense becomes the only interesting thing. Oh, and it runs on coincidences, Steed and Inge finding a body because they wanted to 'go and have a look at a quarry'. The worst ever *Avengers* episode? No contest! Jeremy Lloyd (looking all of twenty) is supposed to be a contemporary of Steed . . . Location filming at Tyke's Water Lake, Elstree, and St Mary's church, Ridge.

French Title: 'Haute Tension'.

156
'My Wildest Dream'
7 April 1969, 10.30pm
Filmed: March/April 1968
US Transmission: 6 January 1969
Writer: Philip Levene
Director: Robert Fuest
Guest Cast: Peter Vaughan (Jaeger),
Derek Godfrey (Tobias),
Susan Travers (Nurse Owen), Philip Madoc (Slater),
Michael David (Reece), Murray Hayne (Gibbons),
Tom Kempinski (Dyson), John Savident (Winthrop),
Hugh Moxley (Peregrine).

When one of the Acme Precision Combine is brutally stabbed,
Steed and Tara are on hand to witness the crime, thanks to a
telephoned warning. But why does somebody want them to see
so many killings, and what does it have to do with Dr Jaeger's
aggresso-therapy clinic?

Wit: ☆ Steed's horse delusion: 'Round about Derby day I do
get a slight twinge in my fetlocks.'

Kinkiness Factor: ☆ Tara in leather jacket and boots. Nostalgia.

Champagne: ☆ A bottle in the tag scene, Steed under analysis.

Fights: ☆☆☆ Tara vs villain in the optics factory, with slides
and tripod attack (a homage to Michael Powell's *Peeping Tom*),
villain in a flat (sword drops from wall and kills him) and female
villain in a car.

60s Concerns: Psychotherapy.

Strangeness: Huge observation room with 'Observation' painted on wall in giant red and white letters. Very therapeutic.

Eccentrics: Jaeger, the aggresso-therapist with a very sinister accent.

With a Young . . . : Edward Fox (Chilcott).

Notes: Tara is starting to be allowed to wear clothes suitable for her age. But still we have the uneasy compromise of shorts (for some reason, Thorson was required to show off her legs). Fuest's Pop Art direction makes an obvious plot enjoyable, and gives the stabbings such force (though most of them are in paper dummies) that the episode was broadcast at the later time of 10.30pm.

157
'Requiem'
16 April 1969, time not known
Filmed: January/February 1969
US Transmission: 31 March 1969
Writer: Brian Clemens
Director: Don Chaffey
Guest Cast: John Cairney (Firth),
John Paul (Wells), Denis Shaw (Murray),
Terence Sewards (Rista), Mike Lewin (Barrett),
Kathja Wyeth (Jill), Harvey Ashby (Bobby),
John Baker (Vicar).

While Steed takes prime witness Miranda Loxton to a safe

house to protect her from Murder International hitmen, Tara is kidnapped and then . . . She escapes to find herself in her worst nightmare. A booby-trap in Steed's apartment kills Mother and Tara may be the only one with the hidden knowledge of where Steed has gone.

Wit: ☆ 'Steed's childhood is simply littered with grand and stately homes.'

Champagne: ☆☆☆ Steed and Miranda have quite a supply at the safe house. While Steed is away from home, Mother raids his drinks cabinet.

Fights: ☆☆ Tara fights the tattooed Murray but is beaten and drugged. Rhonda gets in on the act at the climax, surprising Major Firth and two henchmen.

Strangeness: Two assassins try to kill Miranda in an underground car park but hit her bodyguard instead (he's dressed as a woman having just come from a fancy-dress party). Tara is drugged into believing that she has broken both her legs in a bomb blast at Steed's apartment and that Mother is dead. The mock-up extends to a hospital and Mother's funeral. Steed, meanwhile, finds a soulmate in Miranda who shares his love of toy soldiers.

With a Young . . . : Angela Douglas (wonderfully vulnerable as Miranda).

Notes: 'In loving memory of Mother. The finest chap we ever knew.' A nostalgia trip for Steed, a trip of a completely different nature for Tara. Steed carries a gun on this case. 'Must be important,' Tara says. A partial reworking of *The Baron* episode 'The Maze' and the *Adam Adamant Lives!* episode 'A

Slight Case of Reincarnation'; later remade as *The Protectors*' 'Thinkback'. Location shooting around Letchmore Heath and Totteridge Village.

Trivia: Steed had an uncle who was a chess grandmaster, which explains his passion for the game in many episodes. His cousin 'Demon Desmond Steed' is the world Ludo champion.

158
'Take-Over'
23 April 1969
Filmed: February 1969
US Transmission: 14 April 1969
Writer: Terry Nation
Director: Robert Fuest
Guest Cast: Tom Adams (Grenville),
Elizabeth Sellars (Laura), Michael Gwynn (Bill),
Hilary Pritchard (Circe),
Garfield Morgan (Sexton), Anthony Sagar (Clifford).

The home of Steed's friends Bill and Laura Bassett is invaded by a group of ruthless criminals who implant explosives in their throats. Unfortunately, this is the weekend that Steed is coming to stay.

Wit: ☆☆ Sexton considers the Bassett's coffee awful. 'You'd think people who live in a house like this would at least have some fresh coffee.'

After the dinner, Steed comments: 'I haven't seen a room clear so quickly since Freddie Firman took a live skunk into the Turkish baths.'

Kinkiness: ☆☆☆ Circe flirts with Steed in a baffling duel of

282

strangeness. Later, she cavorts around on the shagpile cutting up a newspaper to spell the word 'Bang!' Damn sexy it is too!

Champagne: ☆☆ Yes, at dinner, and wine.

Fights: ☆☆☆ Tara fights Circe, then Grenville in splendid judo style. Steed uses a catapult to stick one of Circe's phosphor-bombs to Granville's neck, and knocks out Lomax with his own long-distance gun.

Strangeness: Steed and Granville play a musical game by playing records backwards. How very 60s.

Eccentrics: Circe, Granville's beautiful, spaced-out, utterly strange assistant, who punctuates every conversation with surreal comments. She says her name reflects her whole character and spends all her money on new noses.

With a Young . . . : Keith Buckley (Lomax), John Comer (Groom).

Notes: 'February's an awful month for table setting.' A very untypical adventure with Steed and Tara stumbling accidentally into a case. Tom Adams is great as a charming villain, wearing a silk cravat and proud of his 'esoteric knowledge' which Steed plays on brilliantly. A partial reworking of *The Baron* episode 'The Maze'.

Trivia: Steed was held prisoner in Nan King during the war. He must have been there for some time as he and his fellow prisoner Bill Bassett lost track of time and still celebrate Christmas in February.

French Title: 'Noel en Fevrier'.

159
'Pandora'
30 April 1969
Filmed: January 1969
US Transmission: 10 March 1969
Writer: Brian Clemens
Director: Robert Fuest
Guest Cast: Julian Glover (Rupert),
James Cossins (Henry),
Kathleen Byron (Miss Faversham),
John Laurie (Juniper), Anthony Roye (Pettigrew),
Geoffrey Whitehead (Carter),
Peter Maddern (Lasindall),
Reginald Barratt (Xavier Smith),
Raymond Burke (Young Gregory).

Tara is kidnapped, and wakes to discover that it is 1915, and she is apparently called Pandora. Could this be because of the little matter of a dowry and a missing bride? Steed struggles to solve a very old mystery.

Wit: ☆

Kinkiness Factor: ☆ One could allege that Tara's whole situation, including enforced marriage, is very de Sade. But then, it's Tara, isn't it?

Fights: ☆☆ Steed comes to the rescue in old-fashioned style.

60s Concerns: Rupert's villainy is related very specifically to his army background.

Eccentrics: Simon Henry Juniper, far too keen on clocks.

Notes: This story owes a lot to Dickens's *Great Expectations*, including the rooms covered in cobwebs. Miss Faversham (Haversham?) is a nod in this direction. Mother lives in a balloon. And does one even have to say *Prisoner*esque? This is Linda Thorson's favourite episode.

160
'Get-A-Way!'
14 May 1969
Filmed: February 1968
US Transmission: 24 April 1968
Writer: Philip Levene
Director: Don Sharp
Guest Cast: Andrew Keir (Col. James),
Peter Bowles (Ezdorf), Peter Bayliss (Dodge),
Neil Hallett (Paul Ryder),
Terence Longdon (George Neville),
William Wilde (Baxter), Michael Culver (Price),
Michael Elwyn (Lt. Edwards), John Hussey (Peters),
Barry Linehan (Magnus), Robert Russell (Lubin),
Vincent Harding (Rostov), James Belchamber (Bryant).

Two invincible foreign agents escape from the ultimate prison, a monastery run by the security services. They resume their mission, to kill one important person each. Steed and Tara set out to catch them, and to find out how they escaped, before their leader follows suit.

Wit: ☆

Champagne: No. Lizard vodka, actually.

Fights: ☆☆ Tara vs agent in magazine offices (she throws him out of a window). There's a cool final duel between Steed and Ezdorf.

60s Concerns: Psychological debriefing of agents. The monastery is, of course, *Prisoner*esque.

Eccentrics: Professor Dodge, escapology expert.

Notes: The actual means of escape is so far-fetched it's most surprising. Ezdorf, with his Hannibal Lecter-like confined charm, makes a good opposite number for Steed. The difference, as Steed says, is 'I kill when I have to, you because you like it.' At the start of the episode, we meet some of Steed's old colleagues at an early-hours party, and, sure enough, one gets killed on the way home. This, and the espionage-network/threat from the past plot, form a virtual blueprint for *The New Avengers*. The monastery scenes were filmed at Ashridge College, near Little Gaddesden.

161
'Bizarre'
21 May 1969
Filmed: February/March 1969
US Transmission: 21 April 1969
Writer: Brian Clemens
Director: Leslie Norman
Guest Cast: Roy Kinnear (Happychap),
Fulton Mackay (Master), Sally Nesbitt (Helen),
James Kerry (Cordell), George Innes (Shaw),
John Sharp (Jupp), Sheila Burrell (Mrs Jupp),
Michael Balfour (Tom), Patrick Connor (Bob),

Ron Pember (Charley).

When a woman is found walking barefoot in a snowy field, complaining of a dead man who wasn't dead, Steed investigates the Happy Meadows funeral parlour, which doesn't seem to be keeping its clients down under. What connection could that business possibly have with Mystic Tours?

Wit: ☆☆ 'We give trading stamps: save for that funeral now!'
'You won't live to regret it.'
Steed on waking in paradise: 'What would it be like if I'd lived a completely blameless life?'
Mother: 'I wonder if it's too late to hand this case over to another department . . . '

Champagne: ☆ A bottle and two glasses are conveniently left in Steed's home-made rocket in the tag sequence.

Fights: ☆☆☆ Tara tackles a bedside assailant. Steed and Tara vs villains to a chivalric version of the theme music in a farcical final punch-up.

60s Concerns: Paradise is full of acid guitar music.

Eccentrics: Bagpipes Happychap, funeral-director son of a father who was told to expect a 'squeaky little bundle' and got the wrong idea. 'We like to make death fun.' The Master, a gravy-browned guru who can only be woken up by the sound of shuffling banknotes.

Notes: Amazing flashback sequence of a woman falling off a train. Cordell is a proto-Gambit, interviewing Mrs Jupp on his own, and checking out Mystic Tours. Mother speaks to 'Grandma' on the phone. Altogether, an episode with a nice atmosphere, but rather inconspicuous and simple. The episode is a partial reworking of the *Adam Adamant Lives!* episode 'The Terribly Happy Embalmers'. The introductory scenes are similar to the *Danger Man* episode 'The Girl in Pink Pyjamas', and would later be reused in *The Professionals* episode 'Blackout'. 'Bizarre' is a really weak and meaningless title, though. The much-quoted final tag scene has Steed apparently building a rocket in his back garden and taking off with Tara in it, going, as it were, over the top. Mother addresses the camera, the only time anybody in the show ever does: 'They'll be back, you can depend on it. They're unchaperoned up there!'

THE NEW
AVENGERS

First Season

Introduction

In 1975, Patrick Macnee and Linda Thorson were reunited for a French champagne advert. *The Avengers*, like most of the good bits of British culture, had always had a more intellectual appreciation on the continent, where high art and high camp amount to much the same thing. French television executive Rudolf Roffi, on seeing the commercial, was surprised to find out that the show was no longer being made, and approached Brian Clemens. Together they managed to gain French backing for a new series.

Clemens was obviously doubtful that Patrick Macnee could be the focal point for this new venture, and thus chose to give him two sidekicks to do the fighting. Basically, Steed became Mother, working from his stud farm, and the female assistant gained a male partner, as Tara had done on several experimental occasions. The new characters were to be Charley, played by Jenny Lee Wright (from *The Benny Hill Show*) and Mike Gambit, played by Gareth Hunt. In the former case, things changed. Joanna Lumley, who had played Ken Barlow's girl-friend in *Coronation Street*, auditioned successfully for the role of Charley, and moved for the character to be renamed Purdey, either in homage to the shotgun of the same name, or after technical crew member Ron Purdey. She also came up with her own haircut, a functional and dangerous bob that suggests that she was trying to make the character harder from day one. Purdey at least defended herself with a recognised form of self-defence, the French kickboxing art of *panache*, though it was never called that on screen. She was an ex-ballerina, and didn't appear to have a first name. Gambit was more straightforward, a working-class drifter, ex-Navy, who liked chatting up women and enjoyed exactly the flirting relationship with Purdey that Steed had with Emma in the first five minutes of their onscreen partnership.

Working-class? Indeed. For Clemens' anti-realism guidelines had gone out of the window. The show for the 70s had racial minorities (mainly fiendish orientals, still no black people), drug smugglers (albeit done with a hilarious lack of street perspective) and uniformed policemen. It had been reformatted to include all classes, even the homeless, and had a nostalgic feel to it. Much was made of the Britishness of the whole thing, but it was a genuine, European, Britishness, out of step with any notion of quaint old England. Lots of location filming gave us some wonderful seasonal looks at the English countryside, but there were also glimpses of ordinary towns and cities. Foreign powers became Soviets, and the Cold War a bitter reality. All in all, it was a very impressive reformatting, a solid base for success in the disillusionment of the 70s, with a useful new cast. But some aspects jarred.

Much is made of the male characters' desire to 'protect' Purdey, while Joanna Lumley was doing a fine job at appearing deadly and witty. Her dialogue, her tendency to fumble things and lead the others into bad situations, and her wardrobe, a series of party frocks unsuited for action sequences, are real indications that the ideal *Avengers* girl for Clemens is a long way from being an adult woman. Lumley fought long and hard for her dignity. Macnee was engaged in battles of his own, trying to get a bigger part and more action, for which he was still absolutely suited. Thankfully, both actors won their battles to some extent.

Despite the quality of the new format, there is something about *The New Avengers* that makes it . . . silly. Perhaps it's the fact that 70s fashions are laughed at, while 60s ones are appreciated. Perhaps it's that after AIDS, Gambit's swift conquests and Steed's vast number of mature girlfriends seem gauche (and perhaps it was a mistake to turn back to sex after a decade of turning away). Perhaps it's just that the new realism only showed up how unrealistic any *Avengers* character is.

Still, for a certain age group, this is the nostalgic stuff. When you see it again now, it's hard to say why you felt such identification with, or hormonal disturbance because of, Gambit or Purdey. But at least it's not hard to see why Patrick Macnee made you want to own a bowler. If it's got him in it, then this must be *The Avengers*.

Wit: Not a lot. Macnee can still put a spin on the most ordinary lines, but the *double entendre* has become the single. Humorous exchanges between Gambit and Purdey tend to consist of a lot of repetition and crude innuendo.

Kinkiness: Purdey gets thrown into a lot of dangerous and potentially frock-tearing situations, but her surprising tendency to show fear rather takes the fun out of the few occasions when she's actually tied to anything. And was Laura Ashley a dominatrix? We think not.

Champagne: Rather restrained. Seventies economies restricted the trio to only four sipping opportunities this season.

Fights: Joanna Lumley manages to suggest that Purdey's actually more dangerous than we see here, doing her own fighting and delivering her kicks with straight-faced ruthlessness. With Mike Gambit we get a lot of martial-arts mysticism and the same fixed expression. Unlike the playground fights of the 60s, these combats are staged like gladiatorial contests, testosterone-charged fights to the death between ruthless professionals. It all feels very serious when you're twelve.

The Writers: Brian Clemens rather comes into his own here, creating a whole new aesthetic for the series which actually works and has a strange sort of poetry to it. The idea is that Purdey and Gambit are but children, playing spy games with glee under the watchful eye of Steed. To some degree this justifies the treatment of Purdey. Having grown up, Steed is aware that everything isn't such fun, and is really shocked sometimes at the changes that have happened since he was so carefree. He won't show any sign of such pain to his charges, though. Five of the episodes concern threats from the past, as if the carefree 60s had to be paid for in some way. Four of these are by Clemens. The other is Terence Feely's austere 'To Catch a Rat', an unfortunately dull requiem for the past, as indexed by the rise and fall of Ian Hendry's career. His Guest Star status is appropriate for a story of somebody who's lost his memory, literally lost the past, trying to come home to a show which was once his. The theme is, in a word, nostalgia and how Steed manages to hold it at bay. Clemens's writing partner on the whole season is Dennis Spooner, another ITC veteran. He contributes three scripts of his own, all of which are more old-fashioned *Avengers* than the new format, and co-writes two with Clemens, the result of a mutual writer's block which led to them swapping scripts half way through. The order of credits indicates who started and finished what.

Top Five Episodes: 'Faces'
                               'The Eagle's Nest'
                               'Sleeper'
                               'Target!'
                               'Three-Handed Game'

Broadcast Details

Transmission details are as LWT. The season was partially networked until December 1976.

13 colour episodes (60 mins)
Avengers (Film & TV) Enterprises Ltd
and IDTV TV Productions, Paris

Producers: Albert Fennell and Brian Clemens

Music composed by Laurie Johnson

Regular Cast: Patrick Macnee (John Steed),
Gareth Hunt (Mike Gambit), Joanna Lumley (Purdey).

162
'The Eagle's Nest'
22 October 1976, time not known
US Transmission: 5 September 1978
Writer: Brian Clemens
Director: Desmond Davis
Guest Cast: Peter Cushing (Von Claus),
Derek Farr (Father Trasker), Frank Gatliff (Karl),
Sydney Bromley (Hans), Trevor Baxter (Brown-Fitch),
Joyce Carey (Lady with Dog), Neil Phillips (Man),
Brian Anthony (Stannard), Ronald Forfar (Jad),
Jerome Wells (Barker), Trude Van Doorne (Geda),
Peter Porteous (Nazi Corporal), Charles Bolton (Ralph).
Uncredited: Sammie Winmill (Molly),
Maggy Maxwell (Dowager),
Raymond Mason (Man with Suitcase).

Agent Stannard is missing, Von Claus, an expert in suspended animation, has been kidnapped, and Steed is back! Meanwhile, on the tiny island of St Dorca, the monks of the Fourth Reich are rising . . .

Wit: ☆☆ Purdey: 'I need my beauty sleep.'
Gambit: 'There's a lot of things you need, but that isn't one of them!'
Guard: 'You are to be executed immediately!'
Steed: 'Thank goodness you broke it to me gently!'

Kinkiness Factor: ☆ Steed: 'I want Purdey.'
Gambit: 'Who doesn't?'
Purdey's lipstick is called 'Sins of Youth'. 'That's not a colour, it's an accusation,' notes Steed.

Champagne: ☆ Steed got his strong wrists, according to Purdey, by pulling champagne corks.

Violence: ☆☆☆☆ Gambit tips Purdey out of bed. The windscreen of Gambit's speeding car is shot out at point-blank rage. After Gambit has kicked his would-be assassin around a field, the man takes a cyanide capsule. Purdey is menaced by a fishing-rod-wielding local. Steed (in a habit) and Purdey (in a leotard) take on four Nazis. 'I abhor violence and loud gunfire makes me blink,' says Steed, before participating in both.

Porno Funk Music Factor: 4. Nice wah-wah guitars in a chase sequence.

Strangeness: Jack-booted monks. ('Monkey business,' notes Steed, before adding 'You can get into bad habits.' Which he does. . .)

Fashion Victims: Gambit. Definitely Gambit.

Gambit's Conquests: Gerda, a clerk in the German Air Ministry. In a typically efficient German way she wants to bed Gambit, though she believes he must have German blood in him. He has: 'I took three bullets coming over the wall last year.' A meal is arranged for Saturday.

The Enemy: Nazis disguised as the Trappist monks of St Dorca.

Notes: 'It's hideous! It's obscene!' 'It's the future!' 'Avenging is better than ever,' said the *Daily Mail* reporter about this episode. Well, it's not *that* good but it is a fun episode, especially the climax with Steed, Purdey and Gambit whistling 'Colonel Bogey' as they round up the Nazis. A very good performance from the ever-reliable Peter Cushing, too. Excellent location filming at Eilean Donan Castle and Doinie, Ross and Cromerty, Scotland.

Trivia: Steed saws at a violin at one stage (*à la* Sherlock Holmes). Purdey was rejected by the Royal Ballet because she was too tall.

163
'House of Cards'
29 October 1976
US Transmission: 20 October 1978
Writer: Brian Clemens
Director: Ray Austin
Guest Cast: Peter Jeffrey (Perov),
Frank Thornton (Roland), Lyndon Brook (Cartney),

**Derek Francis (The Bishop), Mark Burns (Spence),
Geraldine Moffat (Jo), Annette André (Suzy),
Ina Skriver (Olga), Murray Brown (David),
Gordon Sterne (Prof. Vasil), Don Meaden (Boris),
Jeremy Wilkin (Tulliver), Anthony Bailey (Frederick).**

When Steed had a hoard of screaming teenagers rescue his intended victim, spymaster Perov seemingly commits suicide. But days later his system of sleeper agents, the House of Cards, activates, and Steed, Purdey and Gambit find themselves fighting trusted friends.

Wit: ☆ 'We live in an age of euphemisms!'

Champagne: ☆☆☆ Steed's long-time girlfriend, Joanna, puts poison in his glass, leading to a rather awful emotional scene.

Violence: ☆☆☆ Gambit has an impressive bout with his karate master, Spence, in the dark, and Purdey decks Perov with a right hook when 'He HIT me!'

Fashion Victims: Gambit's pop-star cover is a hoot.

They Need a Haircut: Spence has a fuzzy perm.

The Enemy: Perov and his 13 sleeper agents.

Notes: Joanna inspects Steed's photos of Cathy, Emma and Tara. Steed thinks she's looking at horses: 'Had to take the whip to her on occasion' while on Emma hardly raises an eyebrow, but she pauses at the idea of having Tara shot. Purdey's stepfather is a bishop, who can kick like his daughter, and we learn that her real Dad was shot as a spy. Of the 13 sleepers, we only meet five. Interesting, with some lovely details, but a bit slow-moving, and there's something almost uncouth about Steed having a long-term relationship. Windmill footage shot at Turville, near High Wycombe. In repeat showings, this episode is the most likely to be shown with the US title sequence (a montage of scenes from this season set to the same music).

164
'The Last of the Cybernauts ... ??'
5 November 1976
US Transmission: 9 March 1979
Writer: Brian Clemens
Director: Sidney Hayers
Guest Cast: Robert Lang (Kane),
Oscar Quitak (Malov), Gwen Taylor (Dr Marlow),
Basil Hopkins (Prof. Mason),
Robert Gillespie (Goff),
David Horovitch (Fitzroy), Sally Bazely (Laura),
Pearl Hackney (Mrs Weir),
Martin Fisk (Second Guard), Eric Carte (Terry),
Ray Armstrong (First Guard),
Rocky Taylor (Cybernaut), Davina Taylor (Tricia).

Felix Kane, a villain caught in an explosion a year ago, returns to seek revenge. He picks up Goff, Dr Armstrong's assistant, on his release from prison, and has him reactivate a storehouse of Cybernaut parts, with the aim of building himself a new body.

Wit: ☆ Steed to his cleaning lady: 'Are you a woman of high moral standards? Then I should leave the guest room until tomorrow.'

Kinkiness Factor: ☆☆ Kane drools over Purdey quite a lot.

Violence: ☆☆☆ Gambit vs Cybernaut on stairs. Purdey kicks it down the stairwell.

The Enemy: Felix Kane, wheelchair-bound villain with horribly scarred face and a variety of masks to express emotion.

Notes: Goff was not seen or mentioned in either Cybernauts story previously. Purdey plays piano. Steed gets to play a Stylophone. Much use of a *New Avengers* motif, huge photo blow-ups of the leads. A lot duller than one might expect, but the dark nostalgia of the thing is interesting. Purdey and Gambit once again resemble schoolkids amazed by their elders. Purdey is outclassed by Kane, and is actually scared, rather gauchely. Oh, and Gambit uses a spray can in a corny gun-firing posture. Hee hee hee!

165
'The Midas Touch'
12 November 1976
US Transmission: 1 December 1978
Writer: Brian Clemens
Director: Robert Fuest
Guest Cast: John Carson (Freddy),
Ed Devereaux (Vann),
Ronald Lacey (Hong Kong Harry),
David Swift (Turner),
Jeremy Childs (Lieutenant Henry),
Robert Mills (Curator), Ray Edwards (Gavin),
Gilles Millinaire (Midas), Pik-Sen Lim (Sing),
Chris Tranchell (Doctor), Lionel Guyett (Tayman),

**Geoffrey Bateman (Simpson), Tim Condren (Boz),
Pete Winter (Morgan), Bruce Bould (Froggart),
Bruno Elrington (Choy).
Uncredited: Kenneth Gilbert (Rostrock),
Tania Mallett (Sara), Pola Churchill (Princess).**

Professor Turner is a scientist with a lust for gold. He is also rather friendly with Midas, a man whose touch is death. Mix in Chinese gangsters, a threat to the safety of a visiting royal and a groovy party where everybody dies, and what do you have . . . ? A mess, really.

Wit: ☆☆ Hong Kong Harry: 'I swear to you on my mother's grave.'
    Steed: 'You sold it for development years ago.'
    Purdey: 'Steed, you're becoming a roué.'
    Steed: 'An optimist!'
    The best line in the episode is delivered by a young doctor who arrives at a party in the aftermath of a massacre. Gambit asks what killed the people and; after a lengthy list of diseases (everything from smallpox to beri-beri), the Doctor notes 'Yes, Mr Gambit, they died of *everything*!'

Kinkiness Factor: ☆ Purdey, in a short skirt, clambers over a high wire fence. A bit obvious really.

Violence: ☆ Hong Kong Harry is shot going down the escalator at Heathrow. Gambit takes on a 'Grade A' karate expert and easily beats him. 'Grade C,' he notes dismissively.

Porno Funk Music Factor: 8. Funk guitar accompanies Gambit and Purdey chasing an assassin through a deserted factory. And the party (see below).

70s Concerns: 'The plague' (like this was *Survivors* or something!).

Strangeness: Purdey and Gambit argue about who directed *The Treasure of the Sierra Madre* during a car chase.

Fashion Victims: A kinky fancy dress party with voodoo masks and what sounds suspiciously like Atomic Rooster or some other 'progressive' rock on the stereo. All very decadent. Midas turns up wearing a red cloak and death mask. Shades of *Masque of the Red Death*. Everybody dies, needless to say.

The Enemy: Midas, a man 'whose touch is death'. Turner, the former government scientist.

Notes: 'Have I not discovered the way to turn dross into gold!' Being Fuest, this is beautifully shot, but it's all a bit grim for *The Avengers*. And there's a re-emerging contempt for ethnic actors, casting Ronald Lacey (under heavy make-up, at least) as 'Hong Kong Harry'. David Swift makes a great villain, however. Some filming at the Cock Pit, Eton.

166
'Cat Amongst the Pigeons'
19 November 1976
US Transmission: 17 November 1978
Writer: Dennis Spooner
Director: John Hough
Guest Cast: Vladek Sheybal (Zarcardi),
Matthew Long (Turner), Basil Dignam (Rydercroft),
Peter Copley (Waterlow), Hugh Walters (Lewington),
Gordon Rollings (Bridlington), Joe Black (Hudson),
Patrick Connor (Foster), Kevin Stoney (Tomkins),

Andrew Bradford (Merton), Brian Jackson (Controller).

The warning of a dying man tips Steed off that ecologist Rydercroft is to be killed at noon. All pains are taken to protect the man's aircraft, but it still crashes, dead on time. And what's that strange sound that accompanied both deaths?

Wit: ☆☆ Purdey on an egg: 'If it hatches out, a hostage.'
   Gambit on hearing of someone who really understood birds: 'Sounds like a man I should meet.'

Kinkiness Factor: ☆ Purdey threatened by birds. Err . . .

Violence: ☆☆ Lots of people ripped up by unseen birds. Sorry if that spoils it for you. Steed fights a falcon in a range rover.

Fashion Victims: A number of birdy eccentrics who wouldn't be out of place in a Rigg story.

The Enemy: The wonderfully soft-spoken Zarcardi, who talks to the birds and dresses in artistic black while playing his pipes. His motive is entirely that he doesn't want to see birds hurt, which makes him a rather old-fashioned sort of Rigg villain really.

Notes: Rather well directed, with a nice sunny feel, but suffers from the *New Avengers* problem of Obvious Mystery, i.e. the strange thing that is puzzling our heroes is either immediately obvious to the audience or actually explained to them. Steed hides underwater at one stage and manages to stay unruffled. There's a rather good solution to the problem.

167
'Target!'

26 November 1976
US Transmission: 12 September 1978
Writer: Dennis Spooner
Director: Ray Austin
Guest Cast: Keith Barron (Draker),
Robert Beatty (Ilenko), Roy Boyd (Bradshaw),
Frederick Jaeger (Jones),
Malcolm Stoddard (George Myers),
Deep Roy (Klokoe), John Paul (Kendrick),
Bruce Purchase (Lopez), Dennis Blanch (Talmadge),
Robert Tayman (Palmer).
Uncredited: Suzanna Macmillan (Nurse),
John Saunders (Titherbridge),
Peter Brace (Potterton), Marc Boyle (McKay).

An automated village is a training ground for British agents, where they are shot with dye markers by dummies. But after they've left the place and go on leave, they die in mysterious circumstances.

Wit: ☆☆ Gambit on why holidaying agents are dying: 'Plan to disrupt the tourist board?'
   'That's funny. . . '
   'Not the way I said it.'

Violence: ☆☆ Lots of people shot with poison.

Fashion Victims: Purdey opts for a nice dress to run across rooftops in.

They Need a Haircut: Bradshaw, the lab assistant, has a wonderful perm.

The Enemy: The wonderfully understated Draker and his vertically-challenged assistant.

Notes: An episode with great set pieces, the one that everyone remembers, but it's not constructed very well. The village itself is though, with lookalike dummies, fake graffiti ('I Luv Purdey') and little touches like the postman with his head in the pillarbox, the police box (which gets blown up) and the village signs (like 'Denham – The Middle Churchyard Is a Disgrace', Denham being a village near Pinewood). There's an American-speaking Soviet agent too. A bit of a telefan's delight, with Derek Blanch (Willis from *Strangers*), Keith Barron, Deep Roy and John Paul (out of *Doomwatch*) alongside Frederick Jaeger's smallest-ever mature role. (Jaeger was due to film for a week, but this was ruined by rain. After this he wasn't available and, having only shot one scene, he was then replaced by Roy Boyd playing a new character.) Gambit shows tremendous stupidity: after having the plot explained to him by a dying man, he still fails to get it. Purdey is once again made into someone to be rescued by our heroes. John Paul's line-remembering problems get in the way of everybody else's repartée. It's typical of *The New Avengers* that even this, which would have made a great theme for an Emma Peel story, and has tons of energy, is done in a botched manner, as though we're only going to see it once and it doesn't have to stand up to much scrutiny.

168
'To Catch a Rat'
3 December 1976
US Transmission: 16 February 1979
Writer: Terence Feeley
Director: James Hill

Guest Star: Ian Hendry as Gunner
Guest Cast: Edward Judd (Cromwell),
Robert Fleming (Quaintance), Barry Jackson (Cledge),
Anthony Sharp (Grant), Jeremy Hawk (Finder),
Jo Kendall (Nurse), Sally-Jane Spencer (Mother).
Uncredited: Genevieve Allenbury (Bridgit),
Anita Graham (Helga).

Recovering his memory, Gunner, a veteran of the Cold War, starts to broadcast again on his old frequency. He has information about a double agent, the White Rat, in high places. But who'll get to him first?

Wit: *Nil points*. It's like watching moss grow.

Kinkiness Factor: ✩ Trouser sewing? Nope.

Violence: ✩ Purdey attacks Cromwell from a trapeze.

They Need a Haircut: Cromwell could do with some hair.

The Enemy: The White Rat. But who is he?

Notes: Steed's old codename was The New Doberman, and this week's girlfriend is called Helga. Purdey is rather horridly chatted up by Cromwell after she sews his trousers. No, really. It's obvious who the traitor is immediately. Ian Hendry, who gets guest star status, really earns it, and the role is apt. Steed gets to say: 'I know I'm 17 years too late, but welcome back.' This would seem to be the whole motivation for the story. The churches featured are at Harefield and Fingest.

169
'The Tale of the Big Why'
10 December 1976
US Transmission: 2 February 1979
Writer: Brian Clemens
Director: Robert Fuest
Guest Cast: Derek Waring (Harmer),
Jenny Runacre (Irene), George A. Cooper (Brandon),
Gary Waldhorn (Roach), Rowland Davies (Poole),
Geoffrey Toone (Minister),
Maeve Alexander (Mrs Turner).

Released from prison after nine years for spying, Burt Brandon heads straight for an abandoned well near Neverton containing unspecified secret information. He is soon killed by two agents but has managed to post a package to his daughter. Steed recovers the package, only to find it contains a pulp Western, *The Tale of the Big Why*.

Wit: ☆ 'He needs a phrenologist like he needs a hole in the head' is pretty good, but any story containing a line like 'It's a ghastly plot' really is asking for trouble.

Kinkiness Factor: ☆ The book includes explicit details of 'Bessie the saloon gal's mating habits'. Steed says he's read it. Twice. 'Very badly written,' notes Purdey. 'And anatomically impossible.'

Champagne: ☆☆ Yes, four glasses.

Violence: ☆☆☆ Gambit knocks over an agent with his Range Rover. Steed takes on Roach and Poole in macho style, using his bowler to deflect a shotgun blast. Gambit coolly disarms

Harmer, not knowing that Steed had removed the bullets from the gun. He does it, he says, because he trusts Steed.

Porno Funk Music Factor: 10. Sleazy saxophones, jazz bass, the works. Like a Barry White backing track, in fact.

Strangeness: Poole and Roach cause Brandon's car to crash, then strip first the agent and then the car in search of his secrets. When they find nothing in the car, Poole asks what they should do now, 'put it back together?'

Fashion Victims: Typical mid-70s, Crimplene and suede, big collars, flares, 'That Shirt'. Probably Hai-Karate aftershave too.

The Enemy: Poole and Roach, Russian agents after Brandon's secrets. Harmer, a double agent in the Ministry.

With a Young. . . : Roy Marsden (Turner).

Notes: 'The answer is in the book.' This episode takes a long time to get going, cramming much into the final few minutes. However, there are great directorial touches by Fuest, notably a tracking shot past a pub with a pint of beer in the foreground used to indicate the passage of time.

Trivia: Purdey drives a motorcycle and wears a jacket with 'Purdey' and *The New Avengers* lion-logo on the back. So much for the *secret* service!

French Title: 'La Grande Interrogation'.

170
'Faces'
17 December 1976
US Transmission: 13 October 1978
Writers: Brian Clemens and Dennis Spooner
Director: James Hill
Guest Cast: David De Keyser (Prator),
Edward Petherbridge (Mullins),
Neil Hallett (Clifford), Richard Leech (Craig),
Annabel Leventon (Wendy), David Webb (Bilston),
Donald Hewlett (Torrance), J.G. Devlin (Tramp),
Jill Melford (Sheila), Michael Sheard (Peters),
Robert Putt (Attendant).

Two homeless villains note the resemblance of one of them to
a rich official, kill him and take his place. Are they responsible
for the number of friends and associates that now fail to
recognise Steed? Gambit and Purdey go undercover.

Wit: ☆☆ Steed locks his double in the wine cellar. 'He's got
the same habits as me. I'll bet he's half way through my '61
claret.'

Kinkiness Factor: ☆☆ Purdey in Salvation Army uniform;
plus, she strips off in the mirror.

Violence: ☆☆ Purdey fights a man armed with an arrow. No,
not a bow and arrow. An arrow. He causes her a disproportion-
ate amount of trouble.

Fashion Victims: Petherbridge in flares!

The Enemy: Mullins the archer, Terrison the imposter, and Dr

Prator the plastic surgeon. So much for care in the community.

Notes: The moment that the tramp has taken on the identity of Craig, he knows enough to call Steed 'John'. Gambit and Steed shoot clay pigeons together. 'You can't help your background.' A deserted military base, one of Clemens' obsessions, appears. Joanna Lumley shows her talent in the creation of Lolita ('Naw what I mean?'), a moll with dress sense even worse than her own. And Gambit gets to say 'I can do an Irish accent.' Just as well the remote control hadn't been invented. Great variation on the false identities game that actually keeps the viewer on their toes. Hugely indebted to 'Two's a Crowd', but great fun anyway. Clemens, hitting a writer's block, handed this script to Spooner halfway through.

171
'Gnaws'
21 December 1976
US Transmission: 29 December 1978
Writer: Dennis Spooner
Director: Ray Austin
Guest Cast: Julian Holloway (Charles Thornton),
Peter Cellier (Carter), Jeremy Young (Chislenko),
Keith Marsh (Tramp Joe), Ken Wynne (Tramp Arthur),
Morgan Shepherd (Walters), John Watts (Harlow),
Keith Alexander (Malloy),
Ronnie Laughlin (Motor Mechanic).
Uncredited: Anulka Dubinska (Pretty Girl).

Two scientists are developing, in secret, a new growth drug which could end world famine (and make them a lot of money). Unfortunately, some of the drug has been flushed down the sink, and now there's something nasty in the sewers.

Wit: ☆☆ Purdey: 'I am a woman. Women are allowed their idiosyncrasies.'

Steed tells Gambit to check the sewers: 'It won't be pleasant.' 'That's all right. I normally come up smelling of roses.'

Kinkiness Factor: Purdey in a nightdress. Cute, but hardly kinky.

Champagne: No, scotch and vodka in the sewers instead.

Violence: ☆☆☆☆ Seven men are eaten by a giant rat. Just a nice old-fashioned family show, eh? Purdey has a fight in the sewers with a (red-tracksuited) Russian agent, whilst Gambit gives him the full *Dirty Harry* dialogue: 'If I hit your little finger with this, it'll take your whole arm off...' (What next, 'Do you feel lucky, punk?')

Porno Funk Music factor: 1. Dull. Really dull. Like Emerson, Lake and Palmer dull.

Fashion Victims: Purdey wears a hideous patterned headscarf.

The Enemy: A giant rat in the London sewers.

With a Young...: Patrick Malahide (George Ratcliffe).

Notes: 'What's big enough to drive all the rats away?' An interesting, sometimes amusing episode with a moral scientific dilemma and with Spooner giving even his minor characters some good lines. However, this one was done on the cheap (with virtually no location filming), most of the action taking place in various bits of sewer. The rat itself is a normal rat, dimly lit on a miniature set – with, shall we say, mixed results.

French Title: 'Le Monstre des Egonts'.

172
'Dirtier by the Dozen'
7 January 1976
US Transmission: 22 December 1978
Writer: Brian Clemens
Director: Sidney Hayers
Guest Cast: John Castle (Col. Miller),
Shaun Curry (Sgt Bowden), Colin Skeaping (Travis),
Stephen Moore (Major Prentice),
Alun Armstrong (Harris),
Ballard Berkeley (Col. Elroyd Foster),
Michael Barrington (Gen. Stevens),
Michael Howarth (Capt. Tony Noble),
John Forbes-Robertson (Doctor),
John Labonowski (Keller), David Purcell (Orderly)
Francis Mughan (Freddy).
Uncredited: Richard Derrington (Turner),
John Challis (Soldier).

Gambit tries to meet Travis, a man carrying some secret film, but he's killed before he can hand it over. The film is footage of a unit fighting all over the world, but the unit is commanded by a serving British officer. How can this be?

Wit: ☆ Soldier showing scars: 'Look at this.'
Purdey: 'A hairy forearm?'

Kinkiness Factor: ☆☆ Purdey donates her bra as a sling. 'Bra-vo!' Ahem.

Champagne: ☆☆☆ Purdey is offered a glass whilst dangling from a helicopter over a minefield.

Violence: ☆☆ Lots of people machine-gunned. Gambit fights three squaddies, and is saved by Purdey, who throws one over the roof.

Fashion Victims: Purdey in knee-length boots, safari hat and orange trousers.

They Need a Haircut: The soldiers display a number of very unmilitary collar-length jobs.

The Enemy: 'Mad Jack' Miller (in eyepatch and monocle) and his 19th Special Commando.

With a Young . . . : Brian Croucher (Terry) in an episode featuring a character called Travis (for *Blake's 7* fans).

Notes: Purdey rather wonderfully pumps a pubful of squaddies for information, and we find out that she drinks gin with orange, bitters, ginger ale and ice. The soldiers have a real Armoured Personnel Carrier. Gambit displays his horrid Irish accent again. Another deserted army base, and once again Steed talks to a soldier while he wanders through an assault course. Standard Clemens runaround, seemingly written quickly out of a font of clichés. There's really nothing for Steed to do in it, but at least we get to see his collection of toy soldiers.

French Title: 'Commando Tres Special'.

173
'Sleeper'
14 January 1977
US Transmission: 6 October 1978

Writer: Brian Clemens
Director: Graeme Clifford
Guest Cast: Keith Buckley (Brady),
Arthur Dignam (Dr Graham), Mark Jones (Chuck),
Sara Kestelman (Tina), Gavin Campbell (Fred),
David Schofield (Ben), George Sweeney (Phil),
Peter Godfrey (Pilot/Carter), Leo Dolan (Bill),
Jason White (First Policeman),
Tony McHale (Second Policeman).
Uncredited: Joe Dunn (Hardy),
Denise Reynolds (Woman in Car).

Having witnessed a test on a new sleeping gas, S-95, and been made immune to its effects, Steed, Purdey and Gambit awake one Sunday morning to find the whole of London asleep and an open house on the city's banks and jewellers.

Wit: ☆☆ Purdey, told that the drug they are taking has been tested on rabbits: 'People aren't rabbits.'

Steed: 'An uncle of mine sired nineteen children. He was a keen bicyclist . . . ' Later, Steed picks up a copy of *The Times* and tells Gambit, 'things are worse than I thought, England were all out for 142.'

Kinkiness Factor: ☆☆☆☆ Whilst posing as a shop window dummy ('Today's Biggest Offer') Purdey's pyjama pants fall down. Very Brian Rix.

Champagne: No, Steed and Gambit share a nightcap of whisky. When chasing through London, they find a pub and enjoy a pint of beer ('It *is* an emergency,' notes Steed).

Violence: ☆☆ Purdey is chased in a Mini Cooper by machine-gun-toting thugs in best *Starsky and Hutch* style. Lots of explosions, car chases and gunfire, but strangely few fights.

Porno Funk Music Factor: 8. A nice bit of guitar to accompany Gambit coming upon a semi-naked girl in a taxi. Rather against form, he covers her dignity.

Fashion Victims: 'I like this place,' says Steed about Gambit's apartment, 'it's not my style, but it does have style.' True, a horrible, garish 70s dayglo style. Bright green decor no less. Purdey wears a pair of electric blue silk pyjamas.

The Enemy: Bank robbers using anti-terrorist gas to put London to sleep.

With a Young. . . : Prentis Hancock (Bart), and an uncredited Peter Richardson (Man in Car).

Notes: 'We have the whole of the city to ourselves.' The filming of a deserted London gives the story a sinister edge far removed from normal *New Avengers* stories. The whole tone of the episode is summed up by two minor police characters (in uniform, please note), who are told to investigate why no one north of the river is answering their radios. One asks if they should use their siren, the other replies: 'If it's good enough for *Kojak* it's good enough for us.' Exactly.

French Title: 'Le S-95'.

174
'Three-Handed Game'
21 January 1977
Writers: Dennis Spooner and Brian Clemens

Director: Ray Austin
Guest Cast: David Wood (Ranson),
Michael Petrovitch (Larry),
Stephen Grief (Juventor), Tony Vogel (Ivan),
Gary Raymond (Masgard), Terry Wood (Meroff),
Ronald Leigh-Hunt (General), John Paul (Doctor),
Hugh Morton (Professor), Noel Trevarthen (Tony Field),
Bill Bailey (Cary).

Steed's plan to have three memory experts memorise a third each of the Allied defence plans for courier purposes seems to have been a perfect success. Until, that is, Juventor arrives with a machine that can drain minds.

Wit: ☆☆ Gambit admits a grudging respect for Juventor when discovering he sold the plans for a missile head to four governments on the same day. 'Perhaps it was early closing,' says Steed. Helen Mackay is showing off her modern-art sculptures to Purdey and Gambit. They are all obscurely shaped blocks with titles like 'Napoleon's retreat from Moscow'. Gambit asks if one wire and wood structure is 'Nelson at Waterloo'. 'No, the gardener put that up to support the rhododendrons!' Gambit, as is his function, kicks a door in at one point. 'You do that awfully well,' says Purdey. 'I get a lot of practice,' he replies.

Kinkiness Factor: ☆☆☆ Purdey and Gambit squabble like a married couple over the relative 'sexiness' of Larry, Gambit's rival for Purdey's affections. There's an interesting shot of a busty blonde in yellow hot pants in the pits at Silverstone when Steed visits the racing driver Field. This is the only *Avengers* episode in which one of the regular cast appears nude. Unfortunately, it's Gambit.

Violence: ☆ The pre-title sequence ends with a freeze-frame

315

on 'Taps' Ranson having his face redesigned. It's all rather graphic.

Porno Funk Music Factor: 1.

Fashion Victims: Purdey wears a vile pair of knee-length knickerbockers. Flared ones at that!

The Enemy: Juventor, the spy who possesses a sophisticated machine that can transfer the mind into another body.

Gambit's Conquest: Helen Mackay. In this 'permissive' age, Mike is eager to get to know Helen better whilst supposedly protecting her, and is delighted when Helen asks him to take his clothes off. Sadly, from his point of view, she simply wants to sculpt him.

With a Young. . . : Annie Lambert (Helen).

Notes: 'Deadly, dangerous, ruthless. The master of the double play. You're not related to him by any chance?' Much closer to the spirit of the original series than most *New Avengers* episodes, we have some nice scripting, courtesy of a swop between Spooner and Clemens, and a few character-expanding scenes (Gambit and Steed play snooker, for example). John Paul makes his second *New Avengers* appearance with a one-scene cameo as a doctor. Purdey's background is as a dancer. She could, she claims, 'tap before she could walk'.

Second Season

Introduction

It all began so promisingly, but ended up as a cardboard, cheapskate epitaph. *The Avengers* deserved better.

The first season of *The New Avengers* had been generally well received, being partially networked between October 1976 and March 1977. The second block of 13 episodes was filmed during the spring and early summer of 1977, with the productions team's trip to Canada occurring in July and August.

The first two episodes in production, 'Hostage' and 'Trap', should have told Clemens and Fennell that something was going wrong. The series seemed tired already, although, thankfully, Joanna Lumley had overcome the initial absurdity of her character to produce something charming and eccentric in the vein of her predecessors. However, Clemens was also busy with a new series, *The A Squad*, leading to Dennis Spooner doing much uncredited work on the scripts. Ron Fry, Production Supervisor on the first fifteen episodes of *The New Avengers*, was at this point promoted to Associate Producer.

Clemens and Fennell's original contract with Rudolph Roffi in 1975 had indicated that some episodes would be filmed in France and this was achieved, reasonably successfully, with the two-parter 'K is for Kill' and 'The Lion and the Unicorn', which made good use of their Parisian locations without becoming self-consciously location-orientated. But, according to Brian Clemens, '*The New Avengers* was killed by financing. The French didn't come up with all the promised money and they ended up owing Albert and me the cost of an episode . . . The motto for all this has to be never work with the French production companies, they're all crooks and vagabonds!' Because of this a Canadian company (Nielsen-Ferns Inc. of Toronto), became involved. 'It was supposed to be French-financed, but then they had to take on Canadian money, and we were told we could only have more if we made four episodes in Canada. Canada is the worst place to shoot anything, it's such an empty sort of nothing. I'd rather have shot them in Los Angeles, which at least has an identity, but Canada always looked like Milton Keynes with snow.'

By this stage the series had become *The Avengers* in name only. 'I didn't go to Canada,' Clemens notes. 'Albert went, the leads and the scripts went and it effectively became a Canadian production. They took over and it shows. It also didn't help that the show didn't sell onto the American network until we were in real financial difficulty.' The Canadian episodes carry additional production credits, each episode beginning with 'Albert Fennell and Brian Clemens present *The New Avengers in Canada*'. Clemens and Fennell, in fact, produced only three of the episodes. The fourth, 'Emily', was 'Produced in Canada by Hugh Harlow and Jim Hanley'. Whilst Ron Fry remained Associated Producer throughout the Canadian episodes, director Ray Austin was credited as 'Coordinating Producer (for *Avengers* [Film & TV] Enterprises Ltd)'.

As it was, the Canadian episodes were, by and large, dreadful ('Complex' was the best and even that wasn't up to much). The direction was flat and lifeless, any attempts at wit were usually heavy-handed and the mostly anonymous bit-part players have about as much feeling for being part of an *Avengers* episode as they would for a ten-second advert.

So, what are we left with from this hotchpotch of episodes? Well, we have one of the very best episodes of any *Avengers* era, 'Dead Men Are Dangerous', a story that manages to define Steed like no other. There is the well-structured runaround fun of 'Angels of Death', and 'Hostage', 'Obsession' and a couple of passable French farces. We also have four or five contenders for the worst-ever *Avengers* episode (we'd like to nominate 'Trap' because it's ludicrous, humourless, grim and very ideologically unsound, with 'Chinese takeaway' being probably the worst ever attempt at a witty closing line).

The elements that made previous seasons (including, let's remember, the first season of *The New Avengers*) so watchable – the wit, the strangeness, the eccentricity, all of the categories that we have made so much of in this book – go out of the window. *The New Avengers* became something more akin to *The Sweeney* or (heaven help us) *Target*. The 70s excesses of violence and socio-realism (via drugs and terrorism) take over from the traditional *Avengers* enemies, though thankfully the series pretty much avoided that other 70s excess, sex (despite the presence of so much Porno Funk Music).

Much to the chagrin of Brian Clemens, ITV once again only partially networked the season. They were shown in a different order in different areas (for example, in most regions 'Dead Men Are Dangerous' kicked off the season but in some others it was replaced by 'Medium Rare'). By the time of the four Canadian episodes each region seemed to have its own order. 'Emily' fared worse, not being shown in some parts of the country until a repeat run late in 1978.

So *The Avengers* story ended with a whimper rather than a bang. Patrick Macnee tells a story of being in a hotel in Toronto and bumping into Peter O'Toole who asked him what he was doing in Canada. 'I'm doing *The New Avengers*,' said Macnee to which O'Toole replied, 'Patrick, you're always doing *The Avengers*!' Sadly, since 1977 this hasn't been the case. The respective careers of Joanna Lumley and Gareth Hunt prove that while it is sometimes possible to escape type-casting in television, more often than not, it isn't. Except through retirement. Coffee, anyone?

Perhaps the saddest aspect of the end of *The New Avengers*

is that out of elements present in this season, Clemens and Fennell created *The A Squad*, or, as it came to be called, *The Professionals*, one of the most mindless and crass of television series. As we've said about so many things in this season, *The Avengers* deserved more.

Top five episodes: 'Dead Men Are Dangerous'
                         erm . . .
                         'Angels of Death'
                         'Hostage'
                         'Obsession'
                         'K is for Kill part 1'
                         (because Emma's in it . . .)

Broadcast Details

Broadcast details as LWT. The season was partially networked, with the exception of 'Emily', which was scheduled for 25 November 1977 but was replaced by 'The Gladiators'. 'Emily' was therefore broadcast on different days in the various regions, e.g. 17 December 1977.

13 colour episodes (60 mins)
Avengers (Film & TV) Enterprises Ltd
and IDTV TV Productions, Paris
and Nielsen-Ferns Inc., Toronto (episodes 184–187)

Episodes 184-187 are collectively known as
The New Avengers in Canada.

Producers: Albert Fennell and Brian Clemens
(episodes 175–186),

Hugh Marlow and Jim Handley (episode 187)
Associate Producer: Ron Fry
(episodes 175–179, 182–187)
Coordinating Producer:
Ray Austin (episodes 184–187)

Music by Laurie Johnson

Regular Cast: Patrick Macnee (John Steed),
Gareth Hunt (Mike Gambit), Joanna Lumley (Purdey).

175
'Dead Men Are Dangerous'
9 September 1977, time not known
US Transmission: 24 November 1978
Writer: Brian Clemens
Director: Sidney Hayers
Guest Cast: Clive Revill (Mark Crayford),
Richard Murdoch (Perry), Gabrielle Drake (Penny),
Terry Taplin (Hara), Michael Turner (Dr Culver),
Trevor Adams (Sandy), Roger Avon (Headmaster),
Gabor Vernon (Russian doctor).

Everything Steed cares about is being destroyed or threatened,
including his china, his Bentley, and even Purdey. Who could
possibly bare such a long-lasting and jealous grudge?

Wit: ☆

Kinkiness Factor: ☆☆ Purdey manacled to wall.

Champagne: None, although Steed serves cognac in his remaining glasses when his place is ransacked, and says to Purdey: 'The only thing that can't be replaced is the love and life of an old friend.'

Violence: ☆ Steed is shot on two occasions.

Fashion Victims: The most threatening thing about a potential mugger is his tie.

The Enemy: Mark Crayford, jealous second-place to Steed since childhood, and a Soviet defector.

Notes: This is by far the best episode of *The New Avengers*. The difference is in the fondness with which it's written. We see files labelled Cathy Gale, Emma Peel and Tara King. Steed and Purdey have a bittersweet relationship that has real heart. 'It's a very comfortable shoulder,' she says to Steed, trying hopelessly to flirt with him. She and Gambit get to define their positions in a matey karate bout. We learn things about Gambit in this well-judged season opener: he joined the Navy at 14, and his flat looks barren because 'he never had time to unpack'. But mainly this is Steed's story. We learn whole chunks of biography: he earned a medal for charging a machine-gun post, earned club cricket honours in 1957, was opening bat in the school cricket team, and Victor Ludorum. The damage done to his property is horrifying (especially when the old Bentley is blown up), but he doesn't care a jot as long as the people he cares for are safe. At the end he nearly sacrifices himself, and even reveals that he cared about the villain, too. It's all rather wonderful, and is written with a nostalgia and grace that could have got the show another season if this had been the new format. Rosy glow time. Very special.

Trivia: Steed's house in this season became Fulmer Park,

Gerrard's Cross.

French Title: 'Mefiez-Vous des Mortes!'.

176
'Angels of Death'
16 September 1977
US Transmission: 29 September 1978
Writers: Terence Feely and Brian Clemens
Director: Ernest Day
Guest Cast: Dinsdale Landen (Coldstream),
Terence Alexander (Manderson),
Caroline Munro (Tammy), Michael Latimer (Reresby),
Richard Gale (Pelbright), Lindsay Duncan (Jane),
Annette Lynton (Pam), Moira Foot (Cindy),
Christopher Driscoll (Martin),
Melissa Stribling (Sally Manderson),
Anthony Bailey (Simon Carter),
Hedger Wallace (Col. Thomson),
Jennie Goossens (Mrs Pelbright).

Senior civil servants, MPs and intelligence personnel are all dying suddenly of 'natural causes'. There seems to be no obvious link between the deaths, and the only lead is the mortally wounded agent who talks of angels of death that kill from within.

Wit: ✩✩✩✩ Purdey is helped by Gambit to run a computer program seeking a link between the deaths: 'Gambit, I didn't know you'd read mathematics.'

'I haven't, I do the football pools.' Some good jokes and a nice wit, but it almost loses a point for the 'Amazing' quip at the end.

Kinkiness Factor: ☆☆☆ Caroline Munro and Pamela Stephenson in nurses' uniforms! They then change into something a little more comfortable for the disco scenes! Plus, Purdey in a huge traction machine ('Switch it off,' she says, 'or I'll be playing for the Harlem Globetrotters').

Champagne: None: inexplicably, the dehydrated Steed rambles on about beer.

Violence: ☆☆ A fight between Purdey and Tammy that is so violent that even Gambit winces. (See also Kinkiness Factor.)

Porno Funk Music Factor: 7. Some truly hideous disco sequences complete with 'chicks' who would not have been out of place on early *Top of the Pops* record covers.

70s Concerns: The stresses of 70s living. Health farms.

Gambit's Conquest: Jane, Coldstream's secretary.

With a Young . . . : Pamela Stephenson (Wendy).

Notes: 'It's hideous the work we do.' Steed's comments on the death of his friend Manderson are part of a melancholy hint that is in keeping with the preceding story. His training for what to do when in the hands of the enemy – complete with 'flashbacks' – allows him to combat the mind-bending drugs. It's also a great Purdey story. She wonders aloud why even a bereavement can't 'stop the show', and reveals that she was called 'skinny' at school. Near the beginning she is plucking petals from a flower ('he loves me . . . he loves me not') when Steed walks up. Later, they are forced into each other's arms by a shrinking room, and Purdey says that she has something to tell him. (They are rescued by Gambit, and she doesn't say what it was.) Gambit tries to track down the traitor, and says that the computer has concluded that the Queen and various others, including Steed and himself, are 'above suspicion'. Purdey isn't, so she calls the machine a 'mechanical prig'. Brian Clemens has stated that where ever possible he wanted dialogue scenes to have some action about them, and there's a good example in this episode: Steed's discussion with Colonel Tomson takes place while the two of them are shooting clay pigeons. Purdey says that Gambit has a joke about a plastic fig leaf, but we don't get to hear it. A really rather good episode, all told.

Trivia: Gambit attributes his 'hot blood' to his Irish granny.

177
'Medium Rare'
23 September 1977
US Transmission: 26 January 1979
Writer: Dennis Spooner
Director: Ray Austin
Guest Cast: Jon Finch (Wallace),
Mervyn Johns (Elderly man),
Jeremy Wilkin (Richards), Neil Hallett (Roberts),
Maurice O'Connell (McBain),
Diana Churchill (Dowager Lady),
Celia Foxe (Model Girl),
Steve Ubels (Young Man at Seance),
Allen Weston (Mason).

Mason is the paymaster to a group of informants, but all is not what it seems: the informants are a single man. When Mason suspects this, he is murdered by Wallace, who has been lining his own pockets. Steed begins to investigate, and Wallace decides that the only option left open to him is to frame Steed, and then kill him.

Wit: ☆☆ Purdey extracting the michael from the fake medium: 'I must have absolute silence. It disturbs the vibrations.'

More oo-er humour as Victoria, the medium, assesses Steed's home, but can discern little from its atmosphere. 'Perhaps if you gave me something to hold . . . ' she suggests. (Minus one point for the awful punning title.)

Kinkiness Factor: ☆ Some cross-dressing in the introductory sequence. A rather liberated scene, in which Purdey is seen putting up wallpaper, is ruined by her climbing out of her dungarees a few moments later.

Fights: ☆☆

Porno Funk Music Factor: 4.

70s Concerns: Fake occultic types.

Strangeness: Purdey suggests that Steed should seek political asylum in Scotland (probably intended as a joke). The awful fake medium plot (probably not).

Fashion Victims: Purdey wears a horrid white/red thing at the beginning. She later wears a rather nice white suit and a clashing tartan mini-kipper tie.

With a Young . . . : Sue Holderness (Victoria Stanton), an interesting performance that falls just short of chewing the scenery.

Notes: 'We're going to kill him with extreme finesse.' A slow, dullish episode, which almost until the end seems to be accepting the occult at face value before coming up with a suitably crap reason for Victoria's sudden feats of cognition. *Ghost* it ain't. There's a character called George Cowley (see *The Professionals*), but he's a boring git from accounts who dies in his first scene. Joanna Lumley for once isn't wasted, however, playing the piano in one scene, and later telling Steed that, despite the murder accusations, 'Even if you did do it, I'd still think you were innocent.' It is stated that Steed now abhors guns, and just has a Colt .45 'for sentimental reasons'.

French Title: 'Steed et la Voyante'.

178
'The Lion and the Unicorn'
30 September 1977
US Transmission: 15 December 1978
Writer: John Goldsmith
Director: Ray Austin
Guest Cast: Jean Claudio (Unicorn),
Maurice Marsac (Leparge),
Raymond Bussieres (Henri), Jacques Maury (Riffer),
Raoul Delfrasse (Marco), Gerald Sim (Minister),
Henri Czarniak (Grima),
Jean-Pierre Bernard (First Bodyguard),
Ludwig Gaum (Second Bodyguard).

In Paris, Steed at last captures the Unicorn, his nemesis. But when the Unicorn is accidentally killed by his own men, Steed must use all of his cunning to avoid open warfare.

Wit: ☆☆☆ 'There's only one problem. The Unicorn is a tiny bit dead!'

'Sounds pretty thin.'
'Positively emaciated.'

Kinkiness Factor: ☆ A photographer's model has her clothes torn off by the speed of Gambit's passing car. Yeah. Right.

Champagne: ☆☆☆ Two bottles. Steed and Gambit use the corks as weapons.

Violence: ☆☆ Gambit fights the Unicorn and is saved from a beating by Purdey's timely intervention. A parachutist strangles a policeman with his parachute.

Porno Funk Music Factor: 7.

Strangeness: The Unicorn shoots the minister with a gun disguised as a camera. Steed, Gambit and Purdey discuss ways of replacing the Unicorn for a swap. 'What about a robot?' asks Gambit. 'Science fiction,' says Steed dismissively.

Fashion Victims: Purdey wears a disgusting yellow, red, green and white abomination.

The Enemy: The Unicorn ('in the top five of the *Good Spy Guide*'), a ruthless killer.

Notes: 'Enjoy your little triumph while you can. It will not last long.' Another French farce, albeit one with an interesting plot.

Trivia: Steed has been stalking the Unicorn for years. He once shot the assassin in a hotel in Tangier. Steed taunts the Unicorn over a shared love, Yvette, a ballet dancer.

179
'Obsession'
7 October 1977
US Transmission: 15 December 1978
Writer: Brian Clemens
Director: Ernest Day
Guest Cast: Martin Shaw (Larry),
Mark Kingston (General Canvey),
Terence Longdon (Commander East),
Lewis Collins (Kilner), Anthony Heaton (Morgan),
Tommy Boyle (Wolach), Roy Purcell (Controller).

An old flame of Purdey's reappears when a missile goes
missing from an air display. But what's the connection between
that, a visiting Arab envoy, and a spy satellite photographing
Buckinghamshire?

Wit: ☆ 'You're a good girl.'
　'But we'll overlook that little flaw in your character.'
　'Berlin's a couple of towns in Germany.'

Champagne: ☆☆ On trays at Steed's party. 'It's the only
thing you can get round here today,' says Purdey.

Violence: ☆☆ A despatch rider is swiped off his bike by a
cable. Gambit faces down a truck.

Kinkiness Factor: ☆ Purdey is slapped around by Larry, thus
ending a lovely romance. She slaps him back at the party.

Porno Funk Music Factor: 5. An airbase break-in is accompanied by a drum-based beat that the James Taylor Quartet
would be proud of.

The Enemy: Larry and his chums, seeking personal revenge and not afraid to take out the Houses of Parliament if it gets in the way.

Fashion Victims: Purdey wears an awful hairdo, heart-shaped choker and stack-heeled boots in flashback scenes of 1970, the series commenting on late 60s styles in a definite pot/kettle/ relative albedo comparison.

Notes: The story is built around impressive RAF stock footage, which fits in well with scenes filmed at an actual airbase. Shaw sits in a real Jaguar cockpit. Stock footage of a building on fire detracts from it. Shaw is good, he and Lumley having an emoting contest, but with competition like Wolach (one of a few realistic RAF men rather than clichés) and Larry's dad (who actually manages to *overdo* being tied to a stake and shot), anybody would shine. His partnership with Lewis Collins doesn't sparkle, but there is a hint that Clemens was thinking of the two future stars of *The Professionals* as a team: 'Maybe we should work together again, we're a good team,' says Kilner. Wall-hopping mentioned as a sport again, Steed took three bullets going over (as Gambit did in 'The Eagle's Nest'). Once more Purdey looks stupid holding a gun, and we see her in a tutu ready for a (very minor) part in *Le Lac Des Cygnes* (with no first name even then). Steed solves the problem in a very stylish way, rounding off a rather satisfying episode with that nostalgic 'Dead Men are Dangerous' glow. But then Clemens goes and spoils it with some end lines that actually seem to embarrass the actors. And the papers at the time were full of 'Purdey seen in bed with chap shock'. But she's not.

330

180
'Trap'
14 October 1977
US Transmission: 2 March 1979
Writer: Brian Clemens
Director: Ray Austin
Guest Cast: Terry Wood (Soo Choy),
Ferdy Mayne (Arcarti), Robert Rietti (Dom Carlos),
Kristopher Kum (Tansing), Yasuko Nagazumi (Yasho),
Stuart Damon (Marty Brine), Barry Lowe (Murford),
Annegret Easterman (Miranda), Bruce Boa (Mahon),
Maj Britt (Girlfriend).

When Steed, Purdey and Gambit intercept a drugs drop, oriental villain Soo Choy, taunted by his criminal peers, tricks the agents into being flown to his estate for execution.

Wit: Zero: 'Chinese takeaway.' Arrgh! Arrgh! Arrgh!

Champagne: ☆ On the plane heading for nuclear Armageddon.

Violence: ☆ ☆ ☆ Purdey and Gambit dispose of oriental soldiers with improvised weapons. Gambit is about to fight Soo Choy, but he commits hara-kiri.

Porno Funk Music Factor: 7.

Strangeness: Terry Wood, not even looking oriental, is Soo Choy! One million dollars worth of drugs are in a small packet! Things like drugs, graffiti, council estates in *The Avengers*! Steed and Gambit are both summoned from dates when they get a bogus alert that nuclear Armageddon is about to occur, and they casually tell their partners that they'll see them soon! They believe the agent who takes their guns off them, telling them that they'll set off airport security! The plane crashes and is smashed to pieces, and the only injury is Steed's broken arm! Arrgh! Arrgh! Arrgh!

Eccentrics: Soo Choy, eccentric for being an odd mixture of Japanese, Chinese, but mostly Caucasian, and talking like Baron Greenback out of *Danger Mouse*.

With a Young . . . : Larry Lamb (Williams).

Notes: 'Welcome to East Anglia, one of Britain's loveliest areas.' At least, amongst all this, Purdey is dressed sensibly and gets to be suitably deadly. 'Me Tarzan, no, me Jane. No . . . me Purdey!' Another contender for the worst-ever *Avengers* episode: at least 'Thingumajig' wasn't full of bad puns and vile racism and sexism. Soo Choy's house footage shot at Iver Grove, Shreding Green, and the car park chase in Windsor.

Trivia: Yasuko Nagazumi is otherwise known as Mrs Ray Austin.

181
'Hostage'
21 October 1977
US Transmission: 8 December 1978
Writer: Brian Clemens
Director: Sidney Hayers
Guest Cast: William Franklyn (McKay),
Simon Oates (Spelman), Michael Culver (Walters),
Anna Palk (Suzy), Barry Stanton (Packer),

**Richard Ireson (Vernon),
George Lane-Cooper (Marvin).**

Purdey has been kidnapped. Steed is given the ransom of the Allied attack plans. But has the whole thing been simply a set-up, to make the Department think that Steed is a traitor?

Wit: ✩ Gambit comments to Steed that he has never taken him on at karate and is told 'You're too young to die!' After Steed has kicked Gambit in the gonads he tells him 'I did warn you I never fight fair!' Steed arrives at the rendezvous to find Purdey unable to speak because of an apple stuffed in her mouth. 'Last time I saw something like this was at the Savoy grill,' he notes.

Champagne: No, red wine.

Violence: ✩✩✩ Purdey puts up a hell of a struggle with three (count 'em) assailants in her flat before falling for that old Tara stand-by, chloroform (but not before she has crowned one with a frying pan).

Porno Funk Music Factor: 9. Like a Bachman Turner Overdrive gig, man!

Fashion Victims: Kidnapper Vernon wears a vile, bizarrely patterned tie. Gambit keeps up the show's traditions with a light green silk cravat. Steed's date, Suzy, has a red blouse with the biggest collars in TV history.

The Enemy: A 'rotten apple' in the department, who turns out to be Spelman (born Speltanovich).

Notes: 'It's only paper. You're Purdey.' A good, if somewhat routine, plot which rattles along at a fair pace. Simon Oates plays a variation on his *Doomwatch* character Ridge (a smoothie dandy-about-town) until he is revealed as the villain. Steed's bowler contains a gun and a mini firecracker, both of which are used in rescuing Purdey. Purdey's mother, according to Spelman, is 'fun but beautiful'. Steed tells Suzy that when he was 21 he rode on a cattle drive from Arizona to the Black hills. He was, he notes, 'an unlikely cowboy'. The fact that Steed was prepared to give up state secrets to save Purdey earns him a kiss from his grateful colleague.

182
'K is for Kill – Part One: The Tiger Awakes'

Working Title: 'The Long Sleep'
28 October 1977
US Transmission: 23 March 1979 (with episode 183)
Writer: Brian Clemens
Director: Yvon Marie Coulais
Guest Cast: Pierre Vernier (Col. Martin),
Maurice Marsac (Gen. Gaspard),
Charles Millot (Stanislav), Paul Emile Deiber (Toy),
Christine Delaroche (Jeanine Leparge),
Sacha Pitoeff (Kerov), Eric Desmaretz (Ivan),
Sylvain Clement (Vassili), Krisha Clough (Soldier),
Kenneth Watson (Salvation Army Major),
Tony Then (Monk), Eric Allan (Penrose).

Tibet, 1945: a Russian Captain discovers a monk with the secret of eternal youth. Berkshire, 1965: a Russian soldier bursts into a Salvation army meeting and mows down the band. France, 1977: A group of hippies is killed by a sniper. Is there a link, and if so, does it mean the beginning of World War III?

334

Wit: ☆☆ Purdey: 'Why are we in France?'

Gambit: 'Steed needs to replenish his cellar.'

General Gaspard is angry when Steed is introduced as an Englishman. 'On the Somme, I asked the English battalion to cover my left flank, they never turned up.'

Steed (rather cruelly): 'Perhaps they got lost, have you looked since?'

Kinkiness Factor: Zilch.

Champagne: ☆ After the Russians have attacked a deserted château, Steed notes the day hasn't been a complete disaster. 'At least they didn't get the champagne.'

Violence: ☆ Gambit karate-kicks a tree in which a Russian sniper is hiding accompanied by funk guitar and pseudo-mystical (i.e. garbage) dialogue. Purdey finds the way to a man's stomach is 'to kick him there'.

Porno Funk Music Factor: 7.

Fashion Victims: Gambit (inevitably) in a fawn leather jacket and brown flared slacks.

Gambit's Conquest: Mike chats up Jeanine, the pretty French pathologist, whilst she is examining a dead Russian. He tells her: 'We British do things by the inch.' Oo-er! Later, having shot a Russian who is about to shoot Purdey, she complains that they wanted the Russian alive. 'Conflict of interests,' says Gambit, '*I* wanted *you* alive.'

The Enemy: Crack Russian troops, placed in cold storage in 1945, activated by a faulty satellite.

Notes: The only proper *Avengers* two-parter. The 1965 pre-title sequence is particularly interesting as Steed's Bentley puts in its only appearance in a *New Avengers* episode. Footage of Diana Rigg from 'The Winged Avenger' and 'From Venus With Love' was used. Emma, unsurprisingly, hasn't aged a day in twelve years. There's a very poor cliffhanger (Gambit shoots a Russian in slow motion) which shows, perhaps, why *The Avengers* was never interested in multi-part stories. Pre-title sequence filming at Holy Cross Church, Sarratt.

Trivia: We learn that Emma has changed her name. 'You'll always be Mrs Peel to me,' says Steed. Purdey is insanely jealous of Emma and her past association with Steed. Steed's ancestor, Sir Everington Steed, was a hero at Waterloo.

French Title: 'Le Long Sommeil'.

183
'K is for Kill – Part Two: Tiger by the Tail'

US Transmission: 23 March 1979 (with episode 182)
Writer: Brian Clemens
Director: Yvon Marie Coulais
Guest Cast: Maxence Mailfort (Turkov),
Alberto Simeno (Minister),
Jacques Monnet (Waiter), Frank Olivier (Minski),
Guy Mairesse (Guard), Cyrille Besnard (Secretary).
With: Pierre Vernier, Maurice Marsac,
Charles Millot, Paul Emile Deiber,
Christine Delaroche, Sacha Pitoeff.

Two hundred and fifty of the revived Russian agents have been captured or killed. But two remain, K agents with specific targets. Stanislav has a special interest in one of the men (his father) and a special interest in the outcome (the start of World War III).

Wit: ✩ Purdey and Gambit think Steed has been killed. Then
– Purdey: 'He's alive!'
  Gambit: 'How can he be?'
  Steed: 'Because I'm a gentleman!'

Kinkiness Factor: ✩ Purdey wears short shorts (red ones) and looks angelic chasing around Paris beating up Russians.

Champagne: ✩✩✩✩ In a streetside café in Paris (the *only* way to drink it) and at the end, in celebration.

Violence: ✩✩ After Toy and Steed have been shot, and Purdey held at gunpoint by the assassin, Gambit does the 'stupidest, most ridiculous, most beautiful' thing Purdey has ever seen and knocks a bullet away with the butt of his own weapon whilst thinking Zen thoughts. This enables Purdey to give the assassin a good kicking.

Porno Funk Music Factor: 7. Including some serious *Shaft*-style wah-wah guitar as Gambit and Purdey hunt the K agents.

Strangeness: All of the Russian soldiers, having been captured, rapidly age and die. Steed, Gambit and Purdey are awarded Russia's highest honours, Purdey becoming a 'little daughter of the Revolution'. Steed is horrified about the prospect of MI5 finding out.

Fashion Victims: The two Russian K agents wear 40s fashions in 70s Paris and *don't* look as ridiculous in the 90s as Gambit does. Remarkable!

Gambit's Conquest: Purdey and Steed are in the café until Gambit arrives with Jeanine. Purdey foists the pathologist onto Steed so she can have a 'quiet word' with Gambit. A disgusted waiter comments: 'Wife swopping, in broad daylight. The world is changing.'

The Enemy: Crack Russian K agents hell-bent on assassinating the French President.

Notes: The pre-title sequence is a recap of scenes from part one with a Patrick Macnee voice-over explaining the plot. When he believes Steed has been killed, Gambit comments that he 'taught us everything we know'. Some of the French accents are Peter Sellers-on-speed, which is ironic as most of the actors *are* genuine Frenchmen. The plot rapidly turns into a *Day of the Jackal* variant.

184
'Complex'
11 November 1977
US Transmission: 5 January 1979
Writer: Dennis Spooner
Director: Richard Gilbert
Guest Cast: Cec Linder (Baker),
Harvey Atkin (Talbot), Vlasta Vrana (Karavitch),
Rudy Lipp (Koschev), Jan Rubes (Patlenko),
Michael Ball (Cope), David Nichols (Greenwood),
Suzette Couture (Miss Cummings),
Gerald Crack (Berisford Holt).

Agent X41 (codename Scapina) is the Soviet's most effective spy. But a photograph has fallen into *The Avengers*' hands which may give a clue to his (or its) identity. But it means a trip to Canada . . .

Wit: ☆ Purdey is delighted to be going to Canada. She says she's seen *Rose Marie*. Twice. Gambit, after he's been arrested for the second time, says: 'I'd like to use your phone, if it's not a chargeable offence.'

Kinkiness Factor: No, just a repeat of 'The House That Jack Built,'s nasty voyeuristic games.

Champagne: ☆ Steed and Purdey share a bottle in the hotel.

Violence: ☆☆ A parachuted agent is machine-gunned to death. Gambit dives through a window, kung-fus an agent and shoots another.

Porno Funk Music Factor: 2.

Strangeness: A camera that looks like a rifle, a palm-print reader, etc. As Purdey says, 'technology gone mad!'

Fashion Victims: Canadian fashions are a little more sober than Gambit's.

The Enemy: X41 (Scapina), a top Soviet agent who is actually a building.

Notes: 'Fort Knox is a pushover compared to this place.' The best of the Canadian episodes. A sign says 'Welcome to Kent, the garden of England', which is supposed to convince us that the story begins in the UK. Not a chance! Gambit and Purdey are fully cleared for 'zee' security. Gambit is arrested by hick-constabulary who won't believe he's a secret agent. When

Steed arrives, the desk sergeant tells Gambit he should look more like Steed. 'Him, I can believe. With that crazy umbrella, what else could he be but an agent?'

French Title: 'Complexe X41'.

185
'Forward Base'
18 November 1977
US Transmission: 3 November 1978
Writer: Dennis Spooner
Director: Don Thompson
Guest Cast: Jack Creley (Hosking),
August Schellenberg (Bailey),
Marilyn Lightstone (Ranoff), Nick Nichols (Malachev),
David Calderisi (Halfhide), Maurice Good (Milroy),
John Bethune (Doctor), Anthony Parr (Glover),
Les Rubie (Harper), Toivo Pyyko (Clive),
Ara Hovonessiaan (Czibor),
Richard Moffatt (Radio Operator).

April 1969; Typhoon Agatha rages and, in Toronto, a new piece of coastline suddenly appears. (Why is it that Soviet activity suddenly seems to be directed exclusively against the Canadians? Budgetary reasons perhaps?)

Wit: ☆ Purdey, finding Bailey's injured body: 'Does this qualify as a clue, do you think?'
   Gambit tells Steed he saw a man throw something extrovertly.
   Steed: 'What do you mean by extrovert?'
   Gambit: 'The opposite of introvert!'

340

Kinkiness Factor: Less than zero.

Champagne: No, vodka.

Violence: ☆ Steed fights an agent in a souvenir shop.

Porno Funk Music Factor: 1. More corn than porn.

Strangeness: Gambit and Purdey snog on a bridge whilst keeping tabs on an agent in a motorised boat in the shape of a swan.

Fashion Victims: One of the minor characters wears huge flares and Cuban heels. Gambit has a rather horrible patterned jumper.

The Enemy: Forward Base, a piece of enemy coastline! A 'sub-aquatic community disguised as a peninsula', in fact.

Notes: 'It's a couple of hundred yards that way. Sometimes . . . ' The last story to be filmed, and an inauspicious finale. Purdey's wet-suit again has her name on the back. There's nothing like advertising, is there?

French Title: 'Bastion Pirate'.

186
'The Gladiators'
25 November 1977
US Transmission: 19 January 1979
Writers: Brian Clemens
Director: Claude Fournier

Guest Cast: Louis Zorich (Karl),
Neil Vipond (Chuck Peters), Bill Starr (O'Hara),
Peter Boretski (Tarnokoff), Yanci Bukoveo (Barnoff),
Jan Murzynski (Cresta), Michael Donaghue (Hartley),
George Chuvalo (Huge Man), Dwayne McLean (Rogers),
Parick Sinclair (Ivan), Doug Lennox (Nada).

The Gladiators are super warriors, trained by crack Soviet spymaster Karl Sminski. They can punch through solid steel and deflect bullets with their hands. Now they are in Canada. And so are the *New Avengers* . . .

Wit: ½☆ 'It is one of the crimes of nature that Steed wasn't born Russian.'

Kinkiness Factor: ☆ 'What does Purdey do when Purdey is annoyed?' If she's got any sense it would be to beat the tar out of patronising gits like you.

Violence: ☆☆☆☆ The opening scene has the Gladiators kicking each other to bits in a fight to the death. The climax in which the *New Avengers* take on the Gladiators is *outrageously* violent.

Porno Funk Music Factor: 5.

Strangeness: The Canadian security services have an 'open day' once a year.

Fashion Victims: Gambit drives a red car with a white stripe. Oh dear, even the cars are ugly.

The Enemy: Sminski and his two Gladiators are training a group of powerful killers. 'Honours in anarchy,' as Purdey says.

342

Notes: 'I am going to give you Gladiators, comrade. Men so deadly, so conditioned, their death will be the greatest, most welcome thing they ever experience.' A simply horrible episode. 'Trouble *is* our business,' notes Purdey, which is apt. The most notorious aspect of this episode remains the ability of Sminski and his boys to deflect bullets using their reflexes.

187
'Emily'
17 December 1977 – see Transmission Notes
US Transmission: 9 February 1979
Writer: Dennis Spooner
Director: Don Thompson
Guest Cast: Jane Mallet (Miss Daly),
Les Carlson (Douglas Collins),
Richard Davidson (Phillips),
Brian Petchey (Reddington), Peter Ackroyd (Mirchtia),
Peter Torokvei (Kalenkov),
Jack Duffy (Radio Operator),
Ed McNamara (Chicken Farmer),
Dan LeGros (Mechanic),
Sandy Crawley (First Policeman),
John Kerr (Second Policeman),
Pat Patterson (Third Policeman),
Bill Ballartine (Fourth Policeman).

The *New Avengers* are on the trail of mysterious agent 'The Fox'. Although he escapes, he leaves a palm print on the roof of 'Emily', a car owned by the aged Miss Daly. Cue a deadly cross-country travelogue.

Wit: ☆ There's a yokel who likes Gambit so much he fights him. Not very witty at all. 'I was winning,' says Gambit after Purdey has helped him.

'If you'd won any more you would have hardly been able to stand.'

Kinkiness Factor: ☆ Purdey goes through a car wash clinging to Emily and emerges with her skirt and sweater shrunken.

Champagne: No, some moonshine gin.

Violence: ☆ The slapstick fight at the moonshine still.

Porno Funk Music Factor: 7.

Strangeness: An opening scene of a chase through a fun fair ending with Purdey about to be shot. Secret information is passed from a boat to a passing water-skier.

Fashion Victims: Purdey, undercover, dresses as a cleaner.

The Enemy: 'The Fox' ('his cunning is synonymous with his name'), really Doug Collins of Canadian intelligence.

Notes: 'We need information!' *The Avengers* meets *Deliverance*, only not that good.

Trivia: Emily's number plate is HHP 999.

S and Em

Paul Cornell

Emma Peel, when tied up, does not acknowledge her bonds in the slightest, wearing them as one would wear a fashion accessory. She is not worried, nor is she relieved when Steed rescues her. She treats the whole process as an inevitable inconvenience. This results in three things. One: she is not seen to be the subject of either male power (the villains doing the tying are almost always men) or male fantasy (the male viewers are denied the emotional responses required for bondage fantasies). Two: despite actually being rescued by Steed, she gives the impression that she could simply step out of the ropes at any point, denying the hero the power of being the rescuer. Three: she gives the programme a postmodern sheen of self-awareness by indicating very obviously that she is in no real predicament, that she knows this is all a game.

Put these three together, and the net result is a Diana Rigg wink to the female audience. As she says to the villains binding her in (the otherwise lamentable) 'Epic': 'Just remember who's the star of this picture!'

With the introduction of Cathy Gale, *The Avengers* started to ignore history. This was the Dayglo 60s, a Now that said 'follow this!', and, indeed, it's been difficult. In this sudden, bright, schizoid isolation from historical precedent, anything was possible. So, instead of making a show that challenged sexism, that pushed forward the frontiers of female power, as the BBC might have done, the makers of *The Avengers* simply decided to *end* sexism.

Of course, the way they went about it was damn sexist.

Cathy Gale is given a 'man's lines', meaning that she is given a neutral, ordinary set of adventure hero lines that don't

345

refer to the house and the children. She is also given a costume that allows her to modestly participate in fight scenes. Patrick Macnee, at this point, makes one of a series of wonderful decisions. At the same time as Cathy is being empowered, he starts to put aside elements of his own power as a hero (his gun, his fisticuffs, his wisdom) in order to give Mrs Gale more of the spotlight. I say Macnee rather than Steed, because, from interviews, it becomes obvious that Macnee had very definite and laudable aims in mind, ones that were sometimes utterly at odds with the show's producers. He can do this, of course, because Steed is a Gentleman, and Gentlemen keep their achievements under their hats. Similarly, it is their money that allows Gale and Peel to pursue independent lifestyles. Both have been married, and the suggestion is almost that they acquired their (perceived) male qualities from matrimony. Clearly, the suggestion is that women only gain power by losing their virginity, that is, from men.

But let's get this in perspective. This was the 60s, when a woman couldn't easily go into a pub on her own. Emma Peel does, and is bought a pint. In the world of *The Avengers*, sexism doesn't happen. It breathed its last during the Gale era, when the villain would occasionally sneer at Cathy before she beat his brains out. By the time Mrs Peel came along, nobody said or did a thing about Emma doing what the hell she liked.

Brian Clemens makes much of the fact that the series take place in an 'idealised' England. However, much as the fetishist elements of the series oddly allowed Emma to demonstrate her ability to rise above them, this 'idealised' view allowed her to exist in a universe without the economic and political imperatives that perpetuate sexism. In a very English way, *The Avengers* turned away from sex. If Emma and Steed were friends rather than lovers, then he lost a lot of the traditional 'reasons' for oppressing her. Add to that

Macnee's determination that Gentlemen didn't abuse women, and a picture of freedom emerges.

Of course, Brian Clemens doesn't quite see it that way. His idea is that Steed and Peel have been lovers, and have now ceased to be. (Again, she gains her power through a past sexual relationship.) He thinks the attraction of the series is the 'will they, won't they?' factor. What's really attractive is an image of ideal male/female friendship. Steed isn't the brains (Emma, especially in the black and white era, has far more book-learning than he has) or the brawn (when they fight, they butt head to head after an epic struggle and Steed has the harder head) of the outfit, but simply a facilitator. His bosses (unseen when the show's any good) need him to be perfect, and he achieves this through working with a woman who has everything he lacks. He isn't bitter or jealous about this. He revels in it. The partnership is almost a role reversal of an American cop show of the 80s, male cop with female boss. In such a show, the man would do the heavy fighting, the woman would wander round with folders, organising things, and would occasionally stick out a foot to trip up a villain. In *The Avengers*, that foot is usually Steed's, and Emma is the one who has to tackle the really dangerous fighters. He is nominally the boss, because he's part of the intelligence services, but then, he doesn't pay her. She's an amateur. She chooses to help him.

If only the other attitudes on display were so enlightened. For instance, the apartheid of *Avengers* England, which could so easily have been avoided. *Department S* for one had a black boss, and race was never mentioned in its hip scripts (which, of course, always oppressed women: it seems you can't have two virtues in one show). A black character showing up as one of the ministers *The Avengers* were always guarding would have been a similar statement on race as the show had already made on sex. I think the real nature of the problem was that 60s Britain in general regarded black people as bus drivers, porters, unskilled menial workers. They were a 'problem of the lower classes', as was drug abuse, another taboo area.

There could never be anything lower class in *The Avengers*. We find a one-way crossing of the class gap, aristocrats becoming chimney sweeps, that sort of thing, but we don't meet anyone from the working classes on their way up. When Steed adopts the guise of Gordon Webster, actor and playboy, we're encouraged to see the character as seedy because he doesn't believe in keeping his place. His only goal is money. He pretends to have been a Spitfire pilot when in actual fact he was a cashier. It's a terrible vision of the upwardly mobile, and the fact that it turns out to be a fiction is even more terrible because it's a fiction that Steed invents.

So how much of this changed during the course of the show, and why?

Well, the Tara episodes are stories about a helpless young girl being looked after by a heroic father figure who rescues her from traps that make her scream and panic. In this era – which Brian Clemens believes was the height of the show – everything that was liberating has gone. To top it all, the public generally blame the woman in question, Linda Thorson, for the problems of the season. The world of *The Avengers* still made no reference to sexism, but started to actually practise it instead. And if that world was even farther removed from reality (Steed's appearance was now practically Edwardian, rather than an ultra-correct street look, and he had no Emma Peel to make his squareness hip), it was only because in the real world, change was starting to happen.

The New Avengers then, should have taken note of some of these difficulties, and rebuilt the heroic female image the show had lost. Instead, it went one step further back and put her in high heels and a skirt. Joanna Lumley, like Rigg and

Blackman before her, fought for her character's autonomy and power, but she had more to buck against. Once more, thankfully, she was able to succeed despite (or because of) the sexist directions the show forced on her. She also had to work with the much more old-fashioned notion of holding male attention at arm's length rather than interacting with a man on a friendly basis. We'd gone from empowered equality to flirting. Purdey was plagued by both potential lover and father figures, and the one interesting avenue – that the man she wanted (Steed) was the one man she wasn't allowed to have – was never really explored. But at least by the end of the series she got herself into some sensible shoes.

Some things go backwards, some never change. Right up to when the series ended, its most prominent black man was Honor.

The Medium is the Message

Keith Topping

It is often said that if you can remember the 60s you weren't really there. Certainly, the popular perception of the era via retrospective films and television is of a decade of free-sex, political literacy, anti-establishmentism and a surfeit of mind-bending drugs; all of which has very little to do with the average working-class family living on a council estate on a weekly wage of twenty pounds.

Most works of fiction are governed by the sociopolitical and cultural atmospheres in which they were created, but the works of the 60s have been elevated to such a mythical status that such considerations seem, on the surface, to have little substance. That *The Avengers* was a series shaped as much by the complexities of 60s attitudes to class and sex consciousness as by the Cuban Missile Crisis doesn't change the basic fact that it was a product of its era in the same way that *Coronation Street*, *Z Cars*, *Steptoe and Son* and *Doctor Who* all were. The aesthetics may be different, but the attitudes that shaped all of these fine series were identical.

Possibly because of the social and political barriers that were overturned during the period, and the changes in peoples' lives affected by these, especially amongst the young, the method via which such changes were relayed to the masses, television, has acquired the reputation of being responsible for them.

Which is as false a claim as any ever made about the 60s.

It is certainly true that television *reflected* what was going on. In Britain, movements such as the satirists and naturalism found a niche for themselves by using the populist medium of television. But television's influence was a double-edged sword, creating a fictionalised era based on its drama. This is possibly true of the literature of other eras, but seldom has it been more acute and more counter-productive than in the 60s. Which brings us to *The Avengers* . . .

For many people, *The Avengers* is the 60s – a glorious, camp and technicolour excess of 'swinging' styles and attitudes. The fictional central London, its streets paved with mad scientists, the car chases through green-belt Hertfordshire, the eccentrics whose names reflect their obsessions and the comic-strip wit are all classic elements often cited by fans and critics as reasons for *The Avengers*' longevity. It's a suggestion that the 1960s was one long party to which everybody was invited, but that only those with the correct accent and manners could attend.

In terms of the myth that surrounds it, *The Avengers* could almost be said to have become an icon. Something that transcends its humble, down-beat origins and become a definitive 'statement' on the era and its excesses. It is somewhat ironic that the very mention of *The Avengers* summons up a fixed image in most viewer's minds when, in fact, the series itself was one of television's great chameleons, changing not only with the times, but, in some cases, ahead of them.

The Avengers' mirroring of 60s concerns can be clearly seen in this book. But, though the series sometimes gave the impression of trying to fit a square peg into a groovy hole (notably in its blinkered, and surprisingly jealous, ignorance of youth culture on several occasions), *The Avengers* tended only towards true conservatism when certain televisual norms required it to. Seen in 1961 as a breath of fresh air for the stagnating genre of crime drama, *The Avengers* started off reflecting a world-view still dominated by the 50s and all of that decade's obvious neuroses.

In 1961 the Cold War still raged (it would get a lot colder

within the following year); public perceptions of spies and spying was that of Burgess and MacLean, moles within the ministry, little men in bowler hats and umbrellas whose allegiance was to one 'side' or the other. The Soviet Union was a terrifying nuclear bogey-state, run by madmen hellbent on the dominance or destruction of the world. Those spies who worked for them were either foreign agents, brought up within the party machine, or British double-agents, 'turned' by ideology or greed. In this climate of increasing paranoia and hatred the James Bond books of Ian Fleming flourished, Alfred Hitchcock's sophisticated spy thrillers were hugely popular, and television, sensing a trend that could be followed, created its own branch of this mini-genre.

Originally devised as something which could accommodate a multitude of styles, *The Avengers* began in 1961 as a generic patchwork. There were elements of the standard 'amateur sleuth' adventure, popular with crime novelists for decades. The mysterious quality in Steed's character was straight from Fleming's world, whilst the London that Steed and Dr Keel inhabited was a strange mixture of cod working-class criminality and the twilight shadows of espionage.

From here, it's a huge step to what we had at the end of the decade, a mad mixture of the postmodern, surreal and utterly bizarre. Yet it was a step that was achieved within a framework like all television. As has been noted, television is the business of compromise, and it is sometimes necessary for television to forsake its artistic leanings in search of populism. That *The Avengers* was both critically and commercially successful during the 1960s is a useful indication that such contradictions can also be perfectly compatible.

The reason that *The Avengers* continues to be regarded as some kind of definitive statement on the era that spawned it is difficult to pinpoint, although it is (thankfully) true that the mid-60s episodes have (for the most part) aged very well.

This, in itself, is not particularly important (the kitschness of many episodes is often cited as a reason for the affection with which it is held, yet kitsch normally works only in small doses), but it does begin to highlight how important *The Avengers* is in televisual terms.

The early juxtaposition between realism and the exotic forms of revolt in style and content manifested themselves largely in the third season. The early steps towards kinkiness and strangeness became more pronounced, more focused, more aggressive. By the end of the third season *The Avengers* had begun to develop its own little world: a world where 'the enemy' could no longer be recognised by the accent of a particular political system, but rather by their greed, obsessions and lust for anarchy. At the same time as politics was becoming more a matter of presentation than dogma, so *The Avengers* worked itself into the new structure of power by being aloof to reality.

There was simply no time for any kind of radical worldview in the early seasons. Steed and Keel were members of 'the establishment' (the doctor possibly less so, but, for all of his anger at injustice he was still a 'management stooge' through his relationship with Steed). Ditto Cathy for most of the time. The series took time out to be cynical about politics and politicians (notably 'November Five'), but by the time that Emma arrived a decision had been taken to actively avoid getting into political questions. Steed has a degree of independent thought from within the system ('The Master Minds'), and spent time pondering class consciousness ('Two's a Crowd'), but, hell, if Steed wasn't a Tory then who is? Interestingly, for the entire period from season three until *The Avengers* ended, there was a Labour government in power. Is it possible the series itself was an MI5 attempt to undermine socialism? Nah, that's worthy of a Philip Levene script . . .

True politics, of course, is about far more than narrow Westminster partyism. Cathy's horror at her role in a man's world is manifested in the number she throws over her shoulder with gay abandon. Wonderful, but not very constructive. Emma, on the other hand, has a lack of any form of traditional female concerns. Both women *hate* being patronised and aren't above using strong-arm tactics to get their way (a line in 'Don't Look Behind You', later reused in 'The Joker', indicates both Cathy and Emma's hatred of male smugness: 'How'd you like me to break your arm?'). *The Avengers* certainly kicked a few doors open in the face of bigots, and that was a good thing. The fact that the series is *still* seen as having a significant role in the changing of popular perceptions of women's ability is, without doubt, one of its proudest achievements.

1960s society was developing and evolving not just because of the force of the changed perceptions of individual men and women. Hand-in-hand went an evolving technology and technological consumerism. The third and fourth seasons showed a paranoid edge when it came to the technical advance of knowledge, a Luddite attitude that wasn't uncommon in 60s television, even amongst fantasy programmes. It was, however, unusual to have a series so keenly in tune with the vibes on the streets coming on like a reactionary old git when it came to this week's 'new toy'. Criticising electronic brainwashing techniques like those used in 'The Wringer' may have been hip, but when you start attacking robotics and cybernetics ('The Cybernauts'), computers ('The House That Jack Built') and cool invasions by man-eating plants from outer space, then the kids are entitled to ask just how turned on and tuned in you really are. Any analysis of the 1960s usually has to conclude that whilst the era produced scientific wonder, the public was so frightened of out-of-control technology that such advances were regarded as little more than another step towards Armageddon.

The Armageddon the series railed against was rarely reflected in its landscapes, institutional or architectural. The bent-out-of-shape wide-focus rocket-concrete of most mid-60s feature films may be missing from *The Avengers* (whose London was still vaguely rural, with tree-lined mews and no urban decay), but there is still an element of groovy-angst in *The Avengers* (especially in the fourth season) that lies perfectly in tune with the beat of the era. The lyrics of the Rolling Stones circa 1965 (notably in songs like 'Get Off My Cloud' and '19th Nervous Breakdown') sound like lines of dialogue from *Avengers* episodes. This was life in the fast lane, even if that fast lane was a country one travelling from Smalltown, Hertfordshire to Nowheresville, Bucks. The concerns of 60s living, as well as extreme 60s neuroses, are visible in many episodes: the consumer society in 'Death at Bargain Prices', dating agencies in 'The Murder Market', permissiveness in 'A Touch of Brimstone', dropping out in 'A Sense of History', nightmares in 'Death's Door' and, generally, the pace at which life was going (brilliantly satirised in 'Dead Man's Treasure'). For all its trappings *The Avengers* showed a sense of mistrust with many aspects of modernity.

Analysing these disparate elements gives a hint as to the reasons for *The Avengers'* huge success. The most obvious danger of this success was that of failing to live up to it. Brian Clemens and Albert Fennell between 1965 and 1967 created a television series that will, quite possibly, live forever. The fact that someone, somewhere, in a position of authority decided that this wasn't enough and moved them off the project between seasons six and seven was one of the most crass acts of managerial interference in areas of artistic concern imaginable. Everything went wrong the moment Clemens and Fennell's hands were lifted from the series' tiller. The fact that they were only away for a couple of months doesn't negate the problems they faced on returning. From here onwards, the series could never quite regain its momentum. The seventh season of *The Avengers* is a roller coaster ride of quality. Some of the episodes are great, a lot are quite average, some are pretty bad and one or two are downright bloody awful. In this respect it closely mirrors many other long-running TV series. Despite all I've said, it has to be remembered that that's all *The Avengers* is.

The Avengers reflected the 60s by taking its concerns, its neuroses and its aspirations and painting them in cartoon-esque strokes across the canvas of popular consciousness. It's not always pretty, but it's very London. If the 60s had a face, that face had to reflect the optimism of the age as much as the anger and the confusion. Steed doesn't represent this. His is more the face of the 50s: solid, reliable, multi-talented but, ultimately, belonging very much to a pigeon-hole of established order. But Cathy, Emma and even, to an extent, Tara *do* represent aspects of the 60s face. And in making that face female *The Avengers* changed the world: perhaps only to a tiny degree, but changed it none the less.

Which is as much as any television series has ever done and a damn sight more than many would even dare to try.

Turn! Turn! Turn!

Martin Day

Naturalists tell us that a herd of buffalo can only move at the speed of the slowest in the group, and that when they are hunted the weakest creatures who lag at the back are killed first. Such natural selection is good for the herd as a whole, because the general speed and health of the whole group is improved by the regular culling of its weakest members.

The television industry seems to work along similar lines. Weak animals (unsuccessful pilot episodes or long-in-the-tooth series) are sacrificed for the good of the 'herd', which is forever limited by the speed (popularity) of its weakest members. That a programme like *The Avengers* survived for over eight years during perhaps the most tempestuous decade of the twentieth century speaks volumes for its chameleon-like ability to reinvent itself; that the programme was a qualified success in the altogether different climate of the 1970s – forming a template for the hugely likeable if terminally brain-dead *Professionals* – and again (on the big screen) in the 1990s, is still more remarkable.

When did the 1960s begin? It sounds like a stupid question, especially given that the preceding articles have concentrated on trying to place *The Avengers* into some sort of socio-historical context. *The Avengers* was the 60s – except that, of course, we mean the exaggerated, overblown 60s that began in 1963, as Philip Larkin famously put it, between the *Lady Chatterley's Lover* trial and the first Beatles LP. This Day-Glo, sexually liberated, flower power era stretched well into the early years of the 70s – whereas 1961, when *The Avengers* began, was very much in the cold, grey shadow of the 1950s, as Keith's essay rightly points out.

357

The Avengers was, and is, all about topicality, and transcending that topicality to become timeless, or, rather, ageless. In that sense, Brian Clemens was right to insist upon his stylised vision of 'Little England'. It felt like the past (Steed, his clothing and manners, the programme's overwhelming interest in the upper classes) was shot through with contemporary concerns (feminism, individualism and self-expression) – but certainly was not 'realistic'. *Avengers*land had, at best, only one foot in the real world. After all, the real world can be a pretty dull place – who on Earth wants to live *there*?

The original context of *The Avengers* can be seen by the TV programmes that were also competing for an audience when it began. In January 1961, the last series of the national service comedy *The Army Game* was in full swing, and *Dixon of Dock Green* was in its seventh season. *Coronation Street* had been on the screens for a month. *Steptoe and Son* was over a year away, as was *That Was the Week That Was*. The two big crime series of the era were *Danger Man*, starring Patrick McGoohan, and the BBC's adaptations of Georges Simenon's Maigret novels. Even come the second season of *The Avengers*, and the revelatory introduction of Cathy Gale, it is not surprising that Steed's exploits still have more in common with Len Deighton than *Austin Powers*.

This isn't a criticism, of course. *The Avengers* evolved with every season, but somehow each change of emphasis was an accomplished step forward (would that *Bugs*, the 90s *Avengers* wannabe, had been as successful in re-formatting itself).

'Death Dispatch' is an excellent example of the early, 'realistic' style. A South American travelogue, beginning with the caption 'Jamaica', it feels very much like a *Danger Man* script, albeit on a lower budget. It's a straightforward, but thoroughly successful, spy caper. Certainly, the 'pop art' look of the later episodes (itself a reaction to limited budgets) was nowhere to be seen: 'Intercrime', for instance, features stock footage of HMP Holloway (and an amusing sign inside the prison that says 'All conversations must be in English'!); 'Box of Tricks' goes to the film library to give its re-creation of Piccadilly Circus and Soho more credence. The contemporary viewer can't help but be reminded of the ITC crime series of the 60s and 70s.

There are, of course, occasional nods towards the 'wacky' *Avengers* of the Mrs Peel and Tara seasons, but for every 'Immortal Clay' (unbreakable china) and 'Warlock' (black magic) there was a 'Bullseye' (boardroom intrigue) or a 'Mission to Montreal' (defence microdots) to balance things out. It's not until the third season that the audience is deemed ready for the lunatic surrealism of 'The Undertakers', 'Dressed to Kill', and 'The Grandeur that was Rome' (complete with main villain who wants to be 'Emperor of the World').

Ultimately, it was Cathy Gale (rather than the stories themselves) that set *The Avengers* apart from its peers during 1962 and 1963. Her very presence was like a firecracker set off during a polite dinner party, and, if she was something unique and special, then so was her relationship with Steed.

The sexual tension of their professional relationship – a surprising forerunner of *The X-Files*'s interest in a man and a woman being drawn together by mutual admiration and their essential difference from the people around them – was an undercurrent of 'real world' emotion crackling away in the background. 'Death on the Rocks', with Steed and Cathy pretending to be married in order to investigate a diamond racket, is shot through with a sensual unease and excitement. As with *The X-Files* – or *Moonlighting*, or *Cheers* (why have so few British programmes succeeded in presenting such contradictory attraction?) – much of the mutual fascination comes through teasing dialogue exchanges.

Steed: Are you decent?
Cathy: I shall be by the time you get here.
('Death Dispatch')

Cathy: I've been trying to call you all
morning.
Steed: I've been in the bath.
Cathy: For four hours?
Steed: Some people take longer than others.
('The Golden Fleece')

There's a joking selfishness about Steed and Cathy. In 'Conspiracy of Silence' Steed states, 'First there's the matter of protecting my neck. That's incidental . . .', to which Cathy can but exclaim, 'But of course!' During 'Intercrime', Steed (ever the gentleman) says, 'We'd better not be seen together. You walk, I'll take the lift.' 'Six Hands Across a Table' is a love story for Cathy, although she still finds time to tell Steed that he has 'a voice like a saw'. In the kitchen farce 'Death à la Carte', Steed flirts playfully (and hilariously) with the north-country maid, Josie.

However, 'The Golden Eggs' opens with Steed and Cathy sharing breakfast, and the clear implication is that they are living together. Indeed, their long-standing intimacy, which the viewer sees only in glimpses, becomes almost marital in its familiarity: in 'Concerto' Steed and Cathy play chess while talking about classic music (she slaughters him!).

Occasionally, the real world dared to intrude on the one that they had created for themselves ('The Nutshell' features a discussion on the nuclear arms race, during which Cathy comes across as rather a unilateralist), but little usually disturbs their playful admiration of each other, their unworldly decency, their simple good humour.

'Build a Better Mousetrap' has some of the funniest Steed

dialogue (especially when he tries to convince the old ladies that he is from the National Dis-Trust: 'The National Trust trusts people to look after buildings of national interest. But we don't. We don't trust anybody at all. Dis-trust, you see?'). It is also regarded as a pivotal episode, one of many templates established during the third season in readiness for the fourth. We're only a step away from the bizarrely named ego-maniacal villains of the Emma Peel years, from 'Mother' and the self-conscious oddity of the Tara season. In a sense, the daring and adventurous stories, the exaggerated visual conceits, were just an attempt to catch up with the radical vibrancy of Cathy Gale and her sparkling relationship with Steed.

The 1998 movie has the unenviable task of encapsulating this eight-year progression within a couple of hours of big-screen action. It has to entertain audiences whose sole idea of spy thrillers with a light touch is James Bond; it needs to appeal to fans to whom the simple words 'The Avengers' can mean anything from hard-boiled David Keel spy thrillers to surreal Tara King adventures. In a masterstroke, the film is relevant to the 90s only because everything takes place in 1999. Frankly, it has a damn sight more work to do than the *Saint* movie ever did, and it goes without saying that Jerry Weintraub's *The Avengers* is vastly superior to the Val Kilmer vehicle.

For a start, the film acknowledges its roots, rather than ignoring them. Almost everything that happens has a precedent in the TV series. The introductory scene – with Emma Peel emerging from a Jaguar, entering an old-fashioned red telephone box, and disappearing through a trap door – and the presence of Mother (and Father!) harks back to the seventh season. Emma's costume – the figure-hugging snakeskin-effect leather – is the perfect updating of a 60s style icon. There's a lunatic villain with a lunatic plan, a robotic double

361

of Mrs Peel, and killer teddy bears – all comfortable nods to mid-period *Avengers*. Best of all, there's a dark humour and a sexual tension that, one could argue, pays homage to the early years of the show.

Despite the film's understandable retrospection, there's something new and fresh here, too. *The Avengers* has never stood still. In television and film, more so even than in life, static equates with stagnation. And Steed and his friends are never less than vibrant.

The Avengers Movie

Warner Brothers
Writer: Don MacPherson
Director: Jeremiah Chechik
Producer: Jerry Weintraub
Executive Producer: Susan Ekins
Director of Photography: Roger Pratt
**Cast: Ralph Fiennes (John Steed), Uma Thurman
(Emma Peel), Sean Connery (Sir August DeWynter),
Jim Broadbent (Mother), Fiona Shaw (Father),
Eddie Izzard, Shaun Ryder (Donovan),
Eileen Atkins, John Wood**

Sir August DeWynter is the diabolical mastermind behind the
Prospero Project, a scheme to control the world's weather.
With Trafalgar Square and the Houses of Parliament sub-
merged in snow, and an evil robotic double of Emma on the
loose, Steed and Mrs Peel set out to defeat DeWynter and his
thuggish henchmen.

Wit: ☆ ☆ ☆ Dark and brooding, or resembling a spoof Tara
story? Like the early years, or reminiscent of Macnee's bits in
that Oasis video? Hmmm . . .

Kinkiness Factor: ☆ ☆ ☆ ☆ ☆ It's got Uma Thurman, star
of *Henry and June* and *Pulp Fiction*, in a costume so tight she
needed talcum powder to get into it – said costume then being
stitched together around her. Not sure if that's kinky or just
plain exploitation, but it's gotta be worth five stars for *something*. And she gets to cavort with Sean Connery, too . . .

Fights: ☆ ☆ ☆ ☆ . . . shortly before it all turns unpleasant.

Strangeness: Martial arts killers who look like teddy bears, numerous nods to Andy Warhol (is that taking the whole pop art thing too far?), an agent killed by falling fish, and gas-mask-wearing butlers ... Is that strange enough for you? Plus, a policeman in a uniform!

Notes: The history of this film is almost as fascinating as the end product. It took twelve years for producer Jerry Weintraub to bring *The Avengers* to the big screen, and along the way a vast array of people were rumoured to be involved with it in one capacity or another. In the mid-90s it seemed that Mel Gibson was to star in a film directed by Nicolas (*Star Trek II*) Meyer. Then attention turned to a succession of (variously un-Steed-like) British actors: Sean Bean, fresh from his role in *GoldenEye*, Alan Rickman, and Robbie Coltrane. Ralph Fiennes, having turned down the lead in *The Saint*, seemed at the time very much a fringe candidate. Emma at this stage was to be played by Nicole Kidman. Comedian Eddie Izzard was lined up to portray Mother, with Dawn French as Father (Izzard was later re-cast).

Filming was not without incident, either. On Friday 13 June 1997 there was an extensive fire at Pinewood Studios, which injured one fireman and damaged a $2.4 million set. Shaun Ryder's face was scarred during the shooting of a fight scene. And poor Uma's feet were continually crushed by her stiletto boots ...

The end product certainly understood that the look of the project was going to be key to its success. Director Jeremiah Checick, best known for *Benny and Joon*, had a superb behind-the-scenes crew to make best use of the estimated £40 million budget. Director of photography Roger Pratt had worked on *Shadowlands*, *The Fisher King*, and *Brazil*, which hint at the look of *The Avengers*. Production designer Stuart Craig was a three-time Oscar winner (*Gandhi*, *Dangerous*

Liaisons and *The English Patient*), as was costume designer Anthony Powell (*Tess*, *Death on the Nile*, *Travels With My Aunt*). Set decorator Stephanie McMillan won an Oscar for *The English Patient*, editor Mick Audsley (*Dance With A Stranger*, *My Beautiful Laundrette*, *Prick Up Your Ears*, *Twelve Monkeys*, *Interview With The Vampire*) won a BAFTA award for *The Snapper* and a nomination for *Dangerous Liaisons*. All combined to create a visual *tour de force*, the look of the 'new' *Avengers* being summed up by its elegant old cars: the racing green Bentley, the black Mini Coopers, and, not forgetting, the Rolls Royce with a snow plough.

Says it all, really.

EPISODE TITLE INDEX

The Avengers in bold; *The New Avengers* in normal type